THE MINANGKABAU RESPONSE
TO DUTCH COLONIAL RULE
IN THE NINETEENTH CENTURY

Elizabeth E. Graves

THE MINANGKABAU RESPONSE TO DUTCH COLONIAL RULE IN THE NINETEENTH CENTURY

EQUINOX PUBLISHING (ASIA) PTE LTD
No 3. Shenton Way
#10-05 Shenton House
Singapore 068805

www.EquinoxPublishing.com

The Minangkabau Response to Dutch Colonial Rule
in the Nineteenth Century
by Elizabeth E. Graves

ISBN 978-602-8397-32-2

First Equinox Edition 2010

Copyright © 1981 by Cornell Southeast Asia
Program Publications; renewed 2010.
This is a reprint edition authorized by the original publisher,
Cornell Southeast Asia Program Publications.

Printed in the United States

1 3 5 7 9 10 8 6 4 2

All rights reserved. No part of this publication may be reproduced, stored in a retrieval system, or transmitted in any form or by any means, electronic, mechanical, photocopying, recording or otherwise without the prior permission of Equinox Publishing.

TABLE OF CONTENTS

	Page
Foreword	7
Note on Spelling and Bibliographic Sources	9
Introduction	11

Chapter

I. The Minangkabau World and its Traditional Village Society 17

II. The Village and the World Beyond 41

III. A New Political Configuration: Centralized Rule and a Status Quo 59

IV. Economic Reorganization: Taxation and the Cultivation System 89

V. Secular Education in the 1840s to 1860s: the Era of Local Initiative 127

VI. Educational Reorganization in the 1870s: The Government Elementary Schools and Advanced Education 177

VII. The Genealogy of the New Elite: A case Study 207

VIII. Epilogue: Minangkabau in the Twentieth Century 225

GLOSSARY 233

LIST OF TABLES AND MAPS

Table	Page
1 Sumatra's West Coast Population (1852 and 1920)	82
2 Padang Coffee Exports	101
3 Coffee Warehouse Purchases (1867-1869 in piculs)	109
4 Corvée Labor Levies (1880)	117
5 Rice Harvest, 1867-1868	120
6 Coffee Warehouses: Michiels' Decision October 11, 1847	122
7 Total Pupil Enrollment in Nagari Schools	142
8 Parents' Backgrounds—Highlands Schools 1860s (in percent of total enrollment)	146
9 Parents' Backgrounds—Lowlands Schools 1860s (in percent of total enrollment)	163
10 Geographic Origin of Sekolah Radja Pupils	188
11 Elementary Schools in Sumatra	190
12 Family Background of Pupils: 1872	202
13 Family Background of Pupils: 1873 and 1877	203

Map		Page
1	Minangkabau and the Western Archipelago	15
2	Minangkabau World	19
3	Coffee Warehouses (1847 and 1867)	107
4	Nagari Schools	135
5	Government Elementary Schools, 1880	194

FOREWORD

Despite the considerable expansion of scholarly studies of Minangkabau society in recent years, the paucity of historical research on West Sumatra is still notable. Especially is this so for the nineteenth century, where, apart from the new perspectives provided in Christine Dobbin's series of articles on the Padri Wars,* virtually nothing has been published during the past decade. A significant study dealing with this period that certainly merited publication was the 1971 University of Wisconsin dissertation of Elizabeth E. Graves, which, following her revision, we are now pleased to bring out in our Monograph Series. In this revision Dr. Graves was not able to draw on Dobbin's work and other germane material published during the last few years, but most of the data she has marshaled and analyzed cannot be found in other published sources, and there is no doubt that her monograph fills many of the extensive gaps in our knowledge of nineteenth century Minangkabau society and its interaction with Dutch political and economic power. Moreover, those familiar with Taufik Abdullah's classic study, *Schools and Politics: The Kaum Muda in West Sumatra (1927-1933)*, will find an excellent complement in her chapters on the development of secular education during this earlier period.

In publishing this study, the Cornell Modern Indonesia Project is confident that it provides an important addition to the regional dimension of Indonesian history and illuminating insights into the shaping of nineteenth century Minangkabau society and the way its character set the stage for better known developments in the present century.

George McT. Kahin
Ithaca, N.Y.
July 1981

---

* See, in particular, her "Islamic Revivalism in Minangkabau at the Turn of the Nineteenth Century," *Modern Asian Studies*, 8, 3 (1974), pp. 319-56, and "Economic Change in Minangkabau as a Factor in the Rise of the Padri Movement, 1784-1830," *Indonesia*, 23 (April 1977), pp. 1-38.

NOTE ON SPELLING AND BIBLIOGRAPHIC SOURCES

Spelling of Indonesian words generally follows the new system introduced in 1972. Exceptions include: personal names and titles, which have been spelled according to individual preference insofar as this could be determined; names and titles of organizations and positions which had ceased to exist before 1972; and quotations from contemporary documents.

Footnote references to *Exhibitum*, *Verbaal*, and *Mailrapport* indicate documents in the Ministry of Colonies' archives in The Hague for the years 1814-1849; 1849-1899; and 1900 to the present. Packets of incoming reports and correspondence from Batavia to the Ministry on a particular issue were dated and numbered as received, and then filed as *Exhibitum*. For the Ministry response to Batavia, all the relevant documents on a given problem were collected and refiled, together with the draft of the reply, according to the date and number of the letter. These documents were placed under the heading *Verbaal*. Documents cited as *Mailrapport* are copies of twentieth century reports, correspondence, and decisions sent from Batavia to the Ministry of Colonies. They were filed by serial number, the last two digits of which indicated the year in which the correspondence was received in The Hague.

INTRODUCTION

At independence, Indonesia woefully lacked educated citizens possessing the professional and technical skills critical for the success of the new nation. Many of the relatively small number that did exist in 1945 came from the Minangkabau ethnic group of West Sumatra. Minangkabau representation among the political, intellectual, and professional elite of the new Republic far exceeded their 3 percent of the total Indonesian population.

The roots of the Minangkabau achievement lay in their reaction to the advent of Dutch colonial rule in the mid-nineteenth century. After gaining control of all of West Sumatra in 1837, the Dutch needed a body of local people with rudimentary mechanical skills—reading, writing, and elementary ciphering—to staff their geometrically expanding colonial bureaucratic structure. Nevertheless, the colonial government had no consistent policy for encouraging education in the region, although Dutch officials did occasionally take the initiative in sponsoring individual schools there. This was partly because the Dutch regime's periodic fears of Muslim activity directed against Christian rulers led it to distrust the intensely Islamic Minangkabau. The few schools the government did provide were designed to create an educated class of enlightened hereditary rulers similar to that on Java. When, however, the chiefs themselves showed little interest in education, preferring instead to hire educated clerks, the non-chiefly families, quick to see the unique advantages offered by education, rapidly filled the vacuum. Thus, the schools that sprang up in the nineteenth century in response to Dutch needs owed less to official Dutch support than to local interest. This was particularly the case in areas that were relatively poor agriculturally, where most men had traditionally been forced to pursue occupations as traders or craftsmen away from their home villages. Because these hill areas were often the same ones in which the Dutch established the coffee cultivation system, the villagers early on had direct experience with and access to job opportunities that required some education.

The socio-economic system of the Minangkabau village, with its tradition of *merantau* by which young men left home to seek their fortunes, was uniquely suited to take advantage of the new opportunities offered by access to the Dutch colonial empire. The Dutch administration needed clerks and other semi-literate staff, and many upwardly mobile Minangkabau families had soon established civil service dynasties within the Dutch administration. The Minangkabau family system stressed pooling resources to advance a member of the next generation, who in turn would carry with him proportionately greater numbers from the succeeding generations. Thus, families which blossomed as intellectual leaders in the twentieth century were those with relatives as school-teachers, coffeewarehouse clerks, or petty civil servants in the nineteenth.

The reasons for Minangkabau advancement in the field of education must be sought within the traditional society—the pressures and demands which it made on individuals, the opportunities or restrictions it placed before them. The colonial government chose to organize its own administration of West Sumatra by using existing *adat* (customary law) village institutions, because it wanted to preserve the existing indigenous pattern of local interfamily relationships. But, in fact, the colonial administration blocked the natural rotation in the upper elite positions and thus changed the nature of relationships between families. The lesser, but upwardly mobile, families could no longer expect to gain chiefly status and had to look outside the traditional milieu to find position and prominence.

It is among these middle-level families that one can see "progress" in the sense of a creative response to the colonial presence and its attendant new chances for wealth and prestige, power and position. For many of these middle families, the best path upward lay in attaching themselves to the new government, and for this they had to learn the new skills and techniques which were preconditions for employment.

"Western" education in nineteenth-century West Sumatra represented a largely pragmatic and almost opportunist response by certain groups to the needs of the European administration for trained bureaucratic personnel. Traditionally, education was not considered as the preparation for future employment, but rather learning to recite the Quran and the Muslim commentaries was a religious obligation which gave proof of obedience to God, and hence religiosity. Even those who became village religious teachers did not begin study with the predetermined idea that it would provide them with the tools to earn a living in traditional Minangkabau society, although one could argue that many saw it as a way to achieve enhanced prestige. The new Western-style schools, however, graduated pupils who sought specific benefits in the material world as a result of their education.

In examining the response to educational opportunities on the part of various elements in the population, one gains at the same time insight into the wider impact of colonialism on Minangkabau society. The reaction to education by the different social groups seems to parallel their response to colonial rule in general. The Minangkabau village leaders, the local aristocracy, were catered to by the colonial authority during the early years as the best means to legitimize the new regime, and, as a result, these local notables often made few if any adjustments in the main ordering of their lives. They were anesthetized into acquiescence by the increased security of their high positions, security which accompanied outward cooperation with the new rulers. For them, the relatively small change at the top level did not really effectively threaten their own positions. Former members of the traditional aristocracy who rejected the new rulers were exiled or neutralized through the power of the colonial regime combined with the approval of the other notables. The Muslim component of the traditional leadership of Minangkabau society were victims of continuous Dutch activity deliberately aimed at undermining Islamic influence. The new administration played off the old aristocratic elite against the religious leaders in such a way that any alliance between the two would be unlikely. Dutch academic studies of Minangkabau society focusing on and analyzing the so-called "traditional conflict" between Islam and the adat ultimately led many Minangkabau themselves to accept these "inherent contradictions," formerly unrecognized, as accurate assessments of reality.

For the peasant, life in the new order differed little from that in the old; as a member of the bottom layer irrespective of who was in power, he was engaged in a constant struggle to withstand outside demands and interferences in his daily affairs. The increased efficiency of the Dutch bureaucracy, however, did penetrate Minangkabau life in a way never before experienced. These increasing irritations usually erupted into short-lived cathartic bursts of violence against the regime and anyone else considered associated with the oppression. But, by and large, life for the peasant, as for the aristocrat, continued to follow the path sanctioned by tradition and legend.

It remained for those in the middle to take advantage of the colonial situation. Unlike the aristocrats, they had no guaranteed place in the elite. For them, the colonial government offered a new way to success, and a major theme of Minangkabau history in the nineteenth century is the increasing acceptance by these Minangkabau families of the new means to elite status.

The Minangkabau case demonstrates the importance of local initiative and interest and the part that social system plays in how a people respond to changing circumstance. The Dutch administration was more intensive in other parts of the archipelago and the Dutch educational system more well developed elsewhere as well, but few of these areas responded in the same fashion as did Minangkabau. Moreover, the other areas later known for their educated and professional class during the Dutch era were Christian communities protected and pushed by Dutch missionaries and with preferred access to the benefits of colonial rule. The Dutch always considered the Islamic Minangkabau a potential threat to public tranquility in Sumatra. Because the Minangkabau achieved their success on their own account, they did not believe its continuation depended on a permanent Dutch presence and thus were early members of the nationalist movement and leaders of the new nation in 1945.

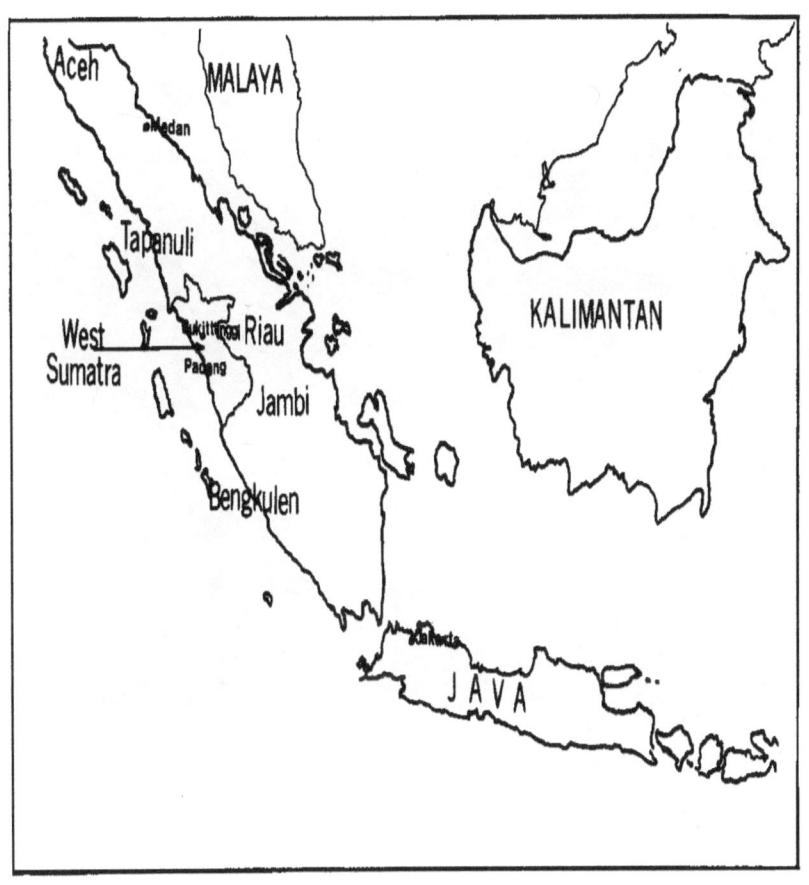

MAP I: MINANGKABAU & THE WESTERN ARCHIPELAGO

CHAPTER ONE
THE MINANGKABAU WORLD AND ITS TRADITIONAL VILLAGE SOCIETY

The island of Sumatra, neatly bisected by the equator, lies with its northernmost tip pointing the way to India and the trading world of the Mediterranean Sea, a world with which Sumatra has been tied in commerce for long centuries. The great mercantile empires of Indonesia—Srivijaya, Melayu, Aceh to name but a few—were based on Sumatra. Movement and competition were the hallmarks of life in these states, and the people of the island as a whole displayed a high degree of personal mobility, travelling far in search of trade or, in times of uncertainty, plunder. Many sailed as far as the eastern coastline of Africa, joining in the Malay settlement of Madagascar.

Sumatra has thus historically been the scene of dynamic and commercially oriented peoples, at home in the arena of international power politics or individual achievement. The Minangkabau of West Sumatra are worthy spiritual heirs of this long tradition. Their homeland, midway along the north/south axis of Sumatra, consists of a series of fertile upland rice plains stretching eastward from the foothills of the Bukit Barisan, the mountainous western spine of the island, to the beginnings of the lowlands which mark the Riau coastal district on the Straits of Malacca. The area is small, comprising some 18,000 square miles which represent only 11 percent of the island's total expanse and less than 3 percent of presentday Indonesia. With the exception of a thin coastal strip, most of the Minangkabau region is over 1,500 feet above sea level.

West Sumatra is the most densely settled residency of Sumatra and, along with the three residencies of Java and that of South Sulawesi, one of the five major population zones of Indonesia. Within the Minangkabau area, the demographic patterns follow the topographical characteristics;

population is not evenly distributed but is concentrated in the four rice-producing plains and, since late colonial times, the area around the capital of Padang. Though the population of Minangkabau has increased over the past two centuries, along with that of the rest of Indonesia, the expansion, relatively speaking, has been slower.

The Minangkabau people are acutely conscious of themselves as a distinct and, in their considered opinions, highly superior ethnic group. The intrusion by the modern world did not shake this self-confidence nor basically alter their fundamental assumptions about themselves as a people or their worth as individuals. They believe that the history of their singular group first began with a settlement on the southern slopes of Mount Merapi, a volcano near Bukittinggi; from this geographic focus, they expanded to fill what is now the province of West Sumatra. The Merapi settlement was divided into three communities, each centered around its own well, called in the language of those days a *luhak*. As time passed, it became necessary to seek new land, and so each of the three groups set off to pioneer and settle a district of its own. The group from the luhak *agam*, the well where the agam plant (used for weaving mats) flourished, travelled to a broad plain north of the Merapi, facing Mount Singgalang. Those from the luhak *tanah datar*, the well on the flat ground, settled on a plain southeast of the Merapi. The people from the third well, of whom there were some fifty (*lima puluh*) families, established themselves on the plain north of Mount Sago.[1]

Henceforth, these three areas of settlement formed the heartland of Minangkabau and were known collectively as the Luhak nan Tigo (The Three Districts)—Luhak Agam, Luhak Tanah Datar, and Luhak Lima Puluh Kota. Although the Minangkabau people continued to expand in all directions from these core districts, the Luhak nan Tigo are considered the real and true Minangkabau country, and all other areas have legends of settlement which tie their ancestors to one of the three original luhak communities.

---

1 Ahmad Dt. Batuah and A. Dt. Madjoindo, *Tambo Minangkabau dan Adatnja* (Jakarta: Balai Pustaka, 1956), pp. 14-16.

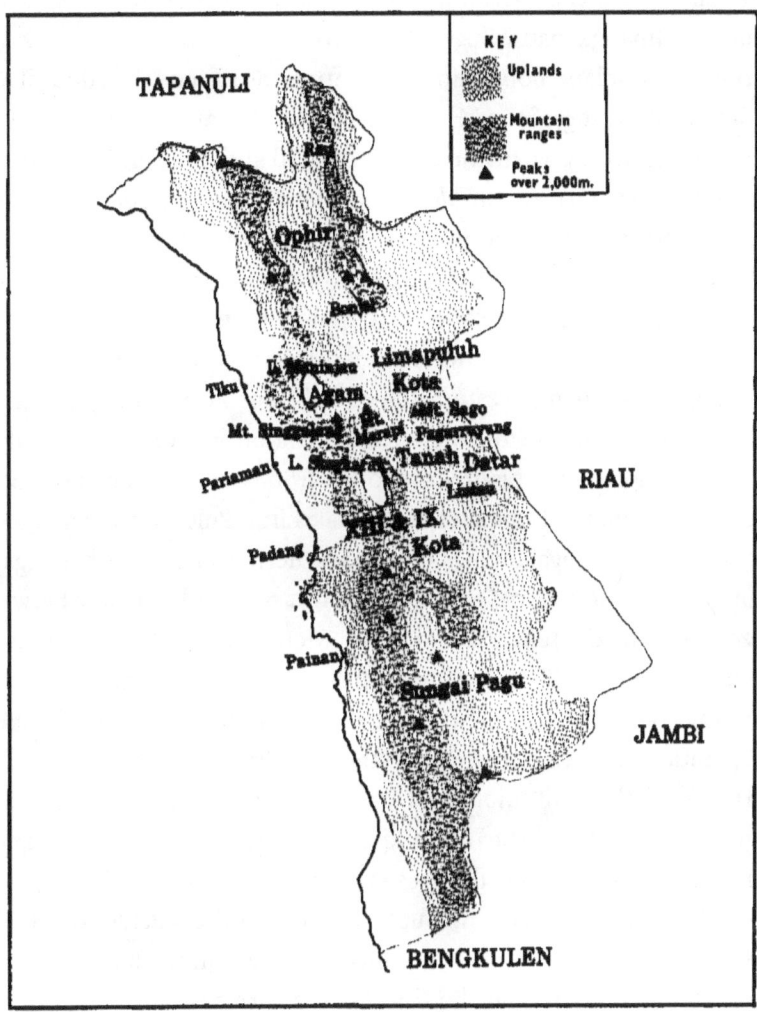

MAP 2: MINANGKABAU WORLD

The main center of Minangkabau development has been four large rice plains which are enclosed within the rugged surrounding hills that divide the Minangkabau from their neighbors. This area is known popularly as the Padang Highlands (after the Dutch term for the area, Padangsche Bovenlanden) or sometimes the Minangkabau Highlands. Each of the four plains sustains a dense population, gathered together on a broad and gently sloping saucer of land, itself carefully demarcated into terraced rice fields which are irrigated by a combination of winter's rains and favorable topography. Artificial irrigation projects have never been an important feature of Minangkabau village agriculture.

These four upland population concentrations include the cultural and historical wellspring of the Minangkabau (the Luhak nan Tigo) plus the district of Solok (known historically as the XIII and IX Kota). Collectively, the districts are termed the *darat* (the land, or more specifically, the upland interior) in opposition to the *rantau*, a term applied to all those frontier, culturally mixed areas which, though perhaps geographically "in" Minangkabau, are not considered quite "of" it.

Each broad plain has its own attendant volcano, constant reminder to the villagers that their ancestors descended from such a mountain in the dimly perceived past before wet-rice cultivation was known and when life on the unprotected plain was too hazardous to contemplate. Mount Sago, now dormant, dominates the Luhak Lima Puluh Kota; an equally inactive Mount Singgalang lies on the southern border of Luhak Agam; Mount Merapi, still active and dangerous, acts as a boundary between Agam and Luhak Tanah Datar; and Mount Talang, only relatively recently returned to life, lies to the south of Solok. These mountains and their rings of foothills girdle the rice plains and provide an atmosphere of separation which has helped isolate and distinguish the men of one district from those of another. Two great crater lakes, Maninjau and Singkarak, provide spectacular and unsuspected breaks in the rugged Barisan Mountains along the western rim of the darat. There are no navigable rivers to connect this upland realm to the outside world. The colonial roads, like the footpaths which predated them, snake along the sides of the mountains and slip through the narrow passes that separate the four plains each from the other.

Life in each of the plains is similar, the regular cycle of the wet-rice farmer, but the inhabitants of each are credited with their own distinctive characters. Agam, in the north, centering on Bukittinggi, is equated with dynamic pragmatism, peopled with men quick to turn any situation to their economic advantage. The Lima Puluh Kota, slightly removed to the east and in closer contact with the traders' world of the Malacca Straits, forms a center for traditional religious studies, especially at the numerous *tarekat* (mystical, Islamic brotherhoods) schools which dot the landscape near the administrative center at Payakumbuh. In the south, the XIII and IX Kota, with their center at Solok, reputedly have the most arrogant and aristocratically minded of all the Minangkabau people. Tanah Datar, in the middle geographically and cosmologically, contains the birthplace for the Minangkabau and their culture as well as their former political center, Pagarruyung, the last visible remains of the reputedly glorious Kingdom of Minangkabau.

These upland plains nurtured Minangkabau culture and were the scene of its most complex and systematic form of development. Here extensive *sawah* (wet-rice fields) holdings allowed the growth of large matrilineal families organized by increasingly intricate adat relationships. The land was sufficient to support all of its people, and few needed to look elsewhere to supplement the rice harvest. An aristocracy of land-based families ruled the villages and preserved the customary law to their advantage. Within the village, each extended family, or lineage, has its own area or compound where large family houses (*rumah gadang*) built on wooden pilings face onto a common courtyard. The most impressive house in the compound belongs to the lineage's main family, the one entitled to hold the family chieftaincy and provide the place for family rituals. Somewhere nearby, but a bit removed from the complex of houses, stands the lineage *surau*, serving as the gathering place of adolescent and adult males for all sorts of social and religious activities.

In the rugged hills which wall in the four rice plains, nestle villages which also belong to the Minangkabau sphere, but where the tempo of daily life is different. Here in the high upland passes, one finds only the occasional narrow plain suitable for wet rice, and the harvests are small. The farmers plant the hilly slopes with vegetables and fruit mixed with a bit of dry-field rice. To survive, these hillside people have developed handicraft or service industries whose products they sell to their compatriots of the plain. Each year, young men from these villages leave for the market towns to become artisans, petty traders, tailors, coffeeshop owners, or bullock cart drivers. The ideal Minangkabau life was evolved by the plains people who could easily sustain it with their extensive rice harvests. For the hill people the ideal is a constantly pursued dream, only partially attainable through the profits of nonagricultural labor.

The image of the Minangkabau as a peripatetic merchant and artisan derives more from the people of these hill villages than from those of the prosperous rice villages of the plains. The bus company owner in Medan, the exclusive antique dealer in Jakarta, the small cloth merchant in Makassar, each comes from an upland village and each represents the financial hopes, and probably significant monetary investment, of an upland lineage.

These hillside villages exist at the fringes of Minangkabau life, but they provide many of the services and goods required to keep the "classic culture" going. Each market day, before dawn, people from the hills begin their journey down to the populous towns of the plains. They bring the cabbages and coffee, the baskets and pottery, the cloth and the jewelry which contribute to the ease of living on the plain. Each hill village is known to the people of the plain according to the service which it can render them.

Along the western coastal lowlands, one finds villages which differ from both of the highlands types. They are in the Minangkabau territorial area, but not completely a part of its culture. Their ethnic composition is mixed; they are trading entrepots and have attracted mercantile elements from as far as India and as near as the Minangkabau darat itself. A Minangkabau resident in the coastal port of Padang, Painan, or Pariaman rarely considers himself a true citizen of any of these places. He belongs instead to the village of his mother's people in the highlands, or, if his mother is part of the coastal population herself, then he takes his father's village as his own, or even that of his grandparents. One may live and work in Padang, one may even be born and die there, but the only people who are really ever "from" Padang are a few "feudal" families, the recognized overlords of the ports who, in a bygone era, collected tribute from the trade conducted in the harbors. Even they, however, can trace their families' origins ultimately to highlands nobility of a not-quite-forgotten past.

On the coast, the cultural conventions of the highlands Minangkabau *adat* (customary law) have become blurred, diluted by years of outside influences, starved by semi-isolation from highlands sources. There is little of the interlineage rivalry which keeps the darat villages in continual cycles of renewal and prevents the development of an entrenched aristocracy.

The small satellite agricultural villages which serve the coastal centers are likewise composed of people who came originally from the Padang Highlands. Their remembered ties to specific villages are important links proving their oneness with the Minangkabau world, for all that their families have resided on the coast for generations. Although their land appears rich, their villages are poor and shabby. Many supplement their livelihood by fishing. The large lineage houses, center and symbol of Minangkabau society in the heartland, apparently did not survive the transition to life on the coast. They were, perhaps, too expensive to maintain, or unsuited to the different lifestyle, or, perhaps, no one who settled here wanted to accept the reality that he had in fact changed his "home village."

Geographically and in terms of life style, therefore, one can divide the Minangkabau *nagari* (extended village units) into three fairly distinct categories. In the Padang Highlands, the main focus of Minangkabau history and culture, two life styles have developed—that based on the sawah-rich plateau with its plentiful harvests, and that centered in the "marginal" villages of the hill country with their handicraft and entrepreneurial interests. The social and political structure of these two types of villages, however, follow the same basic outlines of adat law and custom, differing mainly in their interpretations about how these regulations ought to operate in practice. The third type of nagari are those of the western coast—in its towns and along the narrow surrounding plains. This area was known to the Dutch as the Padang Lowlands (Padangsche Benedenlanden), and to the Minangkabau as the rantau or frontier. Culturally and in terms of social and political organization, the coastal districts often present only a dim reflection of the highlands adat style. These differences in geography, historical experience, and general approach to life would greatly influence the way the various nagari reacted to the events of the nineteenth century and the challenges of the Dutch presence.

Traditional Village Society

A major factor in traditional Minangkabau village society was the constant competition among individuals and their families to attain recognition and status; such position conferred, and at the same time also derived from, lineage power and prestige. Birth, wealth, and prestige in varying combination opened the path to the top for aspiring families and their members. Although, at first glance, the village appears to have been a closely knit oligarchy, organized to benefit the direct heirs of the initial "founding families," a closer examination reveals that a constant circulation took place in and out of this "aristocracy." Birth, though perhaps most important, was by no means decisive. Its importance derived more from the leverage it gave certain families in the struggle to acquire and maintain wealth and prestige than from any recognized preeminence for a particular bloodline. Village life in the Padang Highlands, whether in the plains villages or the hill villages, followed roughly the same general outlines, though it often differed in style, intensity, and the degree to which any given factor was influential or important.

Matrilineal Lineages

The basis of social organization and the arena within which the fundamental power struggles were carried on was the *suku*, a matrilineal lineage group subdivided into large extended branch families. Depending upon the number of its members, and to a certain degree also its importance in the village, a particular lineage might occupy one or more housing compounds in the village.

The composition of each lineage unit, or suku, was based on its members' presumed common descent from the same ancestral mother. Suku were subdivided into large branch families, or *kaum*; here, too, membership was based on descent from a common foremother, usually a great- or great-great-grandmother. The smallest unit, the *sabuah parui*, consisted of all the children of one woman plus the children of her daughters.[2] A sabuah parui was usually the same as the residents of one large family house. Only the women and small children were considered the actual residents of such a house, and only they were entitled to live and sleep there. Men were technically regarded as temporary visitors in the house of their mother. The men either stayed at their wife's house at night, or, if unmarried, they slept in the lineage surau, a combination Quranic school and male clubhouse.

---

2 P. E. de Josselin de Jong, *Minangkabau and Negri Sembilan: Socio-Political Structure in Indonesia* (Jakarta: Bhartara, 1960), p. 10.

Family Property

The main base of operations for the suku was not regional but rather within the village, where it served as the basic political, social, and economic unit. Wealth, and hence power, prestige, and social position, derived from lineage-held lands, properties, and perquisites—known collectively as the *harta pusaka*, or, more usually, *pusaka*.

The most important single item in the harta pusaka were the lineage lands, but the pusaka also included such various items as the central lineage house, individual large family houses and other buildings, jewelry, rights to woodland, and rights to the title of family chief (*penghulu*) and lesser adat positions. The harta pusaka was considered as property "owned" by the whole lineage, branch, or family as a unit. It was inalienable and no single individual could make private contracts concerning it. It served as a "trust fund" for the family members because it could not be sold, and, theoretically, it protected the family from complete poverty. At the same time, as one commentator has pointed out, such a system also made it very difficult for any one family in the lineage to gain control and become very rich quickly.[3]

Family properties were especially important as social security for the family women. Insofar as one could identify "heirs," to the property, these were, properly speaking, women; men were charged, on the other hand, with guarding the inheritance and watching over their sisters' welfare. The male guardian was called the *mamak kepala waris*, which means the "uncle" who controls the legacy or who heads the inheritance unit (*waris* can be used in either sense). The term is usually shortened to *mamak*, meaning uncle or guardian. In theory, the mamak could not make any disposition of family property without consent of the women.[4] He was usually the eldest male who could also claim direct descent from the family's ancestral female founder. He supervised division of family property and its profits and was charged with nurturing it so that its wealth increased.

The most important component of harta pusaka was the wet-rice

---

3   A. W. P. Verkerk Pistorius, *Studien over de Inlandsche Huishouding in de Padangsche Bovenlanden* (Zalt-Bommel: Noman, 1871), p. 58.
4   Batuah and Madjoindo, *Tambo Minangkabau*, pp. 99, 145.

land, the sawah. The mamak supervised its equal division among his sisters. No consideration was given to the relative size of the constituent families to be supported, but rather each received an equal portion. This matrilineality in inheritance practice among the Minangkabau has long confounded outside observers, because the Minangkabau were, at the same time, an intensely Islamic people. Islam has a strong patrilineal bias and, though *Shariah* law divides property among children of both sexes, the males receive the greater share. In Minangkabau, such Islamic concepts of inheritance tended to influence the disposal of a man's personally acquired property, which adat did allow him to leave to his children. But, even here, the matrilineal family exercised a good deal of influence. The problems of inheritance were, and are, so complicated and so intertwined with adat regulations that the Islamic courts in West Sumatra consistently refused to hear inheritance disputes.[5]

Strict regulations prevented alienation of the family's harta pusaka. Movable property, and of that usually only items considered of a "personal" nature such as jewelry, might be pawned on a short term basis to raise money for almost any need, but this still required prior consent from the mamak and anyone else thought to have rights over the item to be pawned.[6] Immovable property, principally sawah, could only be pawned to raise money to meet an adat requirement whose neglect would reflect badly on the whole family or lineage and thereby diminish its reputation within the community. Only four situations were considered important enough to warrant pawning a parcel of family land: burial of a family member; marriage of a spinster sister; repairs to the family house; and installation of the lineage penghulu.[7] Pawning family land required the unanimous consent of all members. Land had to be pawned to some individual or family within the same lineage if possible and preferably within the same branch; as a last resort, however, the land could be pawned to someone from another lineage within the same village. Adat prohibited any alienation of land or its profits to an "outsider."

Adat restrictions governing land alienation had two important

---

5 Nancy Tanner, "Disputing and Dispute Settlement among the Minangkabau of Indonesia," *Indonesia*, 8 (October 1969), p. 51.
6 Batuah and Madjoindo, *Tambo Minangkabau*, p. 91.
7 Ibid., p. 92.

consequences in terms of the continuing competition for power and position. An individual could not own land and, therefore, no one could acquire large tracts of it for permanent use as an independent nonfamily source of personal wealth and power. If one wished to acquire a personal fortune, it was necessary to look elsewhere, usually outside the village to the sphere of the market town. Because land was usually pawned within the lineage, the major focus of the competition for power was contained within a relatively limited circle. Interlineage competition on matters of village importance also existed, but the major energies were devoted to the ongoing intralineage jockeying for leadership and prestige.

Despite the seemingly levelling effect of a system which did not allow permanent alienation of land, branches within the lineage continuously changed economic, and hence social and political, position, relative to each other. If a family were obliged to finance a series of expensive ceremonies in close succession (for example, the funeral of an important family member soon after the wedding of an eldest daughter), accumulated wealth might be exhausted, forcing the family to pawn property to raise the needed funds. This was a double hardship when the property pawned was sawah land, because the family not only owed money but had lost future income from the land as well; this made it that much more difficult to get out of debt. Since the land should not be removed from lineage jurisdiction, other branches or families in the lineage which had not had any major expenditures recently or, alternatively, which had members abroad who earned extra money for the family, would loan the money and acquire the profits from the land. These changes in financial status had political as well as economic ramifications, for wealth acted as an important criterion when it came to choosing the lineage chief, the penghulu. A decline in the fortunes of a penghulu family could cause it to lose possession of the penghulu-ship to a newly emerging, wealthier family.

Every family continually worked to increase its base wealth, the harta pusaka. The main core of wealth, the *pusaka tinggi* (lit. high pusaka) inherited from the original ancestors, was considered the property of the entire lineage, but individual families and lineage branches possessed other property which belonged in common only to their particular unit. Additional land could also be acquired by reclaiming new sawah or *ladang* (nonirrigated, generally hillside, fields). The "ownership" of a given parcel of land belonged to the family (and their heirs) who had first tilled that patch of soil.[8] During his lifetime, the person who had established the plot controlled it and its proceeds, and, theoretically at least, he could freely make decisions concerning it without his mamak's consent.[9] But as it usually happened that the tiller had required family capital to finance his initial operation, he was not entirely free of supervision by the mamak, acting as formal guardian of family investments. Privately acquired property was called the *harta pencarian*, and it too became part of the family's communal harta pusaka at the death of the person who had first acquired it. As a result, the family as a whole would keep a close watch during the "owner's" lifetime to make certain that their potential harta pusaka wealth was not being wastefully used.

Wealth, other than land, which an individual accumulated during his lifetime was also included in his harta pencarian and also reverted to his mother's lineage at his death. Most such additional wealth was earned outside the village by Minangkabau merchants or artisans, two occupations for which people from the region were famous throughout the western archipelago. Such business ventures were usually undertaken with the expectation that the profits would increase markedly the harta pusaka and hence improve the entire family's power position within the lineage.

Father/Son Relationships

The issue of individual property was important because it was often entangled in the more specific problem of a man's relationship to his children vis-à-vis his obligations to his *kemanakan* (his sisters' children). The ambiguity surrounding this question could easily create an atmosphere of intense rivalry between sisters and wives over disposition of property. Worried sisters would accuse a brother of spoiling his own children instead of fulfilling his traditional duties toward his nephews and nieces, who, according to strict interpretation of adat, had first claim on his attentions. Obviously, personal affection could influence the man's

---

8 "Bijdrage tot de Kennis van het Grondbezit op Sumatra," *Tijdschrift voor Nederlandsch Indië* [henceforth *TNI*], 14, 1 (1852), p. 109.

9 Edwin M. Loeb, *Sumatra: Its History and People* (Vienna: Institute für Völkerkunde, 1935), p. 108.

decisions, and thus conditions existed for constant competition among youngsters for attention from their fathers and uncles.

General custom provided that all property, whether individually acquired or inherited, belonged to the matrilineal family, and hence to sisters and their children, upon the death of the owner. But this was not a hard and fast rule. Children, for example, were not automatically excluded from all inheritance of their father's property. They could receive a share of his personally acquired goods if he had so specified before his death and with the prior agreement of his lineage.[10] In general, however, only movable wealth earned through personal labor could be bequeathed.[11]

Minangkabau adat also accepted the right of a person to cede temporary rights over immovable property, similar to provisions in Islamic law. Such grants, called by the Arabic word *hibah*, could be conferred upon a wife, children, or even a total outsider, but they expired on the death of the recipient, and the property returned to the original holder or his lineage heirs.

Personal accounts by Minangkabau tend to support the contention that it was in more intensely Islamic families that patrilineal elements were most pronounced. Hamka [H. A. Malik Karim Amrullah], an important postindependence Minangkabau writer and religious leader, recalled that, although during his childhood he lived first with his mother's people, his father, a noted Islamic scholar, intended from Hamka's birth that he would also become an *ulama* (religious teacher). Thus, when his father divorced his mother, Hamka went to live with his father—an unusual practice since children are considered members of their mother's lineage.[12] Another Minangkabau writer, Muhammad Radjab, related a similar childhood relationship with his father, also a respected religious teacher.[13] In each instance, the Islamic pattern of paternal supervision prevailed on matters concerning the boy's future and his residence.

---

10 A.M. Datuk Maruhun Batuah and D. H. Bagindo Tanameh, *Hukum Adat dan Adat Minangkabau: Luhak nan Tiga, Laras nan Dua* (Jakarta: Poesaka Aseli, n.d.), p. 51.
11 Loeb, *Sumatra*, p. 108. See also letter of the Governor of Sumatra's West Coast, August 15, 1861; Advice of the Council of Justice, Padang; and the Decision of the Governor General, February 15, 1862, No. 27, *Verbaal*, April 23, 1862, No. 9.
12 Hamka, *Kenang-Kenangan Hidup* (Kuala Lumpur: Pustaka Antara, 1966).
13 Muhammad Radjab, *Semasa Ketjil di Kampung (1913-1928): Autobiografi Seorang Anak Minangkabau* (Jakarta: Balai Pustaka, 1950).

Pre-Islamic adat, however, apparently also recognized a bond between father and children. According to tradition, one of the two legendary founders of the Minangkabau adat generally stressed a somewhat patrilineal orientation. The royal families and some of the self-styled nobility of the coastal and highlands areas, who proclaim adherence to this adat interpretation, tend to emphasize the paternal lines of descent. A common proverB, reputed to be of an early origin, described the proper relationship of a man as one which gave protectiveness to his children and guidance to his kemanakan.[14] The social protest novels of the twentieth century depict Minangkabau adat as creating intense and irrational conflicts between men and their sisters over alleged favoritism to children as against nephews.[15] In practice, however, intense conflict occurred only rarely in the village.

The Penghulu Suku

The important position in each descent unit was that of mamak, and as the mamak supervised progressively larger numbers of dependents, called *anak buah*, his own power increased proportionately. A mamak was supposed to foster his dependents, protect them, and provide for their needs. Standing in roughly the same position vis-à-vis the entire suku was the *penghulu suku* (usually shortened to penghulu), designated by the honorific title *datuk* (abbreviated as Dt.). He served also as the pinnacle of the adat hierarchy represented by the suku. As such, he was charged with executing the principles of the adat which affect the suku and which govern the relationship between his suku and others, his suku and the village, his suku and the greater world outside. He represented the interests of the lineage in village government, most importantly in the partition of uncultivated lands and assignments of rights to forest and other communal properties. The position of penghulu, as with that of the mamak, generally passed from mother's brother to sister's son. It is also worth noting here that the Minangkabau adat was not in fact

---

14 The exact proverb reads: Anak di pangku, Kemanakan di bimbing [The child in the lap, the nephew held by the hand]. Darwis Thaib, Dt. Sidi Bandaro, *Seluk-Beluk Adat Minangkabau* (Jakarta: Nusantara, 1965), pp. 78-79.

15 One such novel is: Marah Rusli, *Sitti Nurbaja: Kasih Tak Sampai* (Jakarta: Balai Pustaka, 1965).

matriarchal, though many continue to identify it as such. Power and the administration of family affairs resided not with the women but with the men. The maternal line was important in determining which men.

According to adat tradition, a specific family—one which claimed, whether accurately or not, the closest proximity to the founding female of the lineage in that village—held a hereditary right to the title of penghulu. The penghulu should be chosen, in theory, from among the wisest, most capable, and clearest sighted males of the eligible lineage—a clever speaker, truthful, patient, just, experienced in adat customs, trustworthy, and of reputable family on both his mother's and his father's sides.[16] In reality, the penghulu-designate usually owed his nomination to his family's wealth and personal influence, as exercised in the struggle of intralineage politics. The penghulu-ship often rotated among a specified group of lineage branches. Sometimes this accorded with long-established custom but more often it represented changes in power relationships among branches, as for instance after the gradual decline of a traditional penghulu family and its subsequent replacement by a rival branch.

Wealth played an important role in the rise and fall of penghulu families. The installation of a penghulu involved long and expensive ceremonies, including mass feasts for the lineage members and villagers, lavish popular entertainments and gifts. Obviously, an impoverished family would be unable to maintain its paramountcy in the face of such expenditures and would be forced to surrender the title. Tradition verifies the need for wealth, with the self-serving explanation that a poor penghulu would be a burden to the whole lineage because it would have to underwrite his official and personal expenses.[17]

The total number of penghulu in a given village varied over time. When the number of members in a lineage increased greatly, the lineage often divided into autonomous units, each with its own penghulu. The title of the new penghulu usually contained some element of the original title to indicate the relationship. If the suku Sikumbang, for example, had a penghulu entitled Datuk Narajau, but the suku had outgrown the

---

16 Batuah and Tanameh, *Hukum Adat*, pp. 17-19.
17 Ibid., p. 17. In more recent times, a lineage often leaves the position of penghulu vacant until a suitable candidate comes of age or returns from abroad, or, if the problem is financial, until the family saves enough.

ability of one man to administer, then it would split into two penghulu-ships, each retaining the suku name of Sikumbang. The new chief might be known as Datuk Narajau Mudo (the Younger Daruk Narajau) or alternatively the original chieftain might assume an enhanced title such as Datuk Narajau Besar (the Greater Datuk Narajau).[18] Such actions had to be ratified by the lineage and be approved by the other village lineages. Sometimes, the split in the title represented not increased lineage size but a compromise solution to a quarrel over possession of the title. In order to prevent a permanent and bitter rupture of relations between families, the lineage might decide to recognize each disputant as penghulu over his own faction, but the titles would be changed somewhat to differentiate between them—for example, Datuk Narajau Kuning (the Yellow Datuk Narajau) and Datuk Narajau Hitam (the Black Datuk Narajau).

The opposite process could also occur. A lineage, because of an epidemic or a declining birthrate, might have only a few, or mostly female, descendants, and thus be too small to support a penghulu of its own. The family might then decide to merge its interests with another branch within the same larger lineage. Usually the small family merely kept its own penghulu title in abeyance until it grew large enough to support one again. In the meantime, its members placed themselves under the temporary protection of another lineage. Sometimes they agreed to combine the titles and create a new position; thus Datuk Narajau and Datuk Malekewi might become Datuk Narajau Malekewi.[19]

The pressure was always strong among wealthy upwardly mobile families to capture the position of penghulu. By accumulating much mortgaged land or outside wealth from trade, a new family could, in effect, "purchase" the title from a longstanding but faltering penghulu family. This was not an indication of inherent instability in the adat structure or a symptom of gradual decay; rather expansion and decline in the number of datuk and the shift of the title from one lineage branch to another indicated an ongoing ability to absorb and adapt to changing relationships among various branches or individuals within the same branch.

---

18 Nofian, S. H. Lecturer at the Law Faculty of the University of Andalas, Padang. Interview, July 14, 1967.
19 Stibbe, "Het Soekoebestuur in de Padangsche Bovenlanden," *TNI*, 3 (3rd Series) (1869), p. 33. Such combined titles may later split apart again if the component families increase in size.

In order to wrest the title from the current holder, an emergent family needed strong support among other lineage branches and within the village generally. Other groups had to believe that the aspiring family would be in a better position to exercise authority than the existing penghulu line. Given such support, and especially in cases where the penghulu family had no obviously capable candidate of its own, the incumbent family could be forced to relinquish the title or else compromise and divide the lineage leadership into two penghulu-ships.[20]

Subordinate Lineage Positions

The penghulu usually relied upon subordinates to help administer lineage affairs. Foremost among these was the *malim* (sometimes called the imam) who acted as the suku's highest religious authority and the person responsible for those adat affairs which had religious overtones— for example, marriage and divorce. The *manti* (or *chatib*) acted as a kind of "examining magistrate" and clerk, to hear complaints about adat infringements, and also as a formal communications link between the penghulu and his dependents.[21] The *dubalang* (or *hulubalang*) exercised the "police power" of the penghulu; probably his office evolved from that of the suku *panglima* (military leader), a position more crucial in the days when the lineage was organized on a martial basis, and fighting to maintain its rights vis-à-vis other suku or, combined with other suku, to defend the area against outside incursions.[22] Over time, the dubalang came to act more as an enforcer of decisions by the penghulu or of specific adat provisions governing lineage affairs than as a general.

In addition to these specific offices, there existed a group of petty functionaries called the *pegawai*; they delivered invitations to adat functions, escorted people on ceremonial occasions, and performed other tasks of a bureaucratic or ritual nature, supporting the penghulu or his assistants.[23] The community also included a recognized but

---

20 Report of G. A. Baud to the King, June 18, 1830, *Verbaal*, August 13, 1830, No. 42.
21 Verkerk Pistorius, *Inlandsche Huishouding*, p. 91; Batuah and Tanameh, *Hukum Adat*, p. 28.
22 Batuah and Tanameh, *Hukum Adat*, p. 28; L. C. Westenenk, *De Minangkabausche Nagari* (Weltevreden: Visser, 1918), p. 59.
23 Batuah and Tanameh, *Hukum Adat*, p. 28.

amorphous body of people called the *cerdik-pandai* (lit. the clever ones), best described as the "pillars of the community." Although they did not hold any formal adat office, they were usually consulted on important community decisions. The cerdik-pandai included the skilled, the wealthy, the clever, and the prestigious, in short, anyone who had influence in the community. Their agreement would be essential for village decisions. Consent and cooperation were crucial; the rather loosely structured social and political system and the geographic mobility of the people made coercion difficult. To avoid conflict, as many elements as possible were drawn into the decision-making process, or at least nominally consulted.

The fundamental concept operating both within the lineage and in the supra-lineage sphere was that of mutual obligation. In Minangkabau, the relationship was most generally expressed in the kinship terminology of the mamak (uncle, guardian, or, simply, patron) to his kemanakan (nephew, dependent, or, simply, client), and one's position in the community could be as much a reflection of the prestige and position of one's mamak as of one's own achievements. Any newcomer, called an *orang datang* (lit. person who comes), who planned to settle in a village needed a mamak who could serve as the connecting link in making him a recognized member of village society. He had to belong to someone; someone had to take responsibility for him in the village, and frequently a newcomer would choose a particular village because he had distant relatives there, the result of wandering on the part of a male forebear. Failing the presence of a blood relative, the orang datang sought someone of the same suku name, or a close business associate.

Despite adoption by a local mamak, the orang datang could not hold any office in his adopted lineage because he was not a maternal descendant of the lineage founder. Otherwise, in most matters, he was considered equal to other individual family members. His advice was often sought on family matters, and he was not regarded as a servant or slave in the household.[24]

A common type of orang datang was the ulama (religious scholar) come to study or teach in a nearby mosque school. He might only stay

---

24 Ibid., pp. 16-17.

a few years before moving on again, but, if he was an adult, he usually married a village girl and became, albeit peripherally, a part of village society.

The individual orang datang was usually a transient and thus his "second class" status rarely became an issue. Occasionally, however, whole families moved to new villages. In the late eighteenth century, for example, refugee families were especially common in areas affected by the militant Padri, who sought to purify village society and reorganize it on the basis of revolutionary Islam. Penghulu families often fled in the face of the new force and many never returned, settling permanently in another village. These families had to be recognized by the nagari council in the new village before they could receive rights to use land for building houses and planting crops. Lacking traditional land rights placed new families at a disadvantage, because they had no burial land in the village, a significant factor determining who really "belonged." Possession of land was important in deciding who was a person of "consequence" in local affairs. Even should a new family be wealthy or gain control of enough property by moneylending that other villagers were forced to acknowledge its de facto power, yet for a long time it was considered second class vis-à-vis founding families—a mere transient among the permanent residents.[25]

Slavery and Debt Bondage

The orang datang were treated as full members of society in most matters other than those concerned with inheritance and disposition over family properties and privileges within the adopted lineage. In precolonial village society, there were also people who were definitely regarded as inferior to other villagers—the slaves and bondsmen.[26]

Gradations and styles of slavery varied, depending on the circumstances of entering servitude. Since the advent of Islam in Minangkabau, slaves were supposed to be taken only from among non-Muslim peoples, in this case the pagan people of Nias, Mentawei, Tapanuli, and Riau. Slaves

---

25 Ibid., p. 41.
26 Ibid., p. 17.

and their descendants lived in satellite settlements attached to most of the larger villages, especially the important rice-growing villages of the highland plains. They provided the main source of labor for the fields and households, working as day laborers and sharing the harvested crop.[27] Unable to marry anyone from the so-called *orang patut* (lit. the proper people) of the village,[28] they usually remained dependent on their former masters for their economic and social position. Their best chance of escaping this situation was to seek refuge in the relative anonymity of the coastal towns as apprentices or workers for artisans, traders, or sailors.

In addition to the captured or purchased slaves, the village labor force often included many debt bondsmen, temporarily attached to their creditors in lieu of payment for debts. Such persons became full members of the society again once their period of service was over, although they probably were still considered of rather low status by virtue of their poverty and former "slave" status.[29]

Nagari Government

The basic geographic and political unit in Minangkabau has traditionally been the nagari, generally comprising a large village with its satellite settlements. Nagari size varied widely both in geographic extent and in total population. Numbering perhaps as many as 600, in the precolonial period these districts ranged from a few hundred persons in underpopulated fringe areas and hills to a few thousand in densely settled plains.[30] Actual area covered probably varied inversely to the size

---

27 E. B. Kielstra, *Sumatra's Westkust, 1819-1890,* 1 (The Hague: Bijdragen reprint, 5th series, n.d.), p. 136.

28 J. F. M. de Rooij, "De Positie der Volkshoofden in een Gedeelte der Padangsche Bovenlanden: Hunne Ethnographische en Hunne Politieke Beteekenis," dated Soeliki March 15, 1889, Koninklijke Instituut voor Taal-, Land- en Volkenkunde [henceforth KITLV] Manuscript, H 594.

29 Ibid.

30 The exact size in area and population of the individual nagari for the nineteenth century was not available to me. The Adat Council of West Sumatra issued a list in 1967 which recognized 544 nagari determined according to adat requirements. *Daftar Nama-Nama Kode Kabupaten/ Kotamadya Nomor Urutan Ketjamatan dan Kenegarian Se-Sumatera Barat* (Padang: Lembaga Kerapatan Adat Alam Minangkabau, 1967). The Census of 1920 recorded 578 districts, a colonial district was usually equivalent to a nagari. *Uitkomsten der in de Maand November 1920 Gehouden Volkstelling,* II (Batavia: Drukkerijen Ruygrok, 1922). How far this can be taken to reflect the actual number of precolonial nagari, I am unable to determine, but I would assume there to be a

of the population, there being many fewer nagari in the thinly settled hills where agricultural conditions required more land in the form of ladang and forests. For example, the relatively small region of Agam in 1967 had some 73 nagari while the extensive Pasaman region in the north had only 48.[31]

The satellite settlements included both the colonies of laborers who worked the lineage rice fields and the new villages established by members of the lineages from the core village. Even after they had grown into separate and autonomous nagari, these settlements continued to recognize their historic relationship to the mother nagari (*induk nagari*) in their own *tambo* (histories).[32] Often certain rituals continued to require participation by "observers" from the induk nagari and in quarrels within or among new settlements, the induk nagari might be called upon to mediate.[33]

Presiding over the affairs of the nagari and interactions among its constituent lineages, was a council formed of the lineage chiefs, the penghulu suku. In nagari which accepted the hierarchical and quasi-authoritarian adat style called Koto Piliang, certain penghulu were designated as *penghulu pucuk*, paramount chiefs with greater authority in council sessions. Seating arrangements and other outward marks of superiority set these men off from other penghulu in the council. Even villages belonging to the so-called egalitarian tradition of the Bodi Caniago adat style, which did not formally install penghulu pucuk, still recognized certain penghulu as having greater weight in council decisions by virtue (supposedly) of particular personal qualities and their family's status.[34] The recognized distinction in both cases was generally cited as that between original or founding families, considered the "owners" of

---

close correlation since the nagari are generally adat-organized rather than government-organized divisions.

31 *Daftar Nama-Nama,* pp. 1-4 and 8-9.
32 P.J. Kooreman, "De Rechtspraak in de Burgerlijke Zaken van de Maleiers ter Sumatra's Westkust: Voorheen en Thans," *TNI*, I (NS) (1902), p. 916.
33 J. van den Linden, "Het Inlandsch Bestuur in het Gouvernement van Suma tra's Westkust," *Tijdschrift van het Bataviaasch Genootschap van Kunsten en Wetenschappen* [henceforth *TBG*], 4 (1885), p. 263.
34 Nofian, S. H., interview, July 14, 1967, in Padang; G. de Waal, "Aanteekeningen Betreffende het Adat-Bestuur in de Onder-Afdeeling Soloq," *Tijdschrift voor het Binnenlandsch Bestuur* [henceforth *TBB*], 3 (1889), pp. 67-69.

the nagari land because they had first opened it to settlement, and the relatively recent arrivals, considered merely "occupiers" of land because they had "received" it on arrival from the founding lineages.[35]

The preeminence of particular penghulu in nagari affairs followed more closely their achieved position in society than their ancestors' arrival dates in the area. No two nagari "adat authorities" can ever agree on which families were the original settlers; each asserting that at least one family currently in the ascendant is an upstart heir of a "new arrival." Families on the decline were naturally anxious to retain their hold as penghulu pucuk, but even should they keep the nominal designation, their advice often passed unheeded, once their status in the nagari had otherwise declined. Dutch experience confirmed the occurrence of changes among "paramount chiefs." For example, as part of a twentieth-century reorganization program, a government-sponsored *rapat nagari* (nagari council) was to be established in each nagari. It was to be composed of only the so-called core penghulu (*kern penghulu*). But villagers could not agree upon which families should be included.[36]

Nagari often joined together in loose confederations which acted in concert in cases of mutual need or against outside aggression. In most cases, these federations seem not to have been negotiated political alliances but rather represented a group of nagari which, over time, had come to think of themselves as a single unit. Often, the sense of a common fate represented a believed descent from a common induk nagari; in other cases, they had at some time in the past actually banded together effectively in an alliance for a specific end and had retained the feeling of association.

Changing perceptions about the ranking of families, relations between the nagari, and indeed society in general allowed the traditional Minangkabau village to accept the realities of life without discarding the verities of adat. Adat was vague and ambiguous and some portion of it could always be found to justify any given change when this became desirable, or, perhaps, unavoidable. That is not to imply, however, that change was always accomplished harmoniously or that once one view had

---

35 De Rooij, "De Positie der Volkshoofden."
36 H. S. Stap, "De Nagari-Ordonnantie ter Sumatra's Westkust," *TBB*, 53 (1917), p. 704.

prevailed on a given issue, its adherents could assume that the opposite faction would acquiesce permanently, or even gracefully. But a major function of adat was to help at least smooth over the rough edges and try to prevent any violent explosion which might cause a permanent rupture of relations. For those Minangkabau who could not be reconciled and for those others who wished to regroup their energies for another assault on the status quo, it was always possible to leave the village and thereby avoid the confrontation—or at least postpone it for awhile.

CHAPTER TWO
THE VILLAGE AND THE WORLD BEYOND

Although in many ways the nagari are self-contained units, worlds motivated by the internal play of politics and the struggle to attain wealth and prestige, the villagers are well aware of the world outside. Many rely on that outside world for supplements to their daily livelihood, mainly through a process known as *merantau*, meaning to go abroad. The village society as a whole has also always had relations with the outside. Some of these resulted from institutional arrangements, such as those with the Minangkabau raja, and some are the consequences of historical forces moving in the outer world, for example the Islamic revolution of the early nineteenth century. These different types of outside relationships affected the village in different ways, reflecting, in the course of the interaction, inherent strengths and weaknesses in village society and sometimes in the outside elements also.

The Raja of Pagarruyung

In theory, at least, the various Minangkabau nagari, which otherwise acted much like petty autonomous republics, were joined into one geographic and political entity under the Yang Dipertuan Besar (He Who is Made Great), the Raja of Pagarruyung, the Ruler of Minangkabau. His position, at the supranagari level, in function and design corresponded roughly to that of the penghulu at the nagari level. Two other "raja" were subordinate to him, the Raja Adat (Ruler over Adat Affairs) and the Raja Ibadat (Ruler over Religious Affairs).[1] It has been variously suggested that these two

---

1 P. E. de Josselin de Jong, *Minangkabau and Negri Sembilan: Socio-Political Structure in Indonesia*

represented two major geographic subdivisions within the kingdom or that they served merely as cosmological symbols of the Minangkabau world order.[2] The Minangkabau royal epic, the *Kaba Cindua Mato,* credits these raja with actual jurisdiction over issues within their respective realms of adat and religion. For example, when the hero Cindua Mato infringes on an important adat custom, the Raja Adat convenes a council to hear the case and consider the punishment; then he delivers the council's decision to the Raja of Pagarruyung. This seems to suggest that the ruler did not, or should not, intervene directly in the daily affairs of the kingdom but rather ratify the advice of others charged with investigation and making decisions.[3]

In fact, however, the organization, jurisdiction, and even the origin of the Kingdom and the Raja of Minangkabau have never been satisfactorily explained. According to the most prevalent tradition, the first raja was a Hindu-Javanese prince named Adityavarman. He arrived in West Sumatra only after the system of lineage government under the penghulu and the organization of the independent nagari was well-established. Because the land had already been divided among the nagari, the new ruler could not amass any independent blocks of territory.[4]

It is difficult to know whether the Raja ever exercised important political power, as the first written evidence about the kingdom comes only in the sixteenth century from European observers. By that time, the Raja and his chief ministers exercised only nominal preeminence—and even that was confined largely to Tanah Datar, the district immediately surrounding the royal palace at Pagarruyung.[5] Such physical intervention in village life as did occur was probably limited to periodic visits by the Raja to receive tribute, usually in rice or gold, as evidence of his people's

---

(Jakarta: Bhratara, 1960), pp. 13-14.
2 William Marsden, *The History of Sumatra* (London: J. McCreery, 1811), pp. 282-83; de Josselin de Jong, *Minangkabau and Negri Sembilan,* pp. 107-11.
3 A fuller discussion of the royal myth is contained in: Taufik Abdullah, "Some Notes on the Kaba Tjindua Mato: An Example of Minangkabau Traditional Literature," *Indonesia,* 9 (April 1970), pp. 1-22.
4 A. M. Batuah and D. H. Bagindo Tanameh, *Hukum Adat dan Adat Minangkabau: Luhak nan Tiga Laras nan Dua* (Jakarta: Pusaka Aseli, n.d.), p. 30.
5 A traditional account reports that the court's decline was precipitated by a seventeenth-century succession dispute. Ahmad Dt. Batuah and A. Dt. Madjoindo, *Tambo Minangkabau dan Adatnja* (Jakarta: Balai Pustaka, 1956), p. 42.

veneration and his own presumed imperial rule. One should perhaps view the Kingdom of Minangkabau as in fact merely the collective name for a multitude of independent petty "states," united by virtue of their common origin, language, and custom. The lack of a superior authority meant that nagari quarrels could be solved only by local mediation and, as a last resort, by warfare.

The outer frontiers of the Minangkabau kingdom were ruled by local lords, also termed "raja," who, according to tradition, were descendants of royal viceroys dispatched from Pagarruyung. In these outer areas, one found a pronounced trend toward a more patrilineal, hierarchical, and authoritarian type of society—similar to that associated with the Pagarruyung court—than the usual pattern prevailing in the Minangkabau nagari. The ruling families of Padang, Pariaman, and other coastal towns of the west are also called raja, and they too claim a direct blood kinship and historical political ties with Pagarruyung. They say they are the descendants of viceroys sent to administer the ports and collect customs tolls in the name of the Raja.[6]

The royal preference for patrilineality and formal hierarchical arrangement of rank and status tended to set it even more apart from the general highlands village pattern. It was perhaps intentionally so, a way to affirm royal superiority and prerogative through uniqueness. The existence of the royal-style system in the fringe areas may reflect the late absorption of these settlements into the Minangkabau cultural sphere, that is, that they were incorporated into Minangkabau after the organization of the Pagarruyung court and perhaps at its direct initiative. Whatever the reason, the raja families both in Pagarruyung and on the rantau are the only ones which avowedly and consistently adhere to the more authoritarian and hierarchical of the two Minangkabau adat styles—the Koto Piliang.[7]

Even though the Raja of Pagarruyung was technically supposed to be outside the adat system entirely, the members of his administration

---

6 Padang raja families, interview, August 10, 1967, Alang Lawas, Padang.
7 A description of the two systems and their legendary founders, Datuk Perpatih nan Sebatang (Bodi Caniago) and Datuk Tumenggung (Koto Piliang) can be found in, among others, Batuah and Tanameh, *Hukum Adat,* pp. 20-31, and Batuah and Madjoindo, *Tambo Minangkabau,* pp. 33-38.

were in fact all representatives of the Koto Piliang adat style, and the Raja himself was recognized as the titular head for that system. The traditional supreme representative of the other adat style, the Bodi Caniago, was also located near Pagarruyung; he was the Datuk Bandaro Kuning of Lima Kaum, a small village outside Batu Sangkar. He was not considered a member of the royal court, but the king supposedly would consult him in times of external threat which required concerted action by all Minangkabau.[8]

Insofar as most villagers were concerned, however, the existence of the Raja at Pagarruyung was not a matter of concern in their everyday lives (with the possible exception of the inhabitants of villages in the immediate geographic vicinity of the palace).

Merantau

The most important interaction between the villagers and the outside world was through the process known as merantau, which means to go to the rantau, that is, to go abroad. Rantau, in this context, could be anywhere beyond the village—as near as the local market town or a religious school in a neighboring village; or as far as the ports of Riau or the markets of Batavia.

The rantau was as much an experience as a geographic destination. The village man actively sought out the rantau; he consciously decided to leave home and family and to try and make it on his own. The ease with which this was possible resulted in large measure from the network of relationships represented by the notion of mutual obligation between the mamak and his kemanakan. Common ties of blood, village of birth, or similarity of lineage name set up patterns for geographic movement within Minangkabau and in other areas where groups of Minangkabau had established semipermanent settlements. Families with long-established traditions of merantau could usually locate a kinsman in any major town almost anywhere in West Sumatra (and, since the nineteenth century, almost any major city in Indonesia as well).

---

8 The incumbent Datuk Bandaro Kuning, V Kaum (Batu Sangkar), interviews, August 21 and 22, 1967, in Batu Sangkar.

The families with the most strongly developed tradition of merantau can be divided into two different, though not mutually exclusive, categories—Islamic scholars and petty traders (or artisans). Typically, in the major highlands rice areas, these families had middle (probably lower middle) level socioeconomic status. They had income from rice cultivation which was sufficient for subsistence but not enough to confer importance in village society. In hillside and other marginal villages with insufficient sawah land to support an essentially landed elite, almost every family (except the very poor and the very rich) had a tradition of merantau. The young men would leave home while in their early teens, either as apprentices to someone from their family or village who had gone before or else as freelance artisans or traders. In such villages, one finds that many penghulu were successful traders in their youth and gained prestige as a result; they returned to live in the village as permanent residents only after acceding to their titles. Merantau was an esteemed institution in such villages and was often idealized as the proper road to maturity and success; in some areas, it took on the role of an initiation into adult life.

The Minangkabau social system both facilitated and stimulated the exodus of males; especially unmarried youth. Supervision of agriculture was, to a large extent, in the hands of women. They organized the family's dependent laborers and also assisted directly in the fields themselves when necessary. In a practical sense, young men had no responsibilities directly connected with daily life in the village. Until marriage, they were at loose ends, having no family to look after.[9]

After the age of puberty, young boys could no longer sleep in their mother's house but rather went to the surau at night. Traveling students, religious scholars, and merchants also stayed at the surau when passing through the area. Thus the surau acted as a center for information and contacts about life outside the village. Such experiences created among

---

9 As with most other things Minangkabau, this custom has been honored with a proverb: Keratau medang ke hulu; berbuah, berbunga belum, kerantau bujang dahulu; di rumah berguna belum. The first two phrases set the rhyme scheme, the second two state that the bachelor goes to the rantau first because he is not yet needed (i.e., has no use) at home. Siegel describes a similar process in Aceh. There, the young men leave the village to work on the pepper fields in the rantau because they are not needed at home. James Siegel, *The Rope of God* (Berkeley: University of California, 1969), pp. 48-57.

the young village men an interest in travel.[10] The Minangkabau author Mohammad Radjab, in his reminiscences about life in the hill village of Sulit Air, recalled the tremendous attraction the perantau life had for young boys. They romanticized it as the way to future success, prestige, and a good marriage. Anyone who did not join in merantau, and yet had no particular position or excuse which required his continued presence at home, was ridiculed by his friends.[11]

The perantau usually returned home every year during the fasting month of Ramadan. Initially they came to marry; later, they came to visit wives and children. They also renewed ties with relatives and neighbors. A woman was not permitted to leave her mother's home and thus could not accompany her husband abroad. The returning perantau brought the profits of a year's business to invest in family projects. These profits were used to repair the family house, extend sawah and ladang holdings, repossess pawned lands, and finance marriages or other important ceremonies. Excess money was invested in gold, usually made into jewelry.[12] This extra capital coming from outside enabled the families with small sawah holdings to continue the matrilineal system relatively unchanged by funding the large family house and permitting the continued maintenance of the women and children in it. The profit made on the rantau could be used to rebuild family fortunes, and, if the perantau were really successful, he might use his money to make loans to other families in the lineage, thereby gaining control of more land. Eventually, his family might have enough wealth to take over the lineage penghulu-ship.

Not all families, or even all areas, placed a positive value on the merantau tradition. In the sawah-rich villages especially, the perantau element was fairly small, increasing perhaps in times of general agricultural decline. The perantau's main driving force, despite the "idealistic rationale" that it was initiation into adult life, came from the need for additional wealth to support the family in the village. In most places, with the exception of

---

10 Bahder Djohan, formerly Minister of Education, interview, June 1, 1967, in Jakarta; Iljas Sutan Pamenan, author and teacher, interview, February 28, 1967, in Jakarta.
11 Muhammad Radjab, *Semasa Ketjil di Kampung (1913-1928): Autobiografi Seorang Anak Minangkabau* (Jakarta: Balai Pustaka, 1950).
12 Radjab in his "autobiography" vividly describes the return of the perantau as seen through the eyes of a young boy.

some poorer hill settlements, the families of penghulu and other village notables had sufficient sawah or other wealth to provide for all members adequately. The penghulu, after all, was expected to be a man of means; he was supposed to be able to remain in the village in order to administer lineage affairs. He needed sufficient financial resources to support such a "non-productive" position.

Penghulu families often displayed a definite prejudice against the idea of merantau. Dismissing the idealized values attributed to perantau life by other segments of the community, these men identified it for what it in fact was, an admission of poverty or, at the least, of an inability to live in comfort without extra effort.[13] In a society where others had to find supplements for their yearly income, the penghulu's position was the more lofty because his family could support him without resort to merantau. This "aristocratic" prejudice against leaving home seemed most fully developed in the rich sawah areas of Agam, Tanah Datar, Solok, and Lima Puluh Kota, and also among the coastal nobility. Typical of this attitude was the assertion by a penghulu from the richest rice area in Tanah Datar that no one would want to merantau except in case of direst need—if he were poverty-stricken, or, in later days, because he feared the Dutch.[14]

The young boys in the rich sawah villages also gathered in the surau and also met the traveling merchants and teachers, but disinterest born of aristocratic prejudice and a comfortable life kept such boys from the rantau. These boys perhaps worked off excess adolescent energy in gambling, cock fighting or, if more inclined to quiet pursuits, in Islamic studies. Such young men of means probably married much earlier than those who had to go abroad. The richer and more extensive the sawah land, the greater the number of villagers whose incomes came mainly from rice agriculture, and the more the prevailing attitudes and values were those of the settled farmer rather than the adventurist merchant.

In addition to its economic aspects, however, merantau served as a kind of outlet for tensions which might easily build in the matrilineal family-centered society of village Minangkabau. It provided a kind of an "escape valve" which helped prevent social pressures from exploding.

---

13 Datuk Simaradjo of Simabur, V Kaum (Batu Sangkar), interview, August 30, 1967, in Batu Sangkar; penghulu of Kota nan IV (Payakambuh), interview, November 21, 1967.
14 Datuk Paduko Batuah of V Kaum (Batu Sangkar), interview, August 24, 1967, in V Kaum.

The energies and forces which might create tensions could flow outward. Moreover, they could be channeled to benefit the lineage and even village as a whole. An ambitious youth, tired of being known merely as a "member" of a particular lineage or the "nephew" of some important person, could legitimately build his own life elsewhere and still not cut off ties to his village, family, and adat. The family which desired power and prestige, but was deprived by the existing lineage status quo, could seek to overcome this by sponsoring perantau merchants and artisans. Lineages which had insufficient rice land to support everyone preferred to supplement it with merantau.

Islamic Institutions

The first major threat to the Minangkabau way of life in the nineteenth century grew out of local Islamic traditions. Minangkabau, along with Aceh to the north, had served traditionally as an important area for the study of Islam. Payakumbuh and Pariaman, especially, were noted educational centers which produced many famous religious scholars, ulama. Both areas possessed large and famous surau schools. Marsden suggested that Minangkabau was so important to the Islamic world that Sumatrans who could not make the pilgrimage to Mecca would at least try to visit one of the West Sumatra centers.[15]

Each surau center was closely associated with the prestige of an individual ulama, whose erudition had attracted the pupils to him. Some ulama were successful in transferring their aura to favored disciples, but usually the surau declined with the death of its teacher and either disappeared entirely or perhaps was revived again later by another scholar.

The most famous center in West Sumatra, and a good example of a successful Islamic educational foundation which survived its founder, is located outside the small coastal village of Ulakan near Pariaman. Its focus is the holy grave of Syekh Burhanuddin, an ulama of the late seventeenth century who reportedly first heard about Islam from a Muslim sailor and went to Aceh to study more about it. After returning to West Sumatra,

---

15 Marsden, *History of Sumatra*, p. 278.

he established a training center, in Ulakan, to facilitate the study and propagation of Islam in Minangkabau. But the kind of Islam which he taught was heavily infused with mysticism, and focused on the figure of the Syekh himself.[16]

Most of the other early Islamic centers were also formed as mystic brotherhoods or tarekat. The followers sought a mystical and spiritual experience guided by the ulama who was their leader. The story of the Syekh of Ulakan and that of corresponding syekh in the highlands illustrate also the relative newness and, by orthodox standards, the impurity of Islam in West Sumatra in the seventeenth century. When Islam arrived is not known, but as late as the sixteenth century, the Portuguese traveler Tome Pires reported that the Tiku-Pariaman area (in which Ulakan was located) was still heathen as was also most of the highlands interior; he believed that only one of the "three kings of Minangkabau" had so far been converted to Islam.[17]

The surau study centers were probably the major departure points for the proselytizing of Minangkabau. Advanced students went to Aceh and perhaps the Middle East or India, and, on their return, they either assisted their former mentors or established new centers of their own elsewhere. Many students undoubtedly took up positions in village mosques helping those less learned or practiced to strengthen their belief and to fulfill the basic requirements of Islamic life.

The kind of Islam which spread out from these centers was heavily infused with mysticism and bore little relation to the religion envisaged by the Prophet, but then neither did the religion being practiced in Mecca or Medina during the same period.

The Padri Revolution

A series of individual and highly militant religious campaigns to purify Minangkabau Islam began in the late eighteenth century within the traditional isolated mosque study centers, particularly those located around the northern fringes of the plateau of Agam. It is probably

---

16 Current head of the Ulakan Religious Center, interview, November 15, 1967, in Ulakan, Pariaman.
17 Armando Cortesão, *The Suma Oriental of Tomé Pires* (London: Hakluyt Society, 1944), 1, p. 164.

not coincidental that these areas were also far from Pagarruyung, the traditional cultural and "political" center of Minangkabau and the focus for its adat "religious" rituals. At the beginning, there was no apparent cooperation among the reformers, all of whom sought to cleanse village Islam. They especially directed their attention to the rival Islamic centers, the tarekat, which, they charged, had diverted Islam from the pure religious discipline taught by Muhammad.

In subsequent European and Indonesian accounts, the reformers and their followers have been called Padri, though the origin and first use of the term itself is obscure.[18]

Whether or not there is a direct connection between the timing of the Padri campaign in West Sumatra and the Wahhabi reform movement in Arabia is another often debated issue. The Wahhabi movement like the Padri was a militant and puritanical campaign. The Wahhabi wanted to cleanse Arabian Islam of the accretions it had gained since the death of the Prophet, and those who refused to repent of their impious ways were dealt with summarily. The movement reached its peak about 1810 under sponsorship of the new Saudi dynasty, which rode to power on the crest of the reformist wave by using the awakened religious zeal to drive the Turks from the Arabian Peninsula.[19]

In its broad outlines, the Padri movement certainly pursued the same announced goal as the Wahhabi, that is, ridding local Islamic practice of pagan accretions. Some of the Minangkabau haji who led the Padri could well have been students in Mecca during the beginning of the Wahhabite campaign. According to Minangkabau tradition, local concern about the need for reform had existed already in the late eighteenth century but had only developed into a concerted and aggressive campaign against an "impure" Islam as a result of the catalytic effect of three haji who returned to the highlands in 1803.[20] The translation of their message of spiritual

---

18 An early discussion of the nomenclature problem is contained in H. J. J. L. Ridder de Stuers, *De Vestiging en Uitbreiding der Nederlanders ter Westkust van Sumatra* (Amsterdam: van Kampen, 1849-50), 1, p. 33.
19 R. Bayly Winder, *Saudi Arabia in the Nineteenth Century* (New York: St. Martins, 1965), pp. 1-16.
20 According to widely accepted tradition, the three haji were: Haji Miskin of Pandai Sikat (Agam); Haji Sumanik of VIII Kota (Solok); and Haji Piabang of Tanah Datar. The most complete summary of the conventional version of the Padri wars is in Muhammad Radjab, *Perang Paderi di Sumatera Barat: 1803-1838* (Jakarta: Perpustakaan Perguruan Kementerian P. P. & K., 1954).

reform into one of political and religious revolution was principally the work of four local leaders who had never been to Mecca—Tuanku nan Renceh of Kamang, Tuanku Passaman of Lintau, Tuanku Imam Bonjol of Alahan Pandjang, and Tuanku Rau of Rau.

As with the tarekat leaders, the reformers also gathered their followers into settlements on the periphery of established villages. But unlike their predecessors, these new religious teachers worked aggressively to convert neighboring villages to their ideas about a purified Islam. Asa result, friction grew and often erupted into open warfare.[21]

The absence of a strong central authority to serve as an alternative to the Padri and a rallying point to coordinate efforts against Padri aggression was an important contributing factor to the reformers' initial quick success. Nagari could not agree to cooperate until it was too late, and individual lineages within nagari often used the chaotic and uncertain situation to usurp power from others rather than cooperate in a common defense.[22]

One could argue, as later European observers sometimes did, that the Padri were consciously attempting to evolve a new political centralization using religious ties for bonds of loyalty and directed toward the total abolition of the penghulu by replacing them with a central authority, an imam.[23] The Padri leaders proposed not necessarily an end to the system of family chiefs but rather a closer supervision of it by zealous Islamic monitors. The major conflict arose between two different versions of Islam—the traditional accommodating and eclectic Islam (taught in the lineage surau and the village mosque) and the reformers' less tolerant and more puritanical version. The Padri collided with adat authorities about who should determine correct religious practice and its role in village life.

Adat leaders as well as "establishment" Islamic scholars joined both sides of the religious struggle. Imam Bonjol had as his sponsor and

---

21 The name Bonjol itself comes from one of these religious settlements, a hilltop fortress at Alahan Pandjang, which the local people called *bonjol*. The Dutch re-ferred to the whole village as Bonjol and eventually this became the commonly accepted name. Radjab, *Perang Paderi*, p. 27.

22 Emanuel Francis, "Register der Aanteekeningen en Verigtingen van den Resident van Sumatra' s Westkust, op eene Reis over Pariaman, Tiekoe en de Danouw naar de Padangsche Bovenlanden" (June 20-August 6, 1836), KITLV Manuscript, H 554a/H 554b, esp. the section dealing with the VIII Kota.

23 Report of the Resident of the Padang Highlands van der Hart, 1852, *Verbaal*, July 13, 1858, No. 35.

protector in Alahan Panjang the chief adat official in charge of religious affairs—the Rajo Ibadat. During Imam Bonjol's struggle with the leaders of Alahan Panjang, the major cleavage was not between Islamic scholars per se and adat officials; each side had penghulu as supporters. The split undoubtedly followed the lines of traditional political activity within the village and its lineages. After the Padri movement developed into open warfare against the Dutch, Imam Bonjol was supported by several penghulu in addition to his own religious disciples; he was later betrayed to the Dutch by a religious figure.[24] In Kamang (north of Bukittinggi, in the mountains), Padri chief Tuanku nan Renceh also had penghulu among his most ardent followers.[25]

The force of the Padri campaign to reform the village was partially diverted because they were themselves beyond the institutions of village rule. Most of the principal Padri leaders were men who were not tied by blood to the adat institutions of their village, and thus they had no particular authority according to local custom. Some were newcomers to the village, and others had descended from former orang datang adopted by local penghulu. Such men had no stake in the adat system and, at the same time, local adat officials could not enforce control over them with the techniques which could be applied to suku members. Being outside society also meant that Padri critiques of village life carried correspondingly less weight. They had no effective channel for introducing change short of persuasion or coercion.

The Padri, over the long term, proved unable to establish themselves firmly in the four highlands plains areas. On the other hand, the Padri phenomenon developed rapidly and spread quickly through the fringe areas of Minangkabau—the border areas located in an arc surrounding the northern plains and in the villages of the hills which touched the plains themselves. The movement is perhaps best characterized as one of "outsiders"—marginal people and areas considered traditionally as slightly beyond the pale of Minangkabau civilization. The Islamic scholars in their fortified religious compounds had chosen to remain outside the village and thus the adat community life (at least for the most part). The

---

24 Current Imam of Bonjol, interview, October 27, 1967, in Bonjol.
25 Radjab, *Perang Paderi*, p. 29.

border villages were also "outside," in the sense that they were in areas not fully absorbed into the classic civilization of the heartland. Their exclusion, like that of the hillside villages, partly resulted from a lack of rice land necessary to support a large leisure class of expensive adat functionaries. They were the villages of the highly developed merantau tradition, and their inhabitants may well have resented the smug and only barely concealed superiority complex of their plains kinsmen. The plains people considered these villages as rantau areas and not quite "Minangkabauified." Inside the fringe areas themselves, however, the adat (or at least its outward matrilineal trappings) was often very strongly adhered to and the villagers often far more conservative than the men of the plains.

The Coastal Experience

The Padri uprising was only a brief upheaval in the life of many highlands villages. Another outside force, one which would have a much more pervasive impact, was already developing by the 1800s—but on the coast not in the interior. The consequences of this new force would be foreign penetration of virtually every aspect of Minangkabau life. Historically, culturally, and economically, life on the coast had always been different, so it is perhaps fitting that change when it came, entered via the port towns of the west coast—Pariaman, Padang, and Painan.

The coastal towns had grown up around river mouths or bays, which formed natural trading centers where the products of the highlands could be exchanged for imported goods and sea products, principally salt and salted fish. They had mixed populations but with strong Minangkabau bias, provided by their aristocratic rulers, the numerous itinerant highlands traders and the agricultural families who had migrated to the coast to support the new towns. The ruling lineages, by tradition viceroys of the Raja at Pagarruyung, represented a well-developed indigenous noble class, not found elsewhere outside the immediate vicinity of Pagarruyung itself. They gained control not only of the profitable trading ports but also of the rich rice land located in pockets between the sea coast and the nearby mountains. Although along most of the shore the mountains fall abruptly into the sea, near the areas where the major harbor towns grew, there are broad expanses of fertile rice land (though drainage is often a problem).

The coastal raja followed a greatly modified version of the highlands adat, especially with regard to land ownership; on the coast, land often became concentrated in a few large and privately held tracts. Transfer of title was possible because the nobility had paramount authority and did not have to contend with the traditional suku institutions which had power in the highlands.

The concept of an aristocracy and its perquisites was more highly developed in the coastal areas, in contradistinction to the highlands provinces where the lineage form of government was the most common. Coastal ruling families paid almost no lip service to supposed village democracy; they owned the major portion of local wealth and land and believed themselves above the need to work for a living. They did not conform as closely to the matrilineal aspects of the highlands adat, despite their protestations that their families had originated there, but rather they showed a tendency to favor the male line in distribution and administration of family property. Children did not leave home at puberty to live in the surau, nor was the idea of merantau an important concept.

The hallmark of the coastal nobility was (and is) a system of titles which differed markedly from any found in the highlands interior and which preserved the idea of certain superior bloodlines and the need to recognize them. In the interior, titles belonged to the family pusaka but they did not imply any particular bloodlines of the bearer's father or mother, except that of datuk which implied relations to the previous penghulu, but even that was not certain nor always direct. On the coast, however, when a "raja" (titled Sutan) married a woman of equal rank (titled Puteri), then their children received the titles Sutan and Puteri to connote this heritage. If the woman were not of aristocratic birth, as would often happen with the second wife, the children would be titled Marah and Sitti. Matrilineal aspects still retained importance, however, for the children of a noble woman, a puteri, were always addressed as Sutan and Puteri regardless of the father's social standing. But the puteri rarely married commoners (unless they had very high achieved status such as an important official), and as a result many puteri could find no suitable marriage partner and remained single.[26] A single woman would

---

[26] This was especially true among the Padang nobility, according to current members of the raja's

be very unusual and considered as such in the highlands, but this was not the case among the coastal nobility. A family with many unmarried women was not necessarily at a disadvantage, because family wealth was not being dissipated among an ever-expanding number of descendants.

Except for the raja and their subordinate families of agricultural laborers, there were few really permanent settlers along the coast, no one to establish and preserve the pure traditions of Minangkabau adat. The coastal towns included many and diverse groups: the Nias and Mentawai pagans who served as slave laborers and occupied the bottom of the social scale; numerous non-Minangkabau merchants, such as Indians and Acehnese, attracted by the rich export trade (mainly pepper); and a large group of perantau merchants from the highlands, using the ports as bases for commercial operations which often extended back to the handicraft industries of their home villages. For the perantau merchant, the port town was often the final destination in the peripatetic trading system which funneled the agricultural products, the gold, and the handicrafts of the interior to the coastal exporters.

Because outside powers continually struggled to control the lucrative trade, the coast was often isolated politically from the interior of Minangkabau. Aceh was the principal power in the area in the sixteenth and early seventeenth centuries, and much of the paramount position of the local raja, particularly in Padang and Pariaman, was linked to their direct associations with their Acehnese suzerains, rather than their ties to the Raja at Pagarruyung. Aceh could and did enforce its will on the Minangkabau coast. Pagarruyung probably never exercised more than the influence of cultural leadership and prestige. Aceh itself eventually gave way in the face of superior European naval and political power.

Because the coastal areas were so undefined in terms of their population composition, the adat system and social codes of the interior explain less about the coastal way of life. Because the raja were more powerful and controlled the economic resources so completely, coastal village society did not experience the frequent rise and fall among elite families, such

---

family. Interview, August 10, 1967, in Alang Lawas, Padang. An example of a commoner who was acceptable would be the father of Sutan Sjahrir; he was a wealthy merchant who had good connections to the Dutch regime (he came from Kota Gedang in Agam). Sjahrir's mother was a puteri from Natal.

as occurred in the highlands villages. Because of their secure aristocratic position, the elite rarely participated in trade or sought training in skills to change their way of life. Their social code would not permit the merantau; to leave home was to open oneself to ridicule from one's peers.

Coastal settlements had largely escaped both direct relations with Pagarruyung and interference from Padri attacks—both experiences which had formed the relations between highlands villages and the outside world. But in contrast to the highlands, the coast had had a long, often profitable and sometimes dangerous, contact with non-Minangkabau elements. Although less important at first, European contact proved the most lasting of these. The major cause for European interest in Minangkabau was not its legendary importance as a source of gold (which had attracted the first Portuguese explorers in 1515),[27] but rather competition for its agricultural trade goods. Aceh, the major commercial power along the west coast in the late sixteenth and early seventeenth centuries, held a virtual trade monopoly over the Minangkabau pepper ports, the most important of which were Tiku and Pariaman.[28] The Sultan of Aceh used this monopoly to establish himself as the sole middleman between the producers and the European buyers, and he required traders to buy pepper only in Aceh itself. By the mid-seventeenth century, both the Dutch and the English were seeking a way to bypass the Acehnese middlemen, and both had begun operating their own factories along the western coast.

Already by 1613, the Padang raja, at least some of whom had been acting as Acehnese agents, had decided to invite the Dutch merchants established at Pulau Cingkuk, off the Painan coast, to build a branch factory at Padang. In return, the Dutch had to agree to protect the raja from Acehnese reprisals.[29] European factors dealt with the large local

---

27 The Portuguese interests in Sumatra are discussed in: Ronald Bishop Smith, *The First Age of the Portuguese Embassies, Navigations, and Peregrinations to the Kingdoms and Islands of Southeast Asia (1509-1521)* (Bethesda, Md.: Decatur Press, 1968), pp. 85-88; and Armando Cortesão, *Tomé Pires*, 1, p. 164.

28 Arun Kumar Das Gupta, "Acheh in Indonesian Trade and Politics 1600-1641: (Ph.D. dissertation, Cornell University, 1962).

29 Batuah and Madjoindo, *Tambo Minangkabau*, pp. 41-42. The invitation may have stemmed from an internal power struggle whereby the former Panglima Aceh in Padang was replaced. The new panglima was then recognized by the Dutch as the "Governor of the Malays" and given a percentage of the produce traded.

merchants who had joined forces with the Padang leaders to control the collection and sale of pepper in the coastal ports.[30] By 1660, Padang had become the focus for Dutch operations in the west coast area. Pariaman still remained the major trading center for the Minangkabau highlands generally (at least the major west coast center), and, for some time, it retained its close ties with Aceh.[31]

The Dutch rapidly expanded their control from the headquarters at Padang toward the south, mainly the area called Bandar X, the dependent coastal territories of the interior Minangkabau principality of Sungai Pagu. This southern area not only produced pepper, but also contained a gold mine, at the village of Salida outside Painan. A 1663 contract between Dutch authorities and the chiefs of Sungai Pagu/Salida granted the Dutch trading company, the Vereenigde Oostindische Compagnie (VOC), a trade monopoly without tariffs. In return, the Dutch would defend the town against Aceh and would continue payment to the raja of the customary gifts formerly supplied by the Acehnese. This treaty, known as the Painan Contract, served as the model for future Dutch treaties with other coastal raja.[32] The British, meanwhile, had established their own trading post farther south at Bengkulen, an area often economically and historically tied to the Minangkabau area, though culturally dissimilar.[33]

The British challenge stimulated Dutch efforts to consolidate their position in Padang and gain tighter control over the area immediately surrounding their Padang operations. As a result, in 1685, the VOC made an agreement with the local chiefs by which the Dutch gained full possession of the land where the Company had established its warehouses and over sales of the lands directly across the river from them.[34] By 1775, VOC influence had spread from Padang as far south in the direction of the British as Indrapura.[35]

---

30 Das Gupta, "Acheh in Indonesian Trade," pp. 115-17.
31 W. J. A. de Leeuw, *Het Painansch Contract* (Amsterdam: Paris, 1926), p. 18.
32 Ibid., pp. 22-23.
33 John Bastin, *The British in West Sumatra, 1685-1825: A Selection of Documents with an Introduction* (Kuala Lumpur: University of Malaya, 1965), pp. xii-xv.
34 E. B. Kielstra, "Onze Kennis van Sumatra's Westkust, Omstreeks de Helft der Achttiende Eeuw," *Bijdragen tot de Taal-, Land- en Volkenkunde* [henceforth *Bijdragen*], 36 (1887), p. 530.
35 "Nota over de Statie der Voorname Hoofden Langs de Westkust van Sumatra, van Indrapoera tot Tico, Welke Alhier Zullen Gerangschikt Worden Volgens hunne Classe en Waardigheid," Padang, c. 1820, KITLV Manuscript, H 113.

Dutch presence on the coast had little effect on the interior areas of Minangkabau beyond perhaps encouraging people to trade via the west coast rantau rather than the outlets to the Malacca Straits. The VOC represented more a continuation of the Acehnese system than something new. The Raja at Pagarruyung theoretically still controlled all trade at the coastal ports and received income from customs duties levied there. It is a measure of his lack of power that, despite the theoretical arrangement with his "representatives and customs collectors" (the coastal raja), the latter had signed treaties with a foreign power (the Dutch) which guaranteed to its merchants duty-free trade at the west coast harbors.

In 1795, the English occupied the former Dutch possessions on the west coast as part of their European foreign policy, which was designed to counter the power of Napoleon on the Continent by denying him access to the colonies of the occupied countries. In Padang, the British made no effort to expand beyond the limits of the post as already established, and, indeed, if the Dutch reports are to be believed, they allowed the post to lapse into a state of neglect as part of a deliberate effort to enhance their own operations at Bengkulen.[36] Preferring not to mix in local political affairs, the British interregnum administration dealt with troublesome local leaders by buying them off. Stamford Raffles, the head of the interim administration, expressed a direct interest in the interior of Minangkabau, however, and, in 1818, did succeed in leading an expedition to Solok and establishing a small garrison at Semawang on Lake Singkarak. By and large, however, the British government preferred to spend as little money and effort as possible improving its hold on an area which London (but not Raffles) conceived as but a temporary possession.[37] When, to Raffles' intense displeasure, the territories were returned to the Dutch in 1819, Padang existed as a small headquarters town already under the shadow of Padri bands operating around Kayu Tanam only a few miles along the interior road from the coast.

---

36 E. B. Kielstra, *Sumatra's Westkust, 1819-1830*, 3 vols. (The Hague: Bijdragen reprint, 5th series, n.d.), 1, p. 10.
37 Ibid., pp. 2-6.

CHAPTER THREE
A NEW POLITICAL CONFIGURATION: CENTRALIZED RULE AND A STATUS QUO

When the British surrendered custody of the former Dutch trading posts on the west coast of Sumatra, probably few highlands Minangkabau gave it much thought, even those who were aware of it. Certainly the returning Dutch officials did not anticipate any momentous new developments in their relations with the highlands behind Padang, although they knew about the Padri zealots and their relentless attacks on Minangkabau villages. The government in Batavia, for its part, planned a return to the status quo ante, which meant little more than maintaining a series of entrepots on the coast and making the most commercial profit with the least administrative effort.

The second arrival of the Dutch, however, set in motion a chain of events which ended in the creation of a new relationship between the Minangkabau nagari and the world beyond their borders. Unlike the former supravillage "government" exercised from Pagarruyung, the new, European regime soon penetrated into the village and its affairs—organizing, bullying, and cajoling the inhabitants to the greater imperial glory of The Netherlands. The villages found it harder and harder to escape the demands of the new, more effective outside force. Even the hill villages were now drawn into the same political structure as the rest, because, in the final analysis, they were to prove the mainstay of the new economic order upon which the colonial regime was built.

The changes did not come all at once, nor were they apparent everywhere to the same degree or at the same point in time. Strangely enough, the coastal areas, which had had the longest continuous contact with the European world were the last to be fully absorbed into the new political structure. The first to feel the colonial weight were the populous upland plains, followed in a decade or so by the hill villages and, eventually, the more distant frontier areas to the north and south.

For a time, uncertainty in Dutch plans and bickering between the Padang administration and Batavia preserved the villages from total integration into the colonial regime. By mid-century, all West Sumatra had been absorbed into the Dutch East Indies, and Minangkabau society was slowly being reorganized to fit Dutch perceptions of what it should be. Village political competition was stifled. In an ironic turn of fate, however, the former "outsiders" now came into their own. The hill villages had the natural and human resources which the new regime valued and needed. The agricultural products which the colonial economy valued not only grew well in the hills but also only the hill villages had the available empty land for planting. Moreover, hill villagers needed to supplement their incomes and were thus susceptible to the new colonial needs and enticements. The perantau element both in the hills and in the plains villages found a new outlet for their abilities and energies—the colonial civil service and its supporting agencies. And the Dutch administration soon found itself unable to function without their services. The people whom Indies society came to regard as the representatives of Minangkabau were in fact from the former fringe groups of traditional highlands village life.

The Beginning of the "Colonial" Problem

The Minangkabau participated hardly at all in the opening scenes of the drama which ended in colonial control over their lives. At the most, they played supporting roles which provided the rationale for particular Dutch actions; at the least, they were the colorful backdrop for the main stage whose featured players were Europeans. In the early scenes, however, there was little indication to either side of what was about to happen.

After the British surrendered control of West Sumatra to the Dutch, in May 1819, Batavia officials planned to reestablish the trading pattern which had existed in the late eighteenth century. Cautious about large-scale operations outside Java, the central regime proposed to limit Sumatran activities to the port towns of Padang, Pariaman, Air Haji, and Pulau Cingkuk (Painan). Efforts would thus be directed toward reviving the monopoly trading contracts with the local raja and counteracting

British trading interests, which had become well-entrenched during the preceding years, by opening the ports to American and other ships.[1] Even such modest plans were hindered by lack of personnel. Smaller than the pre-British administration, the new Dutch staff included only the same number of civil servants as had the British interim regime, plus some 150 European infantry and support troops. Attempts to reestablish the trading entrepots suffered, moreover, because the VOC post archives had disappeared; the government had to rely on the memory of the former chief merchant of the factory.[2] Added to this were the disruptions in the interior, which inhibited trade flow to the Dutch ports. By 1819, Padri bands were threatening Padang itself, and it appeared that the town might soon lose its position as a major center for trade and the collection of raw materials from the highlands.[3]

Dutch officials on the spot in West Sumatra took a more expansionist concept of their role than that envisioned in Batavia. They wanted authority to pacify the interior by force of arms and establish a Dutch presence which could assure security and therefore improve trade prospects. To the Governor General, West Sumatra, though important as a source for trade goods, was not sufficiently so to justify a large colonial establishment there. In the competition between the two divergent viewpoints, the Padang local authorities had the advantage because they could commit the government's forces first and create a situation which Batavia was obliged to finish. Authorities in Batavia fumed, but they were usually forced to accept the fait accompli though warning Padang officials not to do it again.

Minangkabau refugee penghulu from the highlands, now living in Padang, thought to use Dutch adventurism to their own advantage. By encouraging the Dutch to ally with them against the Padri and their followers, these penghulu hoped to regain lost powers (or perhaps build new ones) in the highlands nagari. They played upon the expansionist desires of Padang officials who, in turn, knew the arguments best designed

---

1 Report of General de Stuers on the Situation on Sumatra's West Coast, May 17, 1826, *Verbaal*, October 23, 1826, No. 48.
2 E. B. Kielstra, *Sumatra's Westkust, 1819-1890*, 3 vols. (The Hague: Bijdragen Reprint, n.d.), 1, p. 9.
3 Report of General de Stuers on the Situation on Sumatra's West Coast, May 17, 1826, *Verbaal*, October 23, 1826, No. 48.

to overcome central government opposition. A classic example of this process is that used by the first Padang Resident, du Puy. He played on the acute Anglophobia of Batavia officials in order to gain permission to reoccupy the former British fort at Semawang (Lake Singkarak), far in the interior behind Padang. Du Puy went to Batavia, in 1820, armed with a letter from a highlands penghulu which promised popular support for any Dutch military action against the Padri. Du Puy argued that, if the Dutch refused, the penghulu might seek help elsewhere, specifically from the British in Bengkulen.[4]

Batavia approved, though reluctantly, the reoccupation of the post, but only as a measure to restore order to the countryside for the advancement of trade. No further expansion would be countenanced. The Governor General was irate when, in February 1821, the Padang administration made a further agreement with fourteen penghulu, purporting to represent the Raja of Pagarruyung, by which the Kingdom of Minangkabau itself was ceded to the Dutch in return for protection against Padri raiders. Batavia believed, and rightly so, that the penghulu had no authority to cede the territory in question; Batavia also feared that du Puy would use the treaty as an excuse for conducting a war of conquest.[5] In the event, these fears all proved fully justified.

Having committed themselves to protect the interests of those who did not wish to join the Padri, the Padang officials soon found themselves caught up in the task of preserving an apparently disintegrating system against the vigor of the religious revolutionaries. Against the will of authorities in Batavia, the regime was gradually pulled into the maelstrom of Minangkabau internal politics. The highlands plains villages were not under Padri control, as such, but often their inhabitants had been forced to reach an accommodation—tributary, political, or both. Those who could not do so, or whom the Padri considered completely undesirable, had been forced to flee, usually ending up in the eastern or western coastal towns. As a result, when the Dutch and their client penghulu began asserting control over the highlands in the 1820s, they became a third major faction in an already confused local situation. The Dutch

---

4 Kielstra, *Sumatra's Westkust*, 1, p. 18.
5 Ibid., pp. 21-24; Muhammad Radjab, *Perang Paderi di Sumatera Barat: 1803-1808* (Jakarta: Perpustakaan Perguruan Kementerian P.O. & K., 1954), pp. 43-44.

found that local politics was not a question of merely pro- or anti-Padri forces but rather consisted of a variety of elements vying for lineage or village power positions. Moreover, sometimes the Dutch client penghulu proved to be only one of the anti-Padri factions and often not even the paramount one. Often too, they were not the actual penghulu of a given lineage but only the unsuccessful candidate for the job.

Rather than being merely quasi-neutral arbiters between two sides, as they had originally envisioned, Dutch officials began to side wholly with what they identified as the "anti-Padri" elements. Eventually, the Dutch officials determined that it was necessary to take over and reorganize the whole area themselves in order to assure peace and security to the Minangkabau—the necessary preconditions to profitable commerce. Because the Padri forces were concentrated in the hills around the highlands plains, the Dutch were able to establish a presence in the plains areas fairly easily—particularly in the Tanah Datar plain and in the southern parts of the Agam plain. But their position was exceedingly tenuous and depended on local co-operation and Padri indifference.

The leading architect of the concept of economic development in West Sumatra as a product of a Dutch-imposed peace was General de Stuers. He arrived in Padang in 1824 as the newly appointed military administrator for West Sumatra. De Stuers argued that, because Padang's main source of income derived from an export tax on coffee plus the sale of imported trade goods, it was essential that secure routes be maintained connecting the highlands producing areas with Dutch entrepots on the coast. If disorder continued, he believed, the Minangkabau would prefer to trade via the rivers of the east coast, an area less subject to Padri attack, with the result that the British settlement at Singapore would be the main beneficiary of the growing European market for Padang coffee as well as the major supplier of consumer goods to prosperous Minangkabau villages.[6]

The traditional flow of trade from the highlands had always been across the relatively lower hills on the eastern rim. From there these goods traveled by river, usually the Siak or Kampar, to the coastal trading ports such as Siak Sri Indrapura, headquarters of the Sultan

---

6 Report of General Stuers, May 17, 1826, *Verbaal*, October 23, 1826, No. 48.

of Siak. Goods which went to the west had to be transportable by an individual bearer, and thus must be of relatively high value for small bulk, such as pepper, gold, and probably coffee. No rivers and only a few very steep trails connected the highlands with the western coast. To attract goods from farther away than the surrounding foothills, buyers in west coast ports, therefore, had to be very competitive. In the early nineteenth century, the problem was exacerbated by Padri activities in the northern and western hills, including the area where the trails cut through to the coast—especially near Lake Maninjau and just outside of Padang. De Stuers hoped, however, that, if he could make the area secure, the traders would prefer to deal with the Dutch merchants directly rather than continue dealing with the aristocratic middlemen who operated in the Malacca Straits, presumably because it would mean greater profit.

De Stuers' desires to impose peace, however, were hampered initially by troop cutbacks caused by Diponegoro's uprising (known as the Java War) which required available Dutch military force to be concentrated there. As an alternative to military action, de Stuers arranged a negotiated settlement with Bonjol, which he identified as the Padri central authority, based on peaceful coexistence and noninterference.[7]

"Border incidents" continued despite the peace treaty, and de Stuers reported a general state of anarchy in Padri areas caused, in his opinion, by an uncertain and constantly changing leadership. Older leaders, such as Tuanku Pasaman (of Lintau), were apparently losing their hold over their followers.[8]

Caught in the middle between militant or terrorist religious leaders and the might of the Dutch army, Minangkabau villages were often torn apart into quarreling factions. There was no real battleline drawn, but rather villages passed back and forth between the two spheres of influence. Few chiefs were willing to commit themselves fully to the Dutch side. De Stuers complained that, except for those areas actually occupied by government troops (some eight places on the coast and five

---

[7] Report of General de Stuers, November 25, 1825, contained in Kielstra, *Sumatra's Westkust*, 1, pp. 154-56 and 147-52.
[8] Report of General de Stuers, May 17, 1826, *Verbaal*, October 23, 1826, No. 48.

in the interior), one could not depend on the local chiefs.[9] When the Dutch took the offensive, however, people declared themselves subjects of the government and delivered weapons, materials, and foodstuffs to aid the war against the Padri. Popular witchhunts took place in the recently defeated areas, as the victors turned on those who had backed the "wrong side."[10] Many non-Padri penghulu preferred to seek refuge with government forces rather than remain in villages conquered by Padri bands.[11] These penghulu gathered at Dutch posts and agitated for military assistance and support to return them to power.

Meanwhile, by 1830, the Java War had been concluded to Dutch satisfaction, and the new Governor General, van den Bosch, was free to turn his attention to the situation in Sumatra. He had decided that, as a general policy, all peoples and princes should recognize the Dutch regime as the overlord for the entire East Indies archipelago. With regard to Sumatra, he thought it sufficient for the control of trade that, in addition to acknowledged allegiance of the princes, the Dutch should also occupy ports, river mouths, and selected interior market towns. Dutch forts, garrisons, and trading factories would be built on each such site. Because Sumatra (unlike Java) was, he believed, too large to be held by an army, local colonial administrators would necessarily be too weak to intervene directly in the course of native affairs and should confine themselves to encouraging "profitable activity."[12] He did concede, however, that peace would have to be restored to West Sumatra, and, to this end, he sent additional troops to reenforce the campaign to reach a settlement with the Padri and recover "government villages." Van den Bosch agreed that, if all the measures for peaceful coexistence with the Padri should fail, local authorities would be free to prepare for a military campaign. He would accede to Padang's wishes for an all-out conquest of Minangkabau if the Padri could not be coerced into some form of lasting "peaceful association" with the Dutch administration.[13]

---

9 Report of General de Stuers to the Military Department, December 30, 1828, No. 43, contained in Kielstra, *Sumatra's Westkust*, 2, p. 39.
10 Report of Resident MacGillavry, November 20, 1829, *Exhibitum*, May 5, 1830, No. 5/A.
11 Radjab, *Perang Paderi*, pp. 116-17.
12 Letter of Governor General van den Bosch to Resident Elout, December 26, 1830, contained in Kielstra, *Sumatra's Westkust*, 2, pp. 73-74.
13 Instructions of Governor General van den Bosch to Resident Elout, January 14, 1831, No. 56,

West Sumatra officials continued to argue that only total subjugation of Padri activists could assure peace and hence guarantee the commercial prosperity so desired by Batavia.[14] Under their persistent pressure, therefore, van den Bosch finally acquiesced to the proposition that the anarchy in the interior had blocked the energy and killed the trade of an "otherwise very industrious society." He accepted the view that the area must be organized politically, that roads must be built to tie the interior producing areas to the coast, and that supervision must be given to the planting of cash crops for export.[15]

In 1832, therefore, Resident Elout received substantial reenforcements from Java, including a Javanese battalion under Prince Ali Basa Prawiro Diredjo, known as Sentot. The story of Ali Basa must certainly rank as one of the more bizarre episodes in the Dutch war against the Padri. Van den Bosch had developed the idea of establishing a settlement composed of Javanese troops in the heart of the contested Minangkabau area (apparently near Lintau), which could then serve as a permanent auxiliary force aiding Dutch pacification. To this end, in 1832, Ali Basa and 1,800 followers were sent to West Sumatra. Van den Bosch promised to cede him a district of some 5,000 to 6,000 people to rule as a small kingdom—in permanent vassalage to the government on much the same basis as the Pangeran Mangku Negoro in Solo. Van den Bosch counted as negligible any chance of a future Minangkabau-Javanese alliance against the government.[16]

Sentot's company was established in the Lintau/Buo area according to plan but, rather than accept his role as written, Sentot determined to enhance his position and make himself the Prince of all Sumatra. He set about cultivating good relations with local penghulu; he dropped the Javanese portion of his name (Prawira Diredjo); and he began publicly displaying an enthusiastic devotion to Islam. Moreover, in Elout's view, he took a provocative stance vis-à-vis the Dutch regime by traveling outside his territorial district (he celebrated Puasa at Pagarruyung, the royal center)

---

contained in Kielstra, *Sumatra's Westkust*, 2, p. 82.
14 Kielstra, *Sumatra's Westkust*, 2, pp. 95-99.
15 Letter of Governor General van den Bosch, February 20, 1832, contained in Kielstra, *Sumatra's Westkust*, 2, p. 129, see also p. 132.
16 Letters of Governor General van den Bosch, May and June 1832, contained in Kielstra, *Sumatra's Westkust*, 2, pp. 138-39.

and not treating the Resident with proper respect (he began addressing Elout in letters as "brother" instead of "father"). When the Bonjol area suddenly erupted again into full-scale revolt, Elout blamed it on the machinations of Sentot, who was thus subsequently recalled to Batavia.[17]

After 1832, then, both Batavia and Padang were in agreement that all of Minangkabau would have to be pacified and subjected to close control. How this control would be exercised would be a matter of some debate in the future, but, for the Minangkabau, it was now only a question of time before village life would be rearranged to suit a new, more powerful and more organized outside force.

In 1837, Batavia appointed Lt. Col. Michiels as military administrator for West Sumatra. He brought a new determination and vigor to the Dutch forces. He prosecuted the war with a singlemindedness which, by August, had culminated in the occupation of the last Padri center, Bonjol—causing its defenders to disperse into the jungle. The most important symbol of anti-Dutch resistance was gone, and with it the Padri will to fight. Sometime later, the Imam of Bonjol surrendered and was exiled first to Java, and then to Sulawesi. From then on, the Dutch could concentrate on organizing administrative and fiscal matters which hitherto had had to be taken care of on a more or less ad hoc basis. Now, for the first time, Minangkabau villagers really began to understand what it meant to belong to the Dutch East Indies.

Isolated revolts of varying size broke out after 1837—the most serious being in Batipuh in 1841 and Pau in 1844—and incursions from nongovernment areas continued, but, by and large, Dutch control of Minangkabau was an accomplished fact. Working from this geographic base, the Dutch continued their expansion into other areas of central Sumatra. The last major part of Minangkabau to be incorporated was the autonomous southern kingdom of Sungai Pagu (centered at Muara Labuh); it was occupied in 1845 because its inhabitants had allegedly attacked Dutch patrols operating on their borders.

Within the space of less than twenty years, the Dutch operation in West Sumatra had grown from a small series of neutral trading post

---

17 Kielstra, *Sumatra's Westkust*, 3, pp. 5-18. There are still families in the Lintau area who can trace their antecedents to Sentot or his men.

enterprises into the beginning of a conquered empire which, by the end of the century, would absorb all of the island of Sumatra. The logic of the desire to make a profit from the territory had led to administrative control over the producing areas. This in turn would lead to major reorganizations of local society designed to provide the products desired as well as assure their efficient transportation to the West Sumatran market centers.

Indirect Rule: Life as Before (Almost)

After restoring peace and destroying any chances for an Islamic state, the Dutch had originally hoped to return to their fortified garrisons and let the Minangkabau resume the business of agriculture, especially coffee production. Such guidance and control as would be needed could, or so Dutch officials had thought, be exercised through the paramount rulers of Minangkabau—identified by the Dutch as the Raja of Pagarruyung and the Regent (paramount raja) of Padang, along with several lesser coastal and interior overlords who had pretensions to territorial sovereignty. Everything would return to the status quo ante Padri, except that now Dutch protection would be extended over the highlands penghulu in the same manner, and for the same concessions, as formerly with the coastal raja.

For the coastal villages and their raja, relations with the returning colonial regime had at first differed little from the old ties with the VOC and with the Acehnese before them. In 1821, Resident du Puy was authorized by Batavia to provide each coastal raja or regent with documents stating his duties and obligations as a vassal of the government. The raja should encourage careful production of coffee and organize its delivery to Padang, receiving in return f. 0.25 per picul in commission. Diligence in promoting coffee production would form a major factor for continuing official government recognition of them as raja.[18] Most, if not all, of the predecessors of these raja had held similar contracts in the seventeenth and eighteenth centuries, with the VOC; in these earlier contracts they had agreed to recognize the Company's authority in matters of trade and defense. The 1821 agreements reactivated these long-standing

---

18 Kielstra, *Sumatra's Westkust*, 1, p. 15.

relationships and transferred the vassal relationship from the VOC to the government in Batavia. But the situation in 1821 differed from that of 1615 or even 1775, and Dutch perceptions had changed as a result of their new position of strength vis-à-vis the various coastal raja. The two sides no longer confronted each other as relative equals.

The former "company raja," it seemed, had declined considerably in terms of the actual power they could exercise, or, more probably, the Dutch now better understood the exact nature of that power. One report did suggest that, in the seventeenth century, the prince of Indrapura, for example, had had control over the whole southern coast, but by the nineteenth century, this power was completely gone. The heir apparent worked as a clerk for a Dutch official in Pariaman,[19] a measure of how far the family's fortunes had declined. But Dutch officials believed that they could rebuild the raja into the strong rulers they believed them to have been. The perquisites of the coastal "lords" were reconfirmed, and the various raja were divided into first, second, and third class rank, based more on pretensions to grandeur than on the reality of power. The logic of the arrangement was that the control which these chiefs presumably had over trade would now be exercised in the name of the Dutch regime. As a consequence, the raja must be compensated for any financial loss this might entail and be paid as agents of the regime as well. Moreover, they should be treated with proper respect so that their subjects would continue to stand in awe of them and obey. As examples of such super-inflated royal privilege, one can take the Tuanku Panglima Padang and the Prince of Indrapura, both designated by Dutch decree as raja of the first rank. As such, each was entitled to a thirteen-gun salute and a reception by the Resident at the Government House, complete with a twelve-soldier honor guard, not to mention the particular potentate's own elaborate retinue which preceded him.[20] Lower-ranking raja received proportionately less elaborate formal honors.

Despite their impressive entourages, titles, and honors, in terms of authority these chiefs often proved unsatisfactory tools for Dutch

---

19 "Note over de Statie der Voorname Hoofden Langs de Westkust van Sumatra, van Indrapoera tot Tico, Welke Alhier Zullen Gerangschikt Worden Volgens hunne Classe en Waardigheid," Padang c. 1820, 13 pp., KITLV Manuscript, H 113.
20 Ibid.

attempts at a new, more organized administration. Comparing the situation along the Padang coast to that which obtained in Java, one Dutch official wrote that a village chief on Java could exercise more control over his subordinates than the "most conceited monarch" found on the West Coast. But, he added, the Dutch were powerless to replace these "monarchs" with a more "rational" system, because each district had an independence of spirit which would not allow a competing raja to be given a superior position or greater honors. It was impossible to combine the territories under one supreme head. The VOC, he said, had deliberately encouraged this autonomy for political reasons and had treated each district as a wholly separate entity, individually allied to the Company on an equal basis with every other territory.[21]

On the coast, the concept of a series of paramount chiefs each with authority to speak for a specific geographic area did make some sense given the history of political developments there. But in the interior, such a solution was doomed to failure. Nagari were ruled by councils of penghulu and, although certain ones might have more recognized authority in council decisions, no single penghulu could speak for the people of his district. What was more to the point, no single penghulu could give orders to all the people. A penghulu had "authority" only over his own lineage group. But the Dutch did not fully understand this, partly because they had dealt primarily with refugee penghulu or other, often self-appointed, "nagari spokesmen" who had implied that they could in fact exercise full and legitimate authority over a particular geographic area. Under the uncertain and chaotic conditions of the Padri war, such individual penghulu often intrigued with the Dutch to seek recognition as the paramount authority for their area.

In the 1820s and 1830s, when neither the Dutch nor the Minangkabau had a clear understanding of the other, some chiefs were able to gain certificates of office which made them territorial rulers in alliance with the Dutch. In return for guaranteeing the loyalty of their followers, these men received promises of Dutch protection.[22] Two self-styled court notables from Suroaso (near Pagarruyung), were already recognized in 1819 as

---

21 Ibid.
22 Kielstra, *Sumatra's Westkust*, 1, p. 111.

the official representatives in Padang of the Minangkabau court.[23] Early Dutch attempts to maintain their rule over West Sumatra were based on the erroneous assumption that a "court" existed in fact and could command obedience and speak for Minangkabau in relations with the Padang authorities. There were many penghulu who were all too willing to continue this illusion.

Based on the legal fiction provided by the 1821 Cession of the Minangkabau Kingdom, Padang officials proposed to use the Raja of Pagarruyung as the instrument for authority. He would receive an act of appointment and a monthly salary, and, in turn, he would install the district penghulu in their own positions as his vassals.[24] The Dutch would then merely advise the Raja and preserve peace among the nagari. Although the early Residents, du Puy and Raaff, had recognized the weakness of the Raja's position, they had attributed it more to the existing state of unrest than to any inherent qualities of the Minangkabau political style. They believed that, once the Dutch had demonstrated their own reliance on the Raja, the lesser penghulu would respond and place themselves under his power.[25] Although the Dutch had more military force than the former Raja of Pagarruyung, it was still insufficient to forge a strong centralized authority under him. There was also some question about the royal credentials of the man selected as Raja, who, consequently, could not command even the "sacral" authority of the prior Raja. With the possible exception of the districts in the vicinity of Pagarruyung, holding a certificate from the Raja had very little meaning in the traditional competition for village leadership. As a result, each nagari worked out its own "understanding" with the Dutch, who found it all very confusing and a bit irritating.

The Dutch misunderstanding was part of a persistent and general problem which consistently colored their relations with the Minangkabau; previous Dutch experience at direct administration had been, by and large, confined to Java, which had a tradition of strong centralized government. Prior to 1819, their experience with the Minangkabau had been confined to the coast where local raja, for various reasons, exercised

---

23 Ibid., 1, p. 18.
24 Ibid., 1, pp. 84-85.
25 Ibid., 1, p. 84.

almost authoritarian control over population areas. When they found themselves entangled in the interior districts of West Sumatra, then, the Dutch tended to look for similar paramount chiefs around whom to organize their relationship. But the Minangkabau highlands were composed of small independent nagari, some of which belonged to loosely-federated units formed solely for mutual convenience, and the Raja represented a cultural symbol more than a political reality.

It became clear over time that the Cession of 1821, by which the Dutch could supposedly act in the name of the Raja, did not in fact give them a corresponding measure of political control. In the first place, the cession itself was soon recognized as, in the words of one Resident, a "pactum in illicito" by which a group of unauthorized persons had given that which they had no right to give.[26] In the second place, as de Stuers pointed out to the Governor General, it was soon clear that the whole idea of a "cession" was a meaningless concept. Not only were the major signatories to the treaty all refugees, many of whom had been living in Padang since the beginning of the Padri troubles and thus separated from contact with their villages, but, in fact, the so-called kingdom (which purported to include the entire area from the Batak lands to Indrapura, extending between both coasts) had never existed as a centralized strong administration under one overlord.[27]

After the arrival of de Stuers, in 1824, the Dutch administrators began to reexamine their notions of Minangkabau and to realize that its organization and rule would involve more Dutch supervision and hence interference. There was no existing system of paramount chiefs in the highlands which would enable it to be administered simply through the offices of a Raja at Pagarruyung. Because of this, under de Stuers' guidance, a system based on district level rulers was created practically from whole cloth, which therefore represented a major change in village social and political organization. De Stuers contended that by virtue of the Act of Cession, the Kingdom of Minangkabau no longer legally existed as an independent entity. He believed that, in any event, the spirit of the times had already decreed its demise. It should remain in the oblivion into

---

26 Report of Resident MacGillavry, November 20, 1829, *Exhibitum*, May 5, 1830, No. 5/A.
27 Report of General de Stuers to the Governor General, August 30, 1825, *Exhibitum*, August 24, 1826, No. 41.

which it had fallen rather than be resurrected by the Dutch for use as the regional administration for the Padang Highlands. The current Dutch-appointed Prince of Minangkabau (Begagar Shah), in de Stuers' opinion, owed his position solely to the presence of Dutch authority. De Stuers believed, therefore, that the Dutch Assistant Resident for the Highlands could better act as the chief official for the regional administration.[28] He had not abandoned the idea of centralizing authority in the highlands, only the belief that it could be carried out through existing institutions and personnel.

A New Local Administration: Creation of Paramount Chiefs

The political administration designed by de Stuers significantly altered the balance of power within the villages and the relationship between them and the outside political world. The new form of rule was organized hierarchically with the lowest level corresponding roughly with the existing nagari unit; above this, a series of ever larger geographic districts was established ending with the Dutch Resident (later Governor) in Padang. De Stuers had originally envisioned that the three lowest levels would be staffed by Minangkabau chiefs, the highest of whom would be similar to the *bupati* (regent) on Java. But this plan was abandoned as unworkable.

A hierarchical organization of government, according to de Stuers, had proved feasible on Java only because, before the Dutch had arrived, the Javanese had already evolved a form of hierarchic government with powerful chiefs. The Minangkabau , he said, had, on the contrary, maintained an individual freedom so great that there was little discernable difference between chief and follower; rather "all will govern, none be governed." As a result, provisions for large regional conglomerations under paramount chiefs would not only create a series of merely nominal overlords, but, worse, would create unrest, stemming from jealousy on the part of the subordinate leaders. To be successful, de Stuers suggested the administrative organization must recognize the "republican spirit" of

---

28 Instructions of General de Stuers to the Assistant Resident of the Padang Highlands, March 1, 1825, and the Decision of the Governor General, No. 16 of December 20, 1825, contained in Kielstra, *Sumatra's Westkust*, 1, pp. 114-17.

Minangkabau institutions including the numerous egalitarian leaders, or penghulu, who acted more as mediators than judges.[29]

Under the new administrative organization established by de Stuers, the penghulu of each nagari had to select one of their number to serve as the *nagarihoofd*,[30] to act as the community's spokesman in its relations with the Dutch administrators and to relay their orders to his constituents. In de Stuers' view, this would preserve traditional lineage administration from European interference; in all daily affairs, the penghulu suku would continue to function as before. Over the long term, however, more and more of such "daily affairs" were absorbed into the realm of "government (Dutch) affairs."

Above the nagarihoofd, de Stuers created a new position, a chief in charge of a wholly new territorial political unit which he called a *laras*.[31] The nagarihoofd from a given laras district would select one of their number to serve as *larashoofd*.[32] After his selection, the larashoofd was officially installed by the Dutch administration which provided him with a certificate of office and a silver-headed baton. The Dutch believed that conferring upon the larashoofd the official approval of the European authority would increase his power and prestige in the eyes of his followers. When possible, the laras districts were drawn to correspond to preexisting groupings of nagari, and thus many conformed with historic confederations. All larashoofd in the highlands were of equal rank.[33] The next higher level in the administration was wholly Dutch-staffed.

The governmental arrangement first instituted by de Stuers was extended to each new district as it was added to the West Sumatra

---

29 H. J. J. L. Ridder de Stuers and B.C. Verploegh, "Report van Komissarissen voor de Overname der Britische Bezittingen op Sumatra," Westkust van Sumatra, November 30, 1825, KITLV Manuscript, H 543.
30 The Minangkabau term for the office was the *penghulu kapala*, literally the head penghulu. In order to avoid possible confusion between this Dutch-created position and the pre-existing adat paramount penghulu, the penghulu pucuk, the Dutch term will be used in the text.
31 Although de Stuers chose to call these new district units by the term laras, one should not equate this with an older, adat usage of *laras nan duo* which referred to the two adat styles of Minangkabau, i.e., the Koto Piliang and the Bodi Caniago.
32 The Minangkabau term was *tuanku laras*, literally lord of the laras, but the Dutch term will be used as an indication that it was a Dutch-created position and to avoid any possible confusion with pre-existing adat terminology.
33 Report of General de Stuers, January 15, 1827, contained in Kielstra, *Sumatra's Westkust*, 2, p. 29; H. J. J. L. Ridder de Stuers, "Verslag van Padang 1828 (1. 1825)," Padang, May-July 1826, KITLV, manuscript, H 726.

Residency in the course of the nineteenth century. Sometime after mid-century, it was also introduced into the coastal areas, and the former raja were transformed into the same type of administrator as their upland counterparts. Although the larger, Dutch-staffed levels were rearranged and renamed as the regime became larger and more complicated, the Minangkabau-staffed lower units remained essentially unchanged until the major reorganization of 1914.

From the Dutch point of view, in order to provide the best possible atmosphere for increased trade and production, the local society should have a regularized and orderly administration. De Stuers argued that the method of selecting penghulu, based as it was on family and lineage rivalry, was a particularly disruptive element, being on many occasions accompanied by violence. Although Padri activities had exacerbated this condition, he believed it was endemic from pre-Padri times.[34] From the beginning, the Dutch directed their attention to countering any activities or elements in village affairs that could be construed as disruptive of general peace and order. Eventually their desire to prevent disruption and the need to maintain contact with every level of village society, led to Dutch interference in the selection of the penghulu suku themselves.

Dutch imposition of a rigid government hierarchy on top of local society and their interference in local affairs in an effort to smother conflict tended to prevent the free working of traditional politics and to stifle social change.[35] Certain individuals and families received official designation as village leaders, which, more often than not, assured that these families would continue in this position for generations. Persons from lower ranking families, who, in former times, might have hoped to move to the top through changes within existing economic and power relationships, now found themselves effectively cut off from advancement via traditional adat institutions. But, at the same time, the new institutions of the nagarihoofd and larashoofd removed most significant issues from

---

34 De Stuers, "Verslag van Padang."
35 For similar descriptions of the smothering effect of colonial rule, see James Siegel, *The Rope of God* (Berkeley: University of California Press, 1969), esp. Chapter 5; E. R. Leach, *Political Systems of Highland Burma* (Boston: Beacon Press, 1965), esp. pp. 69-71; and Frank L. Cooley, "Village Government in the Central Moluccas," *Indonesia*, 7 (April 1969), pp. 139-64.

the authority of the old nagari council, and thus the position of penghulu suku lost some of its traditional appeal.

Over time, the originally alien institutions of nagari- and larashoofd became thoroughly domesticated. It became accepted as "adat tradition" that the successor to each post would be the incumbent's nephew, although preferably the most able of his nephews. This total absorption of the new administrative positions into the traditional world view of the Minangkabau produced an almost "schizoid" reaction on the part of Dutch officials. They found themselves sometimes resolving succession disputes according to so-called "adat tradition" and, at other times, asserting that, since the positions did not represent true "adat officials" but Dutch creations, matters could be settled without regard to adat custom.

The disputes which arose continuously over selection of the larashoofd indicate the ambiguity of the position vis-à-vis the adat system, as well as the reactions of the Dutch officials who had to resolve the arguments. An 1872 larashoofd election in the IV Kota (Agam) is a good example of the problem. It was invalidated by the Governor because the voters had included everyone with an honorific title (called a *gelar*) rather than solely the penghulu suku "as provided by adat" (that is to say, "adat" as interpreted by the Governor). The election had, in the Governor's view, "contradicted the custom of the Highlands." But, when a new election held "according to adat" returned the same candidate, the Governor still refused to install him. This time, he said that the larashoofd was a government-created not an adat position, and hence he was not obligated to accept the people's choice if he disapproved of the person. The penghulu of the IV Kota sent a delegation to Batavia charging that the government favorite was being chosen only because his mamak was an important Minangkabau official and a close confidant of the Governor.[36] Although the government candidate got the job, at his death the position returned to the lineage of the previous larashoofd which kept it until the twentieth-century reorganization of the local administration.[37]

In the VIII Kota (Agam), when the Governor refused to appoint the local candidate, again the nephew of the incumbent, a delegation

---

36 *Verbaal*, January 22, 1875, No. 39.
37 Village elders of Kota Gedang, IV Kota, Agam, interviews, October 1967.

of penghulu and their followers marched on Padang to protest this interference in "sovereign village affairs."[38] The Governor defended his action on the grounds that selection of larashoofd had no basis in adat history, because the Raja of Pagarruyung had never chosen his officials from among candidates elected by the people.[39] The penghulu were forced to acquiesce and apparently no one bothered to point out that the Raja of Pagarruyung had never chosen territorial officials this way because the position had not existed under the Kingdom.

The above cases were the exceptions rather than the rule, for, in most instances, both Dutch officials and local penghulu regarded the selection procedure as part of established adat tradition and hence protected by a declaration of van den Bosch in 1833 (called the Plakaat Panjang) in which he had guaranteed the Minangkabau that Dutch officials would never interfere with adat institutions.[40] In both disputes cited above, the Plakaat Panjang provisions were used as the legal basis for challenging the Governor's decision, and it is evident from the accompanying documents that the Governor was in the minority of Dutch officials who believed that the man selected by the village penghulu could be denied installation by government administrators. Dutch administration in West Sumatra was rarely conducted by majority vote of even the European officials, however.

In most instances, Dutch officials saw themselves as the upholders of adat tradition, protecting it from erosion caused by contact with either Islamic fanaticism or European modernism. This belief that Dutch administrators should work actively to preserve adat rule had already begun in the 1830s when officials were searching for the best means of pacifying the interior and securing local allegiances. Commissioner van Sevenhoven, sent from Batavia to investigate the problems of West Sumatran unrest, concluded that the basic misunderstandings which had clouded Dutch rule so far must be adjusted and the administration be restored to conform with "correct local adat tradition." Under the wartime conditions, unscrupulous villagers had gained positions as government sponsored chiefs and, he said, had used the cloak of Dutch authority to

---

38 *Verbaal*, February 3, 1875, No. 83.
39 *Verbaal*, December 4, 1875, No. 146.
40 Kielstra, *Sumatra's Westkust*, 3, pp. 99-102.

plunder villages and assert themselves over the "legal adat penghulu," whom he identified as being those from the oldest village lineages. According to van Sevenhoven, a penghulu's rank was predetermined by his lineage, and the Dutch had caused great insults by appointing their own favorites without regard to adat prescriptions. Thus, in his view, the persisting rebelliousness represented Minangkabau retaliation to the unaccustomed affronts they had suffered at Dutch hands.[41] His view of village adat politics and the belief that the Dutch should preserve "tradition" formed the basis for nineteenth-century concepts of what kind of interference was allowable in village affairs.

A highwater mark of the view that the government must support adat was an 1888 circular from the Resident, which proposed a series of regulations to assure that people not become penghulu unless they fulfilled adat requirements. The Resident asserted that, unless the government took direct action soon, the Minangkabau would no longer respect the adat, and consequently the penghulu would decline as an important village institution (a crucial problem since they were the foundation of Dutch rule). To prevent abuses in penghulu elections, a family would have to notify the local Dutch official before it could install a new penghulu, and he would then check the nominee against adat requirements. The final court of appeal in disputed cases would be the Dutch Resident.[42] Dutch influence consistently favored the status quo in village politics. Families holding the title when the Dutch arrived tended to retain it, and other families found it increasingly difficult to challenge the incumbent. Although in traditional society upcoming family branches apparently frequently established separate penghuluships if they were unable to dislodge the incumbent family, the Dutch labeled such new penghulu as "extra-legal" and predicted that, whatever their wealth and cleverness, they would not be regarded as legitimate by the people and would have no influence in the village. Dutch officials feared that such new penghulu might even degrade the office in the eyes

---

41 Letter of Commissioner van Sevenhoven to Governor General van den Bosch, December 25, 1833, No. 205, contained in Kielstra, *Sumatra's Westkust*, 3, pp. 105-8.
42 "Circulaire van den Resident der Padangsche Bovenlanden, 25 September 1888, No. 3383," *Adatrechtbundels*, 11, pp. 91-92.

of the villagers and thus erode the administrative system as a whole.[43] Wherever possible, therefore, Dutch officials worked to prevent the rise of new penghulu.

Perhaps more important than direct Dutch influence in preserving the status quo was the new source of power and wealth to which government-recognized penghulu had access in contrast with other, potential leaders. Traditionally, lineage members had owed a certain amount of assistance, called *serayo*, to their penghulu as leaders of the lineage. This was mainly exacted in the form of labor for the penghulu's fields. But, during the nineteenth century, both the penghulu and the government chiefs (larashoofd and nagarihoofd) were able to expand the scope of personal service by using their new positions as administrators of the Dutch government corvée labor corps.[44] All government chiefs received monthly salaries as well as a commission on the export crops harvested in their area, particularly, in the early years, coffee. Penghulu suku, though unsalaried, also received a commission on the export crops harvested by their dependents in the lineage. The lowlands Residency raja usually received f. 50 per month salary and the highlands larashoofd received f. 80; each also received f. 0.20 commission for each picul of coffee delivered by their dependents. The nagarihoofd received f. 20 per month salary plus f. 0.20 per picul commission. In addition, each chief was entitled to a certain number of bodyguards and freedom from corvée duties for himself and members of his family.[45]

The development of the government chiefs into a class set apart by wealth and power was part of a conscious policy by the Dutch to create a Minangkabau aristocracy where none had existed before—an aristocracy which could command the respect, honor, and obedience of the people. The new chiefs must, or so it was believed in Padang, live on a far grander scale than an ordinary penghulu suku—having horses, houses, and large retinues to add grandeur.[46] The larashoofd's official connections with the government often gave him an advantage in gaining government contracts and other benefits. During the early years of the coffee cultivation system,

---
43 H. W. Stap, "De Nagari-Ordonnantie ter Sumatra's Westkust," *TBB*, 53 (1917), pp. 702-5.
44 Resident Le Febvre, October 8, 1917, *Verbaal*, March 4, 1919, No. 23.
45 *Verbaal*, March 7, 1863, No. 26; *Verbaal*, September 12, 1912, No. 66.
46 Assistant Resident of Padang, August 13, 1858, *Verbaal*, September 24, 1859, No. 7.

for example, almost all transport contractors were government chiefs; over half of them were larashoofd.[47]

Although some expressed the fear that association with the government would decrease the penghulu's prestige,[48] this seems not to have been the case. The villagers realized that the person who had the ear of the colonial regime, had the power to grant requests or make trouble. After the abolition of the quasi-adat village administration in 1914 and its replacement by a merit civil service, there were, for example, complaints from officials that no one paid attention to the new civil servants but instead continued to consult the old nagari- and larashoofd; no one believed that the new officeholders were really in a position to understand complaints or convey them to the regime.[49]

Unlike the penghulu, who gained some benefits from the new regime in terms of wealth and prestige, his assistants in the former lineage government gradually lost most of their real function and significance. During the nineteenth century, for example, the Dutch recognized the religious personnel directly associated with the village mosque as the only legitimate Islamic authorities for the community,[50] at the expense of the adat religious officials, such as the malim, who were connected with the lineage religious institutions, such as the surau. And by the twentieth century, a Minangkabau official noted that, although each penghulu continued to have his own religious "advisor," when a case arose the penghulu tended to settle it himself.[51] The decline in the malim's position may also have been hastened by the renaissance and purification movements which occurred within Islam itself in the late nineteenth and early twentieth centuries.

Under Dutch auspices, a new legal system with a European-style board of justice was introduced to hear complaints in civil affairs. This board eventually superseded village level adat courts, and the chatib was reduced to the role of mediator in a few minor family disputes.

---

47 Governor of Sumatra's West Coast, March 29, 1860, *Verbaal*, March 7, 1863, No. 26.
48 A. W. P. Verkerk Pistorius, *Studien over de Inlandsche Huishouding in de Padangsche Bovenlanden* (Zalt-Bommel: J. Norman, 1871), p. 93.
49 Memorie van Overgave, Resident of Sumatra's West Coast Le Febvre, *Mailrapport*, No. 4904/'19.
50 L. C. Westenenk, *De Minangkabausche Nagari* (Weltevreden: Visser, 1918), p. 58.
51 *Mailrapport*, No. 253/'35.

The dubalang also lost most of his former function, in this case to new, Dutch-appointed village policemen. In all cases, the former adat officials retained ceremonial functions, but, by and large, as adat affairs generally lost importance within the total life of the village, these functionaries also lost relevance. New problems that arose were often handled only in the sphere of the European system.[52]

Supra-Nagari Government: The European Administration

The Minangkabau kingdom was dead and gone by mid-century. The ideal of centralized government, which it had embodied but never achieved, now existed in fact; but it was in the form of a European-staffed bureaucracy. This administration was on top of the Minangkabau larashoofd and connected the local nagari with the central governments representative in Padang. The number of officials and their titles changed over the course of the nineteenth century, but, in general, the bureaucratic outline remained the same.

At the top of the administrative pyramid stood the Governor, with his headquarters in Padang. Next in line were the Residents of the Padang Highlands (with headquarters in Bukittinggi) and the Padang Lowlands (with headquarters in Padang). The first, as suggested by his title, had charge of the areas east of the mountain ridge dividing the coast from the Minangkabau heartland. But the Lowlands Residency, up until 1891, also included the northern hill country, the area between northern Agam and Tapanuli which the Dutch knew as Ophir. Each Residency was divided into Assistent Residencies. The Highlands usually had five to eight and the Lowlands three to five. At the lowest level of Dutch territorial administration was the *controleur*. He dealt directly with the laras- and nagarihoofd and was the connecting link between the Dutch and the Minangkabau administration. The territory of a controleur could be equivalent to one laras district if that district were particularly important, but usually a controleur had several larashoofd under him. The controleur were divided into three grades depending on the relative importance of

---

52 A full discussion of these changes in adat functions is contained in Verkerk Pistorius, *Inlandsche Huishouding*, and Westenenk, *Minangkabausche Nagari*.

the area they administered. They devoted most of their effort, during the early years, toward promotion and care of export crops.

Table 1. Sumatra's West Coast Population (1852 and 1920)*

Political Subdivision	Europeans	Natives	Chinese	Other Asians	Slaves	Total
1852 Census						
Padang Lowlands Residency						
Padang/Environs	662	35,126	1,140	953	2,277	40,158
Southern Division	32	34,075	73	17	8	34,205
Pariaman	48	59,887	223	209	151	60,518
Air Bangis/Environs	9	4,039	3	3	2	4,056
Ophir	1	19,078	7	7	--	19,093
Rau/Environs	3	12,729	2	13	--	12,747
Padang Highlands Residency						
Tanah Datar	21	153,471	12	100	--	153,604
Agam	30	196,927	49	190	21	197,217
L. Kota	9	103,541	3	10	4	103,567
XIII & IX Kota (Solok)	12	70,709	5	24	2	70,752
Totals	827	689,582	1,517	1,526	2.465	695,917
1920 Census						
Padang Lowlands Residency						
Padang/Environs	2,447	136,216	6,909	1,190		146,762
Southern Division	82	124,772	844	79		125,777
Pariaman	335	250,410	1,027	193		251,965
Air Bangis/Environs	4	22,190	79	--		22,273
Padang Highlands Residency						
Ophir	23	46,214	18	1		46,256

Table 1 (continued)

Political Subdivision	Europeans	Natives	Chinese	Other Asians	Slaves	Total
1920 Census (continued)						
Lubuk Sikaping (Rau)	7	38,389	8	--		38,404
Tanah Datar	566	238,741	638	64		240,009
Agam	404	245,736	583	167		246,890
L. Kota	126	220,218	832	56		221,232
Solok	153	182,323	148	48		182,672
Totals	4,147	1,505,209	11,086	1,798		1,522,240

* These figures can give only an approximation of the population growth in each district because boundary lines changed so much between 1852 and 1920; unfortunately, the 1852 subdivisions do not appear on any maps so it is difficult to tell exactly how far they correlate with 1920 divisions of the same name.

Source: 1852 Census, General Report of Governor van Swieten, *Verbaal*, July 13, 1858, No. 35; 1920 Census, *Volkstelling* 1920, pp. 166-74.

As the role of the European administration became more complex, additional officials, both Dutch and Minangkabau, were assigned to the various territorial offices. From early on, there were inspectors to assist in the development of the crops and also the improvement of village agriculture generally. By the end of the century, these had been joined by education inspectors and other officials directly involved in local welfare programs.

The total number of European officials assigned to West Sumatra was never very high, and they were often concentrated in the administrative centers. The European community included nongovernment people. At the beginning of direct colonial rule, after the pacification of Bonjol in 1837, there were only thirty-five European officials assigned to all West Sumatra, and twelve of these were at the Resident's bureau in Padang.[53] A great many more Dutch people resided in West Sumatra, but they were nongovernment personnel; of these, 109 lived in Padang, fifteen more in the Lowlands Residency and sixteen in the Highlands. Most worked for commercial enterprises in connection with the export trade.[54] In 1852, after the initial bureaucratic expansion caused by the beginning of the forced delivery system for coffee, some seventy-six Dutch officials were stationed in the highlands area. They had charge of the more than 400 nagari and 550,000 Minangkabau who comprised the Highlands Residency. Many of these officials were located in the few important market and administrative centers, particularly in Bukittinggi. Another seventy-two private Dutch individuals also worked in the highlands; this compares with some 756 in the Lowlands Residency (of which 662 were located in Padang).[55] By 1882, there were forty-eight territorial bureaus each with its own European and Minangkabau staff.[56] Unfortunately no statistics are given for the exact number of European officials then serving in the West Coast Administration. But the bulk of the administration was still in the hands of the Minangkabau through the offices of the laras- and nagarihoofd.

---

53 *Regeerings Almanak van Nederlandsch-Indië, 1837* (Batavia: Landsdrukkerij, 1838), p. 48.
54 Ibid., pp. 198-200.
55 1852 Census, *Verbaal*, July 13, 1858, No. 35.
56 *Regeerings Almanak 1882*, pp. 51-53.

The Minangkabau territorial chiefs functioned as part of the adat-style political structure in their villages as well as part of the Dutch administration. They were specifically chosen from among the penghulu of their district and could serve only in that district. Because their selection to leadership had been based on their traditional position in the local adat aristocracy, they would have no authority in any other area. Their authority was not recognized even by the inhabitants of a neighboring district, though a visiting penghulu would probably be granted a certain amount of deference.

Supra-Nagari Minangkabau Officials

The territorial administration remained in European hands at the higher levels, but the Dutch did create a set of upper-level Minangkabau officials outside the adat system. These officials eventually formed the nucleus for a merit civil service the members of which could serve anywhere in West Sumatra and later throughout Sumatra, Borneo, and the rest of the archipelago. The emergence of this "non-adat" bureaucracy was of crucial importance, because it provided new outlets through which ambitious individuals could bypass the all-but-frozen village adat power structure.

To support the administrative network being extended across Minangkabau, the Dutch needed a corps of minor civil servants—agricultural inspectors and supervisors, office clerks and secretaries, and petty functionaries to serve as messengers and in other low-level jobs. All of these jobs offered new access to wealth and position for the clever and ambitious man and, for the not-so-clever or ambitious, it was at the least an alternative variant of the perantau, petty trader pattern. Once established in the civil service, a man could find a place for his own kemanakan somewhere on the office staff, in the same fashion that a merchant or artisan would take his kemanakan into his business or place them with a friend. As a result, families who specialized in civil service jobs developed in the same manner as, formerly, merchant, artisan, and religious families had grown up in Minangkabau. One needed only interest sufficient to send a son for training and then a mamak strategically placed to assure the aspiring bureaucrat a job. Among the positions available, some were obviously more important in terms of power and patronage than others.

The most important Minangkabau official in the early period was the *jaksa*, the prosecuting magistrate in the Dutch civil and criminal court system. As the Dutch occupied areas of West Sumatra, they began to introduce a judicial administration similar to that used on Java. It was based on judicial councils called *landraad*, which functioned as courts of first instance for both civil and criminal cases and were intended to smooth the interaction between the new legal demands of colonial rule and Minangkabau society. Judgment was often based on a combination of adat "law" and the newly instituted East Indies civil and criminal codes. The landraad were composed of local Dutch officials and Minangkabau chiefs, and they ranged from small, almost informal village level courts to the large regional landraad at the Assistant Residency and Residency levels. Each of the more important councils had its own jaksa. He was salaried by the government—receiving at first from f. 35 per month to f. 75, depending on the importance of the council he served and the scope of his duties. Minangkabau clerks were also appointed to keep council records; they received f. 15 to f. 30 per month.[57] The jaksa's duties were numerous and varied; for example, those of the Head Jaksa of Padang, in charge of the Residency of the Lowlands, included: serving as public prosecutor and investigator, supervising prisoners, keeping jail registers, arranging delivery of prisoners to court, reporting to the Resident at least twice a week on local conditions generally, and maintaining contact with the top Minangkabau officials of the area.[58] The jaksa was not envisioned by the Dutch as merely another indigenous legal expert. Each judicial council already had its own religious advisor to discuss the Quranic law which applied to the cases under review; the bulk of the council's membership was composed of penghulu and government chiefs who presumably represented adat wisdom.[59] Nor was the jaksa merely an indigenous secretary to the court. He usually acted as the most important advisor to the European presiding official, who rarely knew or cared much about the case over which he was passing judgment and therefore depended on the jaksa to give him both a brief and an informed opinion about the ramifications of the affair.[60]

---

57 Report of General de Stuers, May 17, 1826, *Verbaal*, October 23, 1826, No. 48.
58 Instructions of General de Stuers, March 16, 1825, *Exhibitum*, August 24, 1826, No. 41.
59 Ibid.
60 Governor Sumatra's West Coast Heckler, June 23, 1906, *Verbaal*, September 12, 1912, No. 66.

The jaksa, then, occupied a position which enabled him to modify the demands and influence the decisions of both Minangkabau rulers and foreign administrators. As such, he had many opportunities for personal gain, and although his salary was high relative to that of other officials corruption was a real problem.[61] The jaksa had a great deal of patronage, providing jobs for members of his family and for friends, and in villages where interfamily connections were especially close, he not only attracted a large number of his own dependents into his and related government bureaus, but also many other villagers as well. For example, very shortly after a man from Kota Gedang in Agam was made the jaksa for Riau, the taxcollector, opium monopoly administrator, many minor clerks, and a large number of merchants in the residency capital of Riau all came from the same village.[62] Such an occurrence was especially common in the early years when many clerks and minor officials were recruited as apprentices for the government offices and trained on the job. Influence and connections were more important under such circumstances than if there was a network of schools which could provide a wide variety of well-trained candidates.[63]

The selection of the first few jaksa was apparently very dependent on the opinion of the individual local Dutch administrator concerning the person best qualified, in ability both to perform his function and to command respect from among his compatriots. These jaksa were not penghulu, but many did come from among the important branch families of the major lineages. For example a Head Jaksa of Padang came from the collateral branch of an important penghulu lineage in Kota Gedang, as did the previously-mentioned jaksa of Riau.[64]

Many civil service families date their entry into the upper levels of government administration from the appointment of a relative as jaksa in the 1830s to 1840s. As the criteria of selection to government service changed to emphasize formal education, officials such as the jaksa were able to assure entry of their kemanakan into the secular schools and thus

---

[61] Governor Sumatra's Westcoast Meis, March 29, 1860, *Verbaal*, March 7, 1863, No. 27.
[62] Nj. H. A. Salim of Kota Gedang, interview, March 1967, in Jakarta.
[63] This does not mean to imply that civil servants as a group did not retain a continuous advantage; they could usually guarantee entry for their own children into the government schools.
[64] Elders of Kota Gedang (IV Kota), interviews, October 1967, in Kota Gedang.

guarantee the family's continued access to high level jobs. Next to the jaksa the position of warehousemaster (to be discussed later) was the main building block for the new civil service elite. Of somewhat less importance were the "indigenous secretaries" to the Dutch controleur, Assistent Residents, and Residents. These men by their proximity to authority could often influence policy and its execution and they too had important patronage powers.

As a result, then, of the Dutch administrative presence in the village and the consequent interference in local affairs there was a change in the operation of traditional adat politics. A status quo was created whereby those who already held lineage titles and those who first became laras- and nagarihoofd had both official support and also extralegal opportunities to assure that their families retained such titles. To the Dutch, with their belief that an adat aristocracy did and should exist, this situation was as it should be. But to the families who in traditional society could have hoped to capture the title of penghulu, that possibility was usually no longer open, although Dutch reports about "extralegal" and "illegal" penghulu show that it was still possible for some changes to take place within the adat elite. Fortunately for the middle level families, and probably for the stability of Minangkabau society as a whole, the colonial administration also opened new opportunities outside the hardening village political system. The future success of these families was to be found in the new colonial civil service, and its subsidiary organizations, which rapidly increased in size and importance during the course of the nineteenth century.

CHAPTER FOUR
ECONOMIC REORGANIZATION: TAXATION AND THE CULTIVATION SYSTEM

In the precolonial period, village economic life in the Padang Highlands (and to a lesser extent along the coast) tended to be organized around the major product of a given village. The plains villagers mainly grew rice and did only a little weaving, metallurgy, or trading. These occupations existed but on the periphery, and the local village artisan or merchant was often an orang datang, a perantau from some nearby hill village. Each plains village naturally also grew a little coffee, pepper, tobacco, chili peppers, fruit, etc., but these crops would be confined to the fringes of the rice fields and around the houses. The harvests from such crops would be small and intended mainly for home consumption, although occasionally some could be traded at the weekly market.

In the hill villages, the pattern was reversed. Because their topography was in general unsuited for sawah, the hill villages grew dry rice and proportionately more cash crops, at first mainly pepper, but after the eighteenth century, coffee. Some villagers supplemented the rice harvest by making pots, weaving cloth, or working in gold. With the exception of rice, the products which the Europeans bought in the west coast ports usually came from the hill villages. Most of the coffee sold in Padang, for example, was grown in the northern areas near Bonjol, the hillsides of Lakes Maninjau and Singkarak, and the hill villages outside Solok.[1] The villagers also supplemented their rice income with a highly developed tradition of perantau merchants and artisans whose extravillage activity

---

1 Report by General de Stuers on the Situation in Sumatra's West Coast, May 17, 1826, *Verbaal*, October 23, 1826, No. 48.

not only relieved the pressure on the harvest but also generated outside income.

The institution which integrated the economic world of the highlands, binding the hill villages to the plains, was the weekly market (*pekan* which means both week and market in the Minangkabau dialect). Within a given geographic area, the major market rotated to a different town each day of the week. The markets were not only centers for economic exchange but for swapping information, where traveling merchants and artisans brought news and opinions about events outside the village world. And it was not just established traders who sold at the markets; many local people earned extra income disposing of their surplus fruit, vegetables, rice, or handicrafts there.

The nagari derived an important part of its public income from taxing peddlers who came to trade, with the nagari council charging each tradesman a small sum for the privilege of participating. The taxes thus collected could be used to finance village celebrations, repair the council hall, or compensate the penghulu for their services on the nagari council. (Labor for major projects could be obtained by levies on the nagari lineages, through an extension of the serayo service which the members of a lineage owed their penghulu. But projects requiring massive labor supplies must have been few, if indeed there were any at all.)

The arrival of the Dutch in the highlands changed the economic order within just a few decades. The new rulers had a large standing army and an administrative bureaucracy to support, and consequently needed an organized and regular supply of food, materiel, and revenue. They were, moreover, determined to use their superior power and administrative organization to get what they wanted.

Early Revenue Programs: Excise Taxes, Free Coffee Trade

As with the political institutions, also in the economic sphere the first Dutch officials thought that they would be able to use existing structures and institutions, merely diverting the profits from their prior recipients. Nagari excise taxes would now be organized more systematically; new ones would be instituted, and collections would be made more certain. Establishing a secure and permanent European presence also required major investment in buildings and roads to assure the smooth operation of government. Thus it was decided to recruit labor through corvée levies based on an enlarged and reinterpreted concept of the existing serayo obligations. Such new programs would take care of daily administrative costs and needs. Profits would be derived through sales of coffee and other crops, which, according to the colonial organizers, the now secure and contented Minangkabau could be expected to grow and sell to the Dutch trading concerns in great quantities.

Much of the Dutch economic policy and organization before about 1850 was based on the concept of the Minangkabau as "rational," "economic" people. By definition, therefore, the Dutch expected them to understand, without being coerced , the value of a secure countryside, an orderly government, and a protected export market. An example of this sort of Dutch thinking was the debate in 1823 over the need for a land tax. Batavia authorities suggested that a land tax similar to the one already assessed in Java be imposed in the recently pacified areas of the highlands. Officials recognized that the Minangkabau had never paid direct taxes on property to anyone, but the Director of State Revenue argued that, as they were "so far advanced on the road to civilization," the Minangkabau would certainly understand the need for a tax to finance "good" and "beneficial" government.[2] De Stuers and others on the scene were less convinced; they believed, moreover, that the administrative costs of assessing and collecting such a tax would be too high.[3]

Rather than introduce an entirely new system of taxation, de Stuers thought the government should use existing adat-style levies, specifically the various nagari "excise taxes" on village activities. Some similar taxes were already being collected by de Stuers' predecessors, for example, levies on selling tobacco, working iron mines, installing penghulu, and holding cockfights.[4] De Stuers enlarged the scope of the taxes and, in 1825, instituted a tax on the markets in the highlands areas then under Dutch

---

2 Director of State Revenue, Batavia, October 27, 1823, contained in E. B. Kielstra, *Sumatra's Westkust, 1819-1890*, 3 vols. (The Hague: Bijdragen Reprint, 5th Series, n.d.), 1, pp. 86-87.
3 General de Stuers, Regulations for the Market Tax, March 10, 1825 and the Report of General de Stuers to the Governor General, August 30, 1825, *Exhibitum*, August 24, 1826, No. 41. The so-called Plakaat Pandjang, or Long Declaration (see above p. 41), promised, among other things, that no direct taxes would ever be levied on the Minangkabau or their property.
4 Proposal of Residents du Puy and Raaff, September 1823, in Kielstra, *Sumatra's Westkust*, 1, pp. 84-85.

control. The tax, payable in money or kind, affected everyone who did any business in the market, from the owner of a permanent coffeeshop, to the "housewife" selling her surplus chilies. There was massive local resistance to the tax, but de Stuers believed that this occurred because the Minangkabau had never had a centralized authoritative administration and thus were not accustomed to delivering taxes to any government. He expected resistance would be only a temporary problem. But he encountered a more serious resistance in his dealings with the local penghulu, who were supposed to help encourage their subordinates to pay taxes quietly. De Stuers thought that the penghulu had agreed that the tax was a reasonable exercise of government authority, but he found that, in practice, all cooperation disappeared. Like the Javanese, he complained, the Minangkabau will agree, when asked, with all government prescripts, but, unlike the Javanese who will then obey, the Minangkabau will demur and, if pressed, will flee to the jungle.[5]

Seen from the Minangkabau point of view, the tax was an obvious outside encroachment on their daily lives, and the way in which it was collected only served to underscore this fact. There is no indication from the records just how much or with whom the Dutch consulted before they decided that the market tax was a viable answer to the need for revenue. A few client penghulu in Padang could hardly speak for the nagari councils in the highlands, but one suspects that these penghulu are the ones to whom de Stuers refers. Worse yet, the tax was to be collected by foreigners. The right to collect the tax in a particular geographic area was sold at auction to private individuals; these usually turned out to be Chinese. The Chinese had arrived in the highlands in the wake of the Dutch army, whom they served as contractors or for whom they performed other functions needed by a new administration. Though, in contrast to Java, they never gained an important hold on the economic life of Minangkabau, yet these Chinese must have exacerbated the tensions between the tax-collecting government and the Minangkabau.[6]

---

5 Report of General de Stuers to the Governor General, August 30, 1825, *Exhibitum*, August 24, 1826, No. 41.
6 The 1920 census, for example, recorded only 11,086 Chinese as against 1,505,000 Minangkabau. In Minangkabau, the Chinese remained concentrated in only the largest mercantile centers, dealing in bulk import-export goods or contracting for the government. Of the total mentioned for 1920, almost 10,000 lived in the eight largest towns: Padang (5,985); Bukittinggi

In the first assessment, that of 1825, a total of forty-nine markets were taxed—thirty-four in Tanah Datar and fifteen in Agam.[7] But in the first eight months of operation, only f. 400 had been collected and that only after the greatest difficulty; the collectors had repeatedly been chased away by the merchants and petty traders. In 1826, increased efforts netted f. 800 for the first three months alone, but still de Stuers believed that the amount collected did not justify the effort required. In addition to the difficulties encountered in areas where the tax had already been put into effect, in many other areas, notably along the coast and in the Solok region, it had not even been introduced. Government monopolies on the sale of opium and salt also fared poorly; in the highlands, the concessionaire, again usually Chinese, was often beaten and sometimes killed.[8]

The Dutch in 1825 and 1826 were not really in a position to enforce any very unpopular policy, for the bulk of their armies were in Java fighting Diponegoro's forces. In West Sumatra they had only 263 European troops, under 27 officers, and another 392 Indonesian troops (non-Minangkabau, colonial army forces),[9] mostly stationed in the highlands to protect the six existing government establishments—at Batu Sangkar, Suroaso, Padang Ganting, Tanjung Alam, Bukittinggi, and Guguk Sigandang—all located in Tanah Datar or southern Agam.[10] The Dutch could not afford to antagonize their client villages unduly, and so the issue of taxes on the markets was quietly dropped.

Despite the failure of the effort to raise local taxes, the Dutch regime was not without revenue sources; its major income continued to come from the export tax on coffee.[11] The main economic impetus behind Dutch involvement in the highlands had been control of the coffee trade, and thus de Stuers thought it better to concentrate efforts on increasing coffee production. He anticipated that the profits from this would take

---

(539); Sawah Lunto, mainly mine laborers (534); Payakumbuh (736); Padang Panjang (475); Pariaman (452); Painan (452); and Balai Selasa (296).

7 Report of General de Stuers on the Market Tax, *Exhibitum*, August 24, 1826, No. 41.
8 Report of General de Stuers on the situation in Sumatra's West Coast, May 17, 1826, *Verbaal*, October 23, 1826, No. 48.
9 Ibid.
10 Report of General de Stuers to the Governor General, August 30, 1825, *Exhibitum*, August 24, 1826, No. 41.
11 Report of General de Stuers on the Situation in Sumatra's West Coast, May 17, 1826, *Verbaal*, October 23, 1826, No. 48.

care of administrative costs as well as provide extra revenue.[12]

Coffee was not native to the Indies but in 1699, the VOC had begun a campaign to spread its cultivation in Java, in response to an increasing demand in the European market.[13] It seems reasonable to assume that VOC factors in Painan and Padang did likewise in West Sumatra. The contracts signed between the VOC and the coastal raja in the seventeenth century, though at first directed towards pepper cultivation, were probably revised to stress coffee when this became a more profitable crop. Certainly by the late eighteenth century, coffee had bypassed pepper as the most important export from West Sumatra, and the eighteenth-century trade agreements with coastal chiefs specifically mentioned coffee cultivation.[14] Similar agreements were later reached with highlands villages when they were absorbed into the Dutch sphere of influence. In each case chiefs were guaranteed a commission of about f. 0.25 on each picul produced by their dependents.

Although these agreements did not constitute "forced delivery," yet the government also made it clear that continuation of a chiefs favorable relations with the authorities was largely dependent on the degree of enthusiasm which he showed in supervising coffee cultivation and expanding production in his area. Government directives instructed the chiefs to provide for the careful and ordered arrangement of coffee gardens, to keep records on the number of trees in their districts and to organize delivery to the government depots.[15] The arrangement was quite favorable for the various penghulu. In addition to the coffee commissions, they were also in a position to act as the contractors for sales of coffee to the government or, at least, as the agency through which other contractors must deal if they wished to buy village coffee.

As the Dutch extended their influence into the interior, in the 1820s, they became more aware of the rather casual and haphazard manner in which coffee cultivation was undertaken at the village level. This resulted in low quality beans and in fluctuations from place to place and year to year in the quantity and quality of the crop. General de Stuers

---

12 Ibid.
13 *Encyclopaedië van Nederlandsch-Indië* (The Hague: Nijhoff, 1917), 2, p. 385.
14 Kielstra, *Sumatra's Westkust*, 1, pp. 15-16.
15 Ibid.

experimented with the establishment of regulated plots devoted solely to coffee, hoping that such plantings would result in increased quality and yields. He reported, in 1826, that he had established thirty gardens with some 10,000 bushes. Local penghulu in the Dutch-controlled coffee areas of Agam and the XIII Kota were apparently pressured into allotting nagari grazing or vacant land for coffee and then organizing villagers as a communal labor force.[16] Since it takes coffee trees some five years to mature and bear much fruit, de Stuers' regulated groves could not be an immediate success in any event. No record exists of what happened to them.

Despite endemic warfare in the interior and the fact that the major producing areas in the north were within the Padri sphere of influence, coffee exports increased between 1819 and 1825, from 4,464 piculs to 32,887.[17] Dutch officials interpreted this as evidence of an enthusiastic Minangkabau response to the commercial advantages offered by the new order. According to Padang authorities, if the Minangkabau were interested enough to produce more coffee under existing adverse conditions, what greater results might not be expected if peace and order could be brought to the producing areas and an improved means of transportation found to channel the harvest to Padang.[18] Dutch officials did not apparently contemplate the fact that the increases represented only sales to the government, not production. Moreover such sales might be not in spite of adverse conditions in the interior, but rather because of them.

Irrigated rice requires more intensive and constant attention than other crops. Rice yields would thus be affected drastically by chaotic conditions which kept peasants away from their fields or destroyed dikes and new seedlings. A bad rice harvest would force the plains farmers to rely to a greater degree on sales of other crops, such as coffee, the profits from which could be used to buy foodstuffs. There is nothing in the records which indicates that the Minangkabau were in fact showing a greater interest in planting coffee or improving cultivation techniques.

---

16 Report of General de Stuers on the Situation on Sumatra's West Coast, May 17, 1826, *Verbaal*, October 23, 1826, No. 48.
17 H. J. J. L. Ridder de Stuers, "Verslag van Padang 1828 (1. 1825)," Padang, May-July 1826, KITLV Manuscript, H 726.
18 Ibid.

One could expect, then, that once conditions returned to normal, the peasants would probably return to full-time rice cultivation; coffee sales would drop off unless prices were very favorable. The future should have appeared ominous to the Dutch rather than rosy, for, accompanying the dramatic increase in sales of coffee, was a corresponding decline in its world market price, from f. 30 per picul in 1819 to f. 12 in 1825.[19]

By 1831, Padang authorities were indeed concerned about a general decline in coffee sales, noticeable since 1826; the decline in fact affected the volume and value of the whole import-export trade. Added to the decline in coffee prices, unrest in the interior had increased after 1825 when the troops were withdrawn to Java; this caused an increasing disruption of trade links between the coffee-producing areas and the west coast. Although production apparently continued, much of the harvest was routed toward the east coast.[20] With the renewed hostilities, coffee from Padri areas in the north was no longer brought south to Dutch-controlled market centers such as Bukittinggi or Pariaman. Now it too was moved east through the passes near Payakumbuh and down the Kampar and Siak Rivers to the Malacca Straits. It seemed to Padang officials, consequently, that Dutch political influence over all the producing areas combined with a systematic Dutch-controlled collection network was going to be crucial if the coffee profits were to be guaranteed to Dutch warehouses.

Establishment of a "Protected Price"

Governor General van den Bosch made a fact-finding visit to Sumatra, in 1833, to determine the best way to increase Dutch profits from Minangkabau without a corresponding increase in Dutch administration or military entanglements in the area. As the Minangkabau were an "energetic people devoted to trade," he hoped that the government would need only to establish peace and then build a road network which could channel the fruits of indigenous energy into Dutch warehouses.[21] But the government had to work out some means for encouraging producers

---

19 Ibid.
20 Ibid.
21 Governor General van den Bosch to Resident Elout, February 21, 1832, in Kielstra, *Sumatra's Westkust*, 2, pp. 129-32.

to bring the coffee to government buyers rather than sell it to local, Minangkabau middlemen, who usually went directly to the village to buy. These middlemen were disparaged by government sources because they raised the final price at which Dutch factors in Padang must buy the coffee, thereby reducing the margin of Dutch profit on resale to exporters.

The traditional collection method (still operating in the 1830s) consisted of numerous Minangkabau petty traders gathering the harvests from local growers at the weekly village markets, then usually reselling them to larger merchants in regional marketing centers such as Bukittinggi. From there bearers carried the coffee, and other goods as well, to the west coast over treacherous and unsafe trails, so narrow and steep that not even horses could travel them. Each man carried about 60 pounds, for which he received about f. 0.50 per day in wages. It took about five days to reach Padang from the collection point at Batu Sangkar. In addition, local chiefs imposed tolls on those using the trails through their districts, and this, too, added to the overhead on the coffee.[22]

Van den Bosch reasoned that, if the government could organize its own transport system relying on levies of corvée labor, it could then undersell the private traders in Padang. It could afford to offer the producers in the highlands a higher price because of the money saved in transportation costs. Van den Bosch suggested establishing a protected price of f. 9 per picul for all coffee sold to government warehouses, as against the open market price at the time in the highlands of only f. 6 to f. 8 per picul; local buyers should not be able to offer any more because of their high transport costs.[23] In van den Bosch's view even by paying the higher price the government would still realize almost 100 percent profit on resale in Padang,[24] and under such conditions, he believed, forced cultivation would be neither desirable nor necessary.

The Dutch state trading company, the Nederlandsch Handel-Maatschappij (NHM) contracted with the East Indies government to establish warehouses at strategic points in the highlands, which would serve as exchange centers where farmers sold coffee and bought

---

22 De Stuers, "Verslag van Padang."
23 Governor General van den Bosch, Memorandum to Commissioner van Sevenhoven, October 11, 1833, No. 311, in Kielstra, *Sumatra's Westkust*, 3, pp. 75-76.
24 Ibid.

government salt and opium and also the NHM's imported goods. The NHM contract guaranteed the company a 5 percent commission on the coffee which it delivered to the government and also on its sales of government salt. It could sell imported goods on its own account, and it hoped, in the process, to undersell goods which came via the east coast from Singapore.[25]

The government, for its part, agreed to provide transportation for both coffee and the other commodities the NHM would handle. In this regard, a major road was planned to connect Padang to the highlands at Padang Panjang, which would be cut through the Anei Pass, a small chasm through which the Anei River flows. The road would make possible bulk transport of goods and help cut costs to the government in its ongoing competition with native traders. In the interim, the government bearer service (*kuliedienst*) would be responsible for handling NHM merchandise, in addition to other duties related to transport of war materiel and the property of government bureaus and officials.

The road, through the Anei Pass, constructed as part of this agreement with the NHM, was a major accomplishment, combining Dutch engineering and corvée labor. In many places, it had to be carved out of sheer rock faces. The pass itself is some ten miles long, climbing from 450 feet above sea level at Kayu Tanam to 2,535 feet at its outlet near Padang Panjang.[26] Construction of the road brought great hardship to nearby villages in Agam and Tanah Datar, for villagers ordered to work on the road often had to travel as much as a day's journey to reach the worksite. Corvée laborers had to be brought in from the surrounding areas because the region of the Anei Pass itself was only thinly populated, as there was no land suitable for settled agriculture and hence no villages. The Dutch decreed that all inhabitants in areas under their control were liable for corvée duty, excepting only women, "religious officials," and the aged. The laras- and nagarihoofd, working through the penghulu suku, organized the levies. Each man had to bring his own food. The village had to arrange for the tools and often transportation to the worksite as well.[27]

---

25 W. M. F. Mansvelt, *Geschiedenis van de Nederlandsch Handel-Maatschappij (1824-1924)* [henceforth *NHM*] (Haarlem: Enschede [1924]), 2, pp. 53-54.
26 *Encyclopaedië van Nederlandsch-Indië*, 1, p. 51.
27 A. W. P. Verkerk Pistorius, *Studien over de Inlandsche Huishouding in de Padangsche*

Maintenance of the Anei Pass road proved equally burdensome because frequent heavy rains and flash floods destroyed bridges and caused landslides across the road. To alleviate the burden, the government finally agreed that an individual could pay f. 6 per year, known as the *kloofgelden* (pass money), in lieu of personal service. The government then used these funds to hire labor or to finance the use of convict labor.[28]

Private sales of coffee in Padang continued despite the predicted advantages of selling to the government. Much of this "private" coffee, however, probably came from nongovernment territories. Although van den Bosch had predicted that 50,000 to 70,000 piculs would be delivered to the government each year, the actual potential production of the government-controlled areas was in fact little more than some 40,000 piculs. Another 40,000 piculs was produced annually in areas outside government influence at this time—particularly the XII, XIII and XX Kota, the Danau (Lake Maninjau) area and in the southern districts.[29] Van den Bosch himself did not consider the private sales an immediate problem; the government would not suffer a great loss because it collected a high export tax on private coffee. He counseled patience, believing that later, after gaining full control over the interior and hence all the trade routes, the administration could raise the export duty so high that the private traders could no longer compete, and the entire coffee harvest would fall to the government.[30]

The NHM was not disposed to wait patiently for the above eventuality; the company received a commission only on the coffee actually sold to government warehouses. The government, meanwhile, continued to urge the expansion of NHM posts into newly pacified areas, such as Bonjol in the north and the XIII Kota in the south. NHM officials saw no profit in this, but only an "overextension" of their already scarce resources. It seemed increasingly clear to the NHM that its warehouses were intended

---

Bovenlanden (Zalt-Bommel: Norman, 1871), pp. 169 and 171.
28 *Encyclopaedië van Nederlandsch-Indië*, 1, p. 51; *Verslag van het Beheer en den Staat der Nederlandsche Bezittingen en Kolonien in Oost- en West-Indië en ter Kust van Guinea*, ingediend door den Minister van Kolonien [more commonly known as the *Koloniaal Verslag*], 1863, p. 25 and *1881*, p. 75.
29 Letter of E. Francis, May 8, 1834, in E. B. Kielstra, "De Koffiecultuur ter Westkust van Sumatra," *IG*, 10 (1888), p. 1443.
30 Governor General van den Bosch to Resident Francis, February 16, 1835, in Kielstra, "Koffiecultuur," p. 1444.

to fulfill a political function, that is to serve as concrete symbols of Dutch presence, rather than to meet any specific economic needs. This suspicion was confirmed when government officials suggested that NHM warehouse personnel not be overly critical about the quality of the coffee offered for sale, because to do so might divert even more of the harvest into the private sector. As a result, NHM officials complained, they had to accept coffee deliveries which were a mixture of beans in all stages of maturity and all degrees of quality.[31]

Dutch attempts to establish the NHM as the monopoly supplier of import goods were equally unsuccessful, for import goods from the east coast continued to undersell those carried at the NHM depots. Company officials did not believe they would be able to counteract this situation in the foreseeable future.[32] NHM expenses had continued high because the company could not depend on the government's promise of free transport for the goods. The transportation service and its available wagons and animals had been commandeered to assist in the various military operations in the highlands; transport was only rarely made available for the NHM's commercial ventures. As a result, rather than paying for itself, the combined government-NHM operation in West Sumatra was incurring a yearly debt of almost f. 1 million.[33] The NHM, therefore, refused to extend its commercial activities any farther, and, as the various warehouse contracts with the government came due, the company refused to renew them. The last NHM warehouse, the one at Payakumbuh, closed in 1841. After this in order to sell coffee to the government, growers again had to transport harvests to the depots on the coast—Padang, Pariaman, or Air Bangis.[34]

---

31 Mansvelt, *NHM*, 2, p. 61.
32 Ibid., pp. 55-56.
33 Ibid., p. 62.
34 Ibid., p. 60.

Table 2. Padang Coffee Exports					
Year	Piculs	Year	Piculs*	Year	Piculs*
1826	48,437	1862	135,000	1880	130,000
1827	39,684		9,000		3,400
1828	29,371	1863	124,600	1881	106,400
1829	39,703		5,800		2,600
1830	27,697	1864	164,400	1882	99,800
1831	40,200		8,400		2,000
1832	60,794	1865	116,000	1883	141,200
1833	80,753		6,000		3,600
1834	78,581	1866	132,400	1884	88,920
1835	78,837		6,400		1,600
1836	84,823	1867	121,200	1885	101,225
1837	59,920		6,000		1,600
1838	56,295	1868	174,200	1886	50,345
1839	96,180		7,600		800
1840	90,961	1869	154,800	1887	75,528
1841	93,949		6,800		1,170
1842	83,080	1870	157,000	1888	105,290
1843	100,384		6,800		2,100
1844	74,697	1871	162,000	1889	47,166
1845	81,941		8,000		525
1846	66,973	1872	81,800	1890	50,135
1847	58,224		6,200		640
1848	56,101	1873	97,800	1891	58,975
1849	52,833		4,400		550
1850	71,118	1874	121,800	1892	56,186
1851	84,976		5,600		1,530
1852	122,903	1875	131,400	1893	58,817
1853	137,679		6,800		1,415
1854	131,522	1876	138,000	1894	23,278
1855	127,547		3,200		441
1856	128,259	1877	158,000	1895	43,159
1857	190,947		6,200		650

1858	129, 121	1878	84, 400	1896	45, 664
1859	120, 259		2, 600		1, 290
1860	151, 057	1879	103, 600		
1861	150, 000		2, 600		

* The top number indicates first class coffee and the lower one, second class.

Source: *Encyclopaedië van Nederlandsch-Indië*, 2, p. 275.

Economically, for the Dutch the first two decades of their rule in the highlands were a standoff and perhaps even a setback. They had invested troops and time into creating a sphere of influence which should have assured them control over West Sumatran coffee. But the bulk of the coffee came from the hill villages, still, in the late 1830s, not fully under Dutch suzerainty. The Dutch adventure was proving lucrative mainly to the perantau traders who now not only handled export crops and local sales but also acted as the intermediaries in provisioning the new European forces. Farmers in the government areas often found it more profitable to grow foodstuffs to supply the government's military and civilian personnel than to grow coffee. This was especially true in the period around 1837, when the final assault on the Padri dissidents in the north was being carried out and the Dutch had secure control over the plains.[35]

The Dutch tried to halt the trend away from coffee growing by raising the protected price, but in 1838 less coffee was being sold to the government than in 1835, before the price increase. Part of the problem was the continuing drain of coffee to merchants from the east coast in exchange for imported goods from Singapore.[36] Coffee exports from Padang fluctuated throughout the 1830s, and an important factor in the fluctuation was apparently the degree of pressure exerted by the laras- and nagarihoofd to channel the coffee harvests to government dealers. In 1833, after the announcement of a drive to encourage production, local chiefs thought to ingratiate themselves with the authorities by coercing

---

[35] Report of General Michiels on Coffee Cultivation, February 4, 1839, in Kielstra, "Koffiecultuur," pp. 1450-51.
[36] Ibid., p. 1450.

their dependents into making large deliveries to the warehouses. But this caused unrest, especially in areas where private dealers offered higher prices or where other crops were more profitable. The Dutch were already busy fighting the Padri and did not want revolt to erupt behind their lines, so officials cautioned the chiefs against undue pressure. The precipitous drop in deliveries between 1836 and 1837 was attributed by General Michiels, the new Resident, to the decrease in pressure on local growers.[37]

General Michiels himself conducted a full-scale investigation of the coffee problem in 1838 and 1839, and he concluded that forced cultivation and delivery were the only answer. He believed the government should directly control the growers themselves by establishing links to the penghulu suku. Production could then be organized by lineage group, making each one responsible for a certain amount. Forced delivery would have the additional virtue of ridding the countryside of the thousands of petty traders whom Michiels dismissed as unnecessary "parasites" and "swindlers," whose only contribution was to raise the ultimate cost of goods. They should be "forced to return to agriculture."[38]

The Governor General delayed action on Michiels' proposals because of the cost involved and also because such a program would be impractical until all pockets of Padri resistance were eliminated and the territory closely organized directly under the new Dutch administration. Meanwhile, exports had increased again, reaching a new peak in 1843, which probably represented the surge caused by Dutch control over all the producing areas. The government then felt delay had been justified. But by 1844, exports began declining again, and they continued dropping until the end of the decade. In 1847, Batavia gave Miehiels a free hand to reorganize coffee production and collection along the lines he had suggested in 1839.[39]

---

37 Ibid.
38 Ibid., p. 1455.
39 Decision of Governor General Rochusen, March 30, 1847, No. 8, in Kielstra, "Koffiecultuur," p. 1485.

The Coffee Cultivation System

The 1847 decision by Batavia represented a symbolic watershed in Minangkabau relations with the outside world and in their historical development as well. The Dutch had been establishing a skeleton administration in the nagari before 1847, but there had been no real effort to use it for much more than peacekeeping, occasional corvée levies, and general administration. Some government chiefs had pressured their dependents into growing more coffee, but no specific government policy had sanctioned such interference in the daily round of village affairs because the government had believed it unnecessary. In 1847, the government changed its mind.

Control of cultivation and delivery, however, required a more permanent and differentiated colonial bureaucracy. It also increased the pressures on the villages to provide goods and services for the new establishment as well as to satisfy the specific demand to grow more coffee. Both kinds of pressure were detrimental to village interests as their inhabitants saw them. Large government establishments grew up in the important regional centers, especially in the highlands plains areas. Alongside the burden which this represented, however, it did also provide new markets for foodstuffs, new needs for transport services, and new bureaucratic job opportunities. The burden was not the same for everyone, nor for anyone all the time.

The expansion in the coffee cultivation system directly affected the hill villages more than the plains. Partly this resulted from the availability of open land in the hill areas, but also it was a reflection of the nature of coffee itself. Arabica coffee, a prime coffee much in demand in the European market, came originally from the Ethiopian highlands. It grew best in areas with cool weather, good rainfall, and well-drained soil. The sloping hillsides of highlands West Sumatra were thus ideally suited for its cultivation. The hillsides facing on the Indian Ocean near the coastal plain proved less suitable, especially those in the southern districts near Painan. In most of these areas, the hillsides were too steep and rocky, or else they were too close to the sea so there were no villages nearby to provide labor. In other areas the soil and climate were apparently unfavorable, as in the Painan area and farther south.

Most of the hill villages in the highlands had grown coffee since before

1847, but not in the quantity or with the intensity of care and interest which the Michiels' plan envisioned. In descending order, pressure would now be applied from the Dutch controleur (who had general supervision over all cultivation in his region), to the larashoofd (who coordinated Dutch demands with local leaders), to the nagarihoofd (who had to apportion the cultivation tasks among the various suku), and finally to the penghulu themselves (who, as the mamak for their lineages, worked to deflect as much of the government pressure from their followers as possible). Politics and clever maneuvering were at a premium at all levels in this operation; cultivation tasks often reflected the relative power position of a family in the village rather than their ability to spend time growing coffee.

The Dutch offered a commission to the various chiefs at all levels in an effort to buy their loyalty, but the chiefs, especially the nagarihoofd and the penghulu, were also susceptible to direct pressure from their dependents because they depended on their consensus to rule. The individual grower might suffer more or less interference in his daily life in accordance with the relative position of his suku within the village power structure and the relationship of his particular branch within that suku to the penghulu. Much depended upon whether an individual chief were more interested in protecting his clients (whether from humanitarian reasons or because his position was insecure) or advancing his career with the Dutch (whether from personal ambition or fear). The opportunities to play politics or participate in extortion and corruption were many and varied.

Under direction of the controleur, land had to be set aside for coffee groves, preferably a few large plots worked by family groups rather than the former style of scattered individual plantings.[40] The farmer had to terrace the land and clear it to suit the particular notions of the controleur, who closely inspected each September to check on the progress of new seedlings and to make certain that an appropriate cover crop had been planted.[41] The penghulu were encouraged to pledge to plant a certain number of seedlings each year; Michiels suggested that a reasonable

---

40 C. L. Hasselman, "Gouvernement's Koffeecultuur," *Encyclopaedië van Nederlandsch-Indië*, 1, p. 274.
41 General Michiels, Decision on Coffee Deliveries, October 11, 1847, in Kielstra, "Koffiecultuur," p. 1475.

figure would be 100 trees per year per family unit in each suku, at least over the first five years.[42]

Statistics sometimes became more important than reality in deciding how much or where to plant. The villagers and their opinions were often ignored, as was the suitability of a particular area for cultivation. The driving force of many authorities (especially the controleur and larashoofd) was the need to plant more and more trees. In some cases, overzealous officials ordered new groves in areas where the soil was unsuitable, in others in places too far from the villages. New plots were laid out every year, but many never matured—sometimes they had been planted on bad soil; sometimes the cover crop had been poorly selected and had choked off the new seedlings; sometimes officials had ceased close supervision after the initial planting, and the plots were subsequently neglected. The villagers struck back at the increased interference by evading work on the coffee fields whenever possible. A major irritant to them was the continuing government pressure for planting large regular stands of coffee to be worked in common by all members of the village. To the Minangkabau, it made more sense to plant coffee in the time-tested manner and areas—intermixed with other crops, near other fields, in short, on ground proven suitable by past experience.[43]

Planting was not the end of the coffee system's demands on the growers. The trees had to be topped when they reached six feet in height (usually in the first year or so) and afterward carefully and continuously pruned. Otherwise, the tree could develop a tall scraggly growth which bore sparse fruit. The controleur spurred the government chiefs and the penghulu to supervise these operations. In March, he himself had to inspect the new trees, count and grade them, and order the culling of inferior ones.[44] Despite all the time demanded by the young trees from the growers, they did not bear fruit for three years, and produced no sizeable yields for another two after that. Once mature, however, a coffee tree could be expected to produce good crops for about ten years before the yields would begin to decline and the tree had to be destroyed.

---

42 General Michiels, Report on Coffee Cultivation, February 4, 1839, in ibid., p. 1453.
43 *Koloniaal Verslag, 1853*, p. 176.
44 General Michiels, Decision on Coffee Deliveries, October 11, 1847, in Kielstra, "Koffiecultuur, p. 1485.

MAP 3: COFFEE WAREHOUSES

During his March inspection tour, the controleur estimated the expected yield; the chiefs would then be held to this estimate. The Dutch soon discovered that otherwise much of the harvest never reached the government warehouses—it was sold privately, consumed by the family themselves, or merely neglected on the tree while growers pursued other interests.[45] The government announced that it would accept only processed beans—that is, those which had been dried and hulled. Laxity in processing by growers had been a primary complaint by the NHM in the 1830s, and the government was determined not to repeat it. Now the controleur held the chiefs to account for the quality of the beans delivered—broken, green beans mixed with stones and soaked in water to make them heavy would no longer be acceptable. The NHM had been in no position to argue about the quality of the beans it received because, at that time, the government was unable to exert consistent pressure on the growers. But now the regime had the capability to supervise, and the determination to do it. This quality control made life for the grower that much more difficult because he could no longer discharge his cultivation responsibilities merely by picking all the beans at once and selling them. Now he had to wait for each successive set of beans to ripen, and then process them. It was a long drawn-out process which required much effort. According to one estimate by a Dutch observer, for each picul of coffee delivered to the government warehouse, a family spent some 120 days of labor.[46]

Obviously, if coffee were profitable, the farmers would willingly spend the time required to grow it according to government specifications. The record indicates that the peasants did not in fact find coffee especially profitable, unless alternative sources of livelihood failed. All the force of government sanction had to be applied to keep up production statistics. The Michiels' regulations provided for a commission on deliveries not just to the laras- and nagarihoofd, who had received commissions during the era of the "protected price," but also to the penghulu suku. These chiefs received, respectively, f. 0.20, f. 0.20, and f. 0.50 per picul delivered

---

45 Ibid.
46 J. van Vollenhoven, *Padang en het Gouvernement "Sumatra's Westkust": Losse Gedachten over de Oorzaken van Verval en Middelen tot Herstel der Welvaart* (Rotterdam: Bladergroen, 1872), pp. 6-8.

by their constituents.[47] This brought the focus of attention and pressure much closer to the individual grower than had been the case under earlier coffee programs; indeed villagers complained constantly about the undue interference. Although publicly described as a "popular culture," in which cultivation was freely organized[48] and only delivery compulsory, in operation, coercion pervaded the whole system. As shown above, the controleur and the various chiefs were expected to interfere in order to organize a more efficiently grown and better quality crop.

The Dutch, from Batavia to Batu Sangkar, viewed West Sumatra in terms of the coffee it could produce. The administrative apparatus was organized from the very beginning to assure more coffee. More coffee brought the chiefs more money; the Dutch believed this would make them more vigilant and enthusiastic. After the 1840s, as the coffee-cultivation system developed, the debate was less about whether or not to supervise cultivation than how to do it and who should do it. Entries in the daily

Table 3. Coffee Warehouse Purchases (1867-1869 in piculs)

Warehouse Locale	1867	1868	1869
Bukittinggi	14,205	13,182	11,011
Baso	9,634	8,784	6,263
Maninjau	4,319	3,836	1,919
Matur	3,618	3,817	2,756
Palembayan	3,830	3,355	2,459
Pisang	805	520	281
Batu Sangkar	20,513	15,910	25,021
Singkarak	10,389	6,659	11,425
Jambok	5,508	6,994	5,578
Sijunjung	453	388	315
Tanjung Ampalo	1,618	1,324	1,710
Rao-Rao	10,281	12,765	12,388
Buo	3,144	3,221	3,532

---

[47] General Michiels, Report on Coffee Cultivation, February 4, 1839, in Kielstra, "Koffiecultuur," p. 1453.
[48] Report of Governor van Swieten, 1852, *Verbaal*, July 13, 1858, No. 35.

Warehouse Locale	1867	1868	1869
Solok	7,796	6,747	8,420
Supayang	4,735	4,740	3,831
Alahan Panjang	2,657	3,240	2,349
Lolo	1,744	1,825	1,045
Padang Panjang	2,659	2,269	2,396
Batu Buagang	3,423	2.692	4,739
Payakumbuh	3,773	3,810	3,259
Guguk	5,423	4,714	4,061
Situjuh	1,649	1,999	1,797
Lari Lamah	332	510	386
Halaban	3,140	2,543	2,219
Puar Datar	4,107	3,426	3,310
Suliki	3,761	3,192	3,251
Total	133,516	122,462	125,721

Source: *Verbaal*, January 3, 1872, No. 10.

registers of local Dutch and Minangkabau officials for the 1860s indicated that punishments were imposed for neglect of duties associated with coffee cultivation in the same way as for failure to perform corvée tasks.[49] From the very beginning, the Michiels system was considered, at least by local-level authorities, as similar to a corvée requirement. A Dutch high official of the 1860s interpreted the farmers' evasion of coffee work as a result of the "independent nature" of the Minangkabau, combined with the lack of an existing tradition of corvée labor; he did not view their reluctance as the result of any economic hardship. He regarded the "sheer obstinacy" of the Minangkabau as the major obstacle to increased coffee production, saying that they tried to circumvent any regulation whatever, if the government initiated it. The police rolls were filled with the names of villagers charged with failure to perform required labor duties—a situation which the official regarded as without equal elsewhere in the Indies.[50]

---

49 C. Lulofs, "Koffiecultuur en Belasting ter Sumatra's Westkust," *IG*, 26, 2 (1904), p. 1642.
50 *Verbaal*, June 3, 1863, No. 2.

The peasants had real economic grievances, however—the Dutch officials to the contrary. The coffee system, at the least, prevented them from spending time on other more profitable or necessary endeavors, and, at worst, it caused severe economic dislocation. In the 1860s, for example, an epidemic of cattle sickness killed a large proportion of the buffalo and cattle herds in the highlands, animals important to the Minangkabau farmers not only for food but also as draft animals. The rapid spread of the disease, which affected mainly the highland plains areas, was attributed to government insistence that cattle be penned in communal corrals to free open grazing land for planting coffee.[51]

In an effort to include the plains villages in the coffee-cultivation system, the government had wanted to open the nagari nonsawah land for coffee planting. Since that land was already being used as free pasture for cattle, officials decided that the cattle could be corralled and food could be brought to them. The plains areas grew most of the rice produced in West Sumatra, and the death of the cattle and their consequent loss as draft animals meant that less land could be cultivated as sawah. Rice harvests declined.[52] Even without such major disasters, time spent on coffee cultivation generally cut into the time needed for growing food or for other activities crucial to the farmer's daily existence—for example, weaving or part-time peddling. Not only did the peasant often have to neglect his rice crop because he worked in the coffee groves, but even worse, the money earned from the final sale of the coffee harvest would probably not be sufficient to cover the cost of the extra rice or other products he had to buy as a result of his lost time.[53]

In the hill villages, peasants grew little wet rice anyway, but they had to rely on their other crops to provide enough income to buy rice from the plains. For them, the time spent on coffee might better be spent on a more profitable crop or on an activity such as metallurgy or trade. Moreover, the government coffee price was often too low compared to its open market value as well as compared to the relative cost involved in producing it.[54]

---

51 Van Vollenhoven, *Padang en het Gouvernement*, p. 3; Lulofs, "Koffiecultuur," p. 1643.
52 *Koloniaal Verslag, 1869*, p. 145. The harvests dropped from 4,689,000 piculs in 1867 to 3,500,000 in 1868.
53 Van Vollenhoven, *Padang en het Gouvernement*, pp. 6-8.
54 Z. H. Kamerling, "De Vroegere en Tegenwoordige Toestand van Handel, Nijverheid en Landbouw op Sumatra's Westkust, en de Vooruitzichten daarvan voor de Volgende Jaren," *IG*, 17,

As a result, even after the system of forced delivery was instituted, coffee continued to be sold to private merchants who offered better prices than the government warehouses.[55] Other crops were also in increased demand as export items, in particular, nutmegs, tobacco, gambir, gutta percha, and cassia. These were handled by the private sector.

The numerous petty traders and middlemen who had previously dealt in coffee, and who van den Bosch and Michiels had predicted would be forced to return to more "useful" (i.e., agricultural) pursuits, merely switched their attention to the other exportable crops. If government coffee prices were relatively low, the peasants preferred to concentrate on other crops. This process widened the export base of West Coast agriculture (which the government considered a good thing) but at the same time decreased the production of coffee (which the government did not like).[56] The major coffee areas, the hill villages in the highlands, were also the areas of the greatest merantau activity. Many young men left these villages every year, thereby increasing the burden on those remaining. Pressure from local chiefs to keep such men on the land would only have caused intense economic hardship and contributed to local discontent and unrest.

Reorganizing the Economic Infrastructure

The coffee-cultivation system disrupted village life not simply through its demands for greater harvests, but also because it was part of an intensified administration which needed roads, buildings, and transportation facilities in order to operate effectively. To this end, the new administration required a guaranteed and available labor force, organized to serve the government through corvée levies. At the same time that the various village and district chiefs had agreed to encourage greater production among their dependents, they had also agreed to provide labor and materials to construct the warehouses needed to store

---

2 (1895), p. 1070.
55 Ibid. By the end of the century the open market price was f. 30 per picul compared to the government price which had remained at f. 15.
56 Report of the Governor for 1853, *Verbaal*, March 22, 1858, No. 53.

that harvest and the roads to bring it to the regional collection centers.[57] The local residents were already liable for building homes and offices for the Dutch bureaucrats who were the mainstay of the new regime.

The villages of the highlands plains might be able to escape most of the interference in daily life which the coffee cultivation itself entailed because they rarely had enough land suitable for coffee. But they could not avoid the demands for corvée service which were connected with the new coffee-directed administration. The populous rice villages had the human resources upon which a corvée system is based. Also, the major Dutch building projects were located in the administrative capitals—Batu Sangkar, Bukittinggi, and the others—each located in the heart of a sawah plain.

As with the first major work project, the Anei Pass road, so too the rest of the transport network relied heavily on labor recruited from the plains villages. A second road to Padang was constructed along the former main trail to the highlands, that heading east behind Padang, over the hills to Lubuk Selasih (near Alahan Panjang), and then north to Lake Singkarak. It was planned to tie the potential coffee producing areas of the southern highlands to Padang. Though not so difficult a construction job as the Anei Pass road had been, nonetheless, the new road followed a long and difficult path which stretched some thirty-six miles through relatively unpopulated area before reaching the highlands plateau.[58] The other roads constructed about the same time were also built between important (or potentially important) highlands coffee areas and the west coast ports—from Rau to Air Bangis; Maninjau to Tiku, and Pulot-Pulot to Painan. These roads made possible bulk transport of coffee and other items to Dutch-controlled ports in the west; the government confidently predicted that henceforth the bulk trade would be diverted away from the Malacca Straits.[59]

The first traffic along the roads consisted mainly of vehicles on government business. During the early years, few private individuals contracted for the services of the *pedati* (buffalo cart) and packhorse

---

57 General Michiels Report on Coffee Cultivation, October 26, 1847, in Kielstra, "Koffiecultuur," p. 1475.
58 *Encyclopaedië van Nederlandsch-Indië*, 1, p. 51.
59 Report of Governor van Swieten, 1854, *Verbaal*, March 22, 1858, No. 53.

corps which had been organized in response to government needs for transportation of provisions, coffee, import goods, and military materiel. Minangkabau merchants from the highlands or Padang not only lacked the resources to hire the new services, they as yet operated on a scale too small to make bulk transport worthwhile. The old trails were more convenient and were faster than the new roads, which detoured around hills and canyons. Individual travelers and petty traders, who walked to market, continued to use these old paths (and still do today). But larger Minangkabau merchants soon began to appear, and they had an interest and a capacity for using the improved transportation for bulk produce. Moreover, the titled aristocrats created by government design no longer walked but rode.

As new export products developed in response to world demands, private traders needed the carts and horses to get their goods to the harbors. The Minangkabau officials of the new regime rode horseback when touring their areas.[60] Transportation itself, therefore, became an important business as the coffee delivery system and private enterprise extended into all parts of West Sumatra. Large numbers of pedati plied the roads between the coast and the upland producing areas, bringing coffee to the sea and import goods to the highlands. Subsidiary businesses appeared all along the routes in order to service the transport network—coffee houses and rest stations for the drivers, grass-sellers and water carriers for the animals.[61] All of these small business ventures were run by Minangkabau, many of whom, no doubt, had formerly eked out a living in the forests through which the roads passed. Now they could supplement a meager living earned from selling firewood, fruit, resins, and other forest crops by providing services to travelers and traders. In addition, they could sell their own produce more easily because they did not have to carry it all the way to a market town to find a buyer; they sold to one of the traders who passed by on the new roads.

The availability of transport and the development of other export

---

60 Report of Governor van Swieten, 1852, *Verbaal*, July 13, 1858, No. 35.
61 Memorie van Overgave, Governor Heckler, *Verbaal*, April 21, 1911, No. 8. When the railroad was constructed from Padang to Bukittinggi, Payakumbuh, and Sawah Lunto at the turn of the twentieth century, it created much economic dislocation in those areas which had become dependent on servicing the *pedati* transport system for their livelihood.

crops besides coffee benefitted highlands merchants as well. Although slower to enter the field of dealing in wholesale, bulk commodities, Minangkabau families from hill villages, especially in Agam, began to emerge as large "merchandising firms." By pooling family resources, both capital and expertise, and using the influence exerted by relatives in the government service, these families managed to amass great wealth and create regional merchant dynasties. The dynasties were maintained through carefully managed marriage alliances which brought together the necessary resources, both human and financial, into one large family cluster of interests.[62] As Dutch rule spread into other areas of Sumatra, the wealthy merchant families, closely allied to civil service families which ran the administration, followed in the colonial wake.

In addition to roads, the Dutch needed to have numerous buildings constructed to serve as offices, homes, warehouses, and covered market places. As part of the agreements they had exacted from local penghulu in the 1820s and later, the Dutch required that the villagers build these buildings free of charge. The government did not even provide materials or tools beyond certain specialized items, such as the iron works and scales for coffee warehouses. The coffee warehouses had to be built to exacting specifications; at the laras level, for example, they had to have a storage capacity for at least 2,000 piculs (roughly 274,000 pounds) of dried coffee beans. This represents a good-sized structure, as coffee beans are bulky. At the Assistant Residency level, warehouses had to hold 6,000 piculs (about 822,000 pounds). The government agreed, for its part, to build the main highlands warehouse at Padang Panjang, a project which would probably have burdened local villagers beyond the point of endurance. As it was, the first building program called for fifteen major and sixty-six minor warehouses.[63]

The Dutch needed not only warehouses but also homes and offices for the officials who supervised the cultivation system and the regional administration. Each larashoofd demanded his own residence and office in the territorial center for when he had to confer with Dutch officials.

---

62 An example of this is found among several merchant families in the IV Kota district of Agam—particularly among families in Koto Tuo and Sianok. Elders of IV Kota, interview, October 1967, in Koto Tuo.
63 Kielstra, "Koffiecultuur," pp. 1483 and 1485.

To make matters worse, local officials, both Dutch and Minangkabau, often misused the corvée levies, demanding in some cases extravagant architectural styles and decorations which increased the already onerous task.[64] Laras- and nagarihoofd were guilty of using corvée labor to work their personal fields or improve private property.[65]

The burden of this compulsory construction fell hardest in relative terms, on only a few geographic areas and social groups in Minangkabau. In the underpopulated districts, which typically were the hillside areas where coffee was cultivated most intensively and also where roads were more difficult to maintain, villagers might have to spend four times as many days on corvée duty as in the more populated plains areas.[66]

People in the lower socioeconomic groups were the most affected, both because they could not take advantage of the loopholes available to upper-level people and also because they could least afford the time lost to their daily struggle for existence. Bureaucrats and government chiefs, rich merchants with connections, and important adat dignitaries escaped corvée themselves and could also use their influence to gain exemptions for many members of their families. Toward the end of the century, records show that 25 percent of all the ablebodied men in the highlands who were liable for corvée duty had obtained legal exemptions from service.[67] Those who could afford it, hired someone to work in their stead. Traders and merchants in urban centers usually paid a fee to the government in lieu of actual service. Many of the perantau traders and artisans doubtless managed to avoid both service and payment because they moved around so much.[68]

---

64 Verkerk Pistorius, *Inlandsche Huishouding*, pp. 158-59.
65 *Koloniaal Verslag*, 1863, p. 21.
66 Ibid., *1881*, p. 76. The only available figures are those from 1881 which is rather late in the century but at the same time there was less new construction then so the figures may err in the direction of being too low. These figures show that each corvée laborer in Padang served two to three days; whereas each man in Rau served twelve days.
67 Ibid. The total number of ablebodied men was listed as 174,000.
68 Ibid., *1858*, p. 18; *1881*, p. 75. The option of buying off corvée was initiated on a regular basis in Padang in 1858, but de Stuers had allowed it earlier through individual arrangements with the government.

Table 4. Corvée Labor Levies in 1880

Location	Number of Men		Number of Days for Each Type Work				Total	Average Days Work per Laborer for the Year 1880
	Able-bodied Males	Owers of Corvée	Bridge Maintenance	Road Maintenance	Public Works	Military Works		
Padang Lowlands								
Southern Division	20,113	16,413	9,094	60,616	234	--	69,944	about 4
Padang Environs	6,800	6,259	3,290	12,447	--	--	15,737	2 to 3
Air Bangis/Rau	11,282	8,732	--	104,250	1,260	--	105,510	12
Pariaman	30,550	24,077	28,024	135,650	6,472	--	170,146	7
Padang Highlands	173,937	130,317	--	1,295,961	--	--	1,295,961	about 10

Source: *Koloniaal Verslag, 1881*, p. 76.

Another aspect of the reorganization of the economic infrastructure was government attention to increasing food production, in particular rice. This resulted in interference in the affairs of agricultural families in the highlands plains in much the same manner as coffee cultivation had bothered the hill villagers. The Dutch viewed the sawah of Minangkabau not only as sources of food for the members of the new West Sumatra administration but also for Java. Feeding West Sumatra itself was not a major problem because the number of new nonagricultural residents was never very large. These consisted mainly of Dutch government officials and merchants, Chinese contractors, military forces, and all the related families. As foreigners to Minangkabau, they had no land nor could they get any to provide them with rice. Added to these aliens were the numerous Minangkabau traders and others who flocked to the urban centers hoping to profit from the new colonial order. The increase in the nonfarming population raised the prices for rice. The farmers, however, did not react to the increased market as favorably as the Dutch had expected. Through the 1840s, long after the end of the Padri war, whose disruptions had made farming difficult, Padang continued to import as much as 70,000 piculs of rice per year. This occurred despite a fairly high local market price for rice in the highlands.[69]

Dutch officials were determined to reverse the rice-import trend by forcing growers in the highlands plains to pay more careful attention to their sawah. During the early years, therefore, the Dutch pressured Minangkabau chiefs to extend ricefields into hitherto unclaimed wasteland, to improve irrigation, and to supervise planting more closely in order to increase harvests. Dutch officials argued that close government supervision was necessary because otherwise the Minangkabau peasant would not be careful about the best planting times or the proper use of fertilizer.[70] More important than supervision over growing methods was control over marketing. Although Padang had been importing rice from outside West Sumatra in the 1840s, during the same period the highlands were, in fact, exporting rice, but to the eastern ports.[71] As the Dutch gained more control over the highlands and its markets (partly as a result of the new road system), they could channel a much greater percentage of the rice harvest to the west coast. Consequently, by 1850, the government reported that Padang was exporting rice—some 90,000 piculs, most of which went to Java.[72]

Lack of sufficient cheap transportation made it difficult for dealers to offer prices which would attract more peasants to work for increased rice yields. During the early years, much of the available transportation was taken up by the coffee deliveries.[73] Later, in the 1860s, just when it seemed that rice might become an important export crop, the highlands were hit by the cattle sickness which devastated the supply of draft animals and cut down on the rice harvest.[74] Subsequently, rice never recovered its importance as a major export crop. Between 1858 and 1866, rice exports

---

[69] Ibid., *1850*, pp. 81-82.
[70] P. Th. Couperus, "Aanteekeningen Omtrent de Landbouwkundige Nijverheid in de Residentie Padangsche Bovelanden," *TBG*, 5 (1856), pp. 286-96.
[71] Ibid., p. 294.
[72] *Koloniaal Verslag, 1850*, pp. 81-82.
[73] Report of Governor Arriens, *Verbaal*, June 3, 1869, No. 2.
[74] *Koloniaal Verslag, 1869*, p. 145.

had reached as much as 130,000 piculs in one year, but this had declined to only 20,000 in 1878 and to 10,000 by 1881.[75] By the early twentieth century, West Sumatra was a rice-importing area.[76]

Like the hill village farmers, those of the plain apparently turned their attention to other pursuits than those which the government wanted. Perhaps the cultivation requirements of such crops as copra, cassia, and tobacco made them more profitable for the time spent when compared to clearing more land for rice (or coffee). Whatever the reason, as rice cultivation declined these crops were increasing.[77] Other peasants preferred to leave agriculture entirely and pursue different occupations.[78] Apparently, many villagers preferred to buy rice with the profits made from other forms of enterprise.

Absorption into the Indies economic sphere, for all the burdens it brought, also opened new horizons for many Minangkabau. In addition to an enlarged export market for local produce, there was a demand for local skills elsewhere in the archipelago. Many village gold and silver smiths joined the swelling ranks of the perantau who left West Sumatra

---

75 Kamerling, "De Vroegere," p. 1074.
76 Memorie van Overgave, Governor J. Ballott, *Verbaal*, April 5, 1916, No. 15.
77 Ibid.
78 The wide variety of Minangkabau occupations is displayed in some statistics contained in *Koloniaal Verslag, 1875* (pp. 12-13); out of a total population of slightly less than 850,000 there were:

salaried government chiefs	874	handicraftsmen	4,278
unsalaried government chiefs	148	agriculturalists (includes	
adat chiefs	2,380	fishermen and cattlemen)	242,040
recognized religious men	5,903	shipbuilders	215
village headmen	15,349	shippers	1,190
haji	4,010	miners	68
wholesale merchants	111	salaried officials	568
retail merchants	10,983	wage earners	12,155
artisan (entrepreneur)	1	household servants	951
artisans (self-employed)	2,463	soldiers	0
pachter (state monopoly contractors)	59	miscellaneous	5

Table 5. Rice Harvest, 1867-1868

Locale	Piculs of Padi		Rice Price per Picul	
	1867	1868	1867	1868
Padang Highlands	4,089,000	3,138,000	f. 3.35-7.50	f. 3.00-8.50
Padang Environs	121,000	87,000	5.35-6.90	6.26-8.00
Southern Division	377,000	421,000	5.50-7.00	7.00
Pariaman	429,000	275,000	7.09-7.67	8.66-9.66
Air Bangis/Rau	192,000	191,000	2.25-8.00	2.61-7.00
Total	5,208,000	4,112,000		

Source: *Koloniaal Verslag, 1869*, p. 145.

and set up businesses in Java, Borneo, and other parts of the Dutch East Indies. The wares of those who remained home were collected by these adventurous villagers and then carried to places beyond West Sumatra where there was a great demand for fine jewelry, woven gold cloth, and other items of the Minangkabau cottage industries.[79] Local industries sometimes suffered because of the ties to the colonywide economic system; for example, Minangkabau preferred cheaper imported coarse cloth goods to those produced locally.[80] But there were two sides even to this problem, for the weavers of Silungkung and elsewhere could now obtain high quality European thread and dyestuffs which improved the quality and value of the better grades of cloth which they wove. While the cheap European yardgoods might undersell local coarse goods, the market position of the higher-quality local cloth improved.[81]

The benefits of the new markets and transportation accrued mainly to those able to organize relatively large-scale collection and distribution businesses. Many families located in or near important market towns developed profitable merchandising businesses using connections which reached into numerous administrative levels and geographic areas. Their massive wealth, relative to that of other families and sometimes even of chiefs, assured them of position and power within the colonial society

---

[79] Report of the Resident of the Padang Highlands, van der Hart, *Verbaal*, July 13, 1858, No. 35.
[80] Report of Governor van Swieten, 1852, *Verbaal*, July 13, 1858, No. 35.
[81] Verkerk Pistorius, *Inlandsche Huishouding*, p. 37.

and thus enabled them to take advantage of the benefits which that society offered.

New Bureaucratic Opportunities

The coffee delivery system was the most important aspect of Dutch activity in Minangkabau. For the Minangkabau themselves, in addition to the economic opportunities and disruption which it created in the village, the coffee system also opened new bureaucratic positions. Jobs in the local coffee administrative and supervisory apparatus were staffed almost entirely with Minangkabau civil servants. A whole bureaucratic organization began developing as a result of the coffee system, with the warehouse as its focus. From the beginning, the warehouses and their subsidiary collection places were run by Minangkabau; the only European was at the headquarters warehouse for the highlands, located in Padang Panjang. The initial Michiels decision had created five district warehousemasters (*pakhuismeester*), eleven subdistrict warehousemasters, and forty additional clerks to be distributed among the various warehouses.[82] All were Minangkabau.

The warehouses were not only the visible core of the coffee system but also central institutions within the towns and villages where they were placed. Schools were often housed temporarily in them, as were government offices. In the smaller villages the warehousemaster was usually the first, and often the only, man in the village who was literate in Malay, the bureaucratic language of the Indies. For this reason, he often gave lessons to local children, either individually or as part of an organized local school. The warehousemaster had to be at least partly literate and have a rudimentary knowledge of bookkeeping because he kept all the records for coffee production in his district. Local European officials in nearby administrative centers usually kept separate tallies of their own, but this was merely to provide a double check on the honesty of the warehousemaster—his books were the master set.

---

82 Kielstra, "Koffiecultuur," pp. 1484-85.

Table 6. Coffee Warehouses: Michiels' Decision October 11, 1847

Number of Warehouses		Location	European Warehouse-master	Minangkabau Personnel		
Major	Minor			Warehouse-master	Assistant Warehouse-master	Clerks
	1	Padang Panjang		1		2
1		Padang Panjang	1		1	6
2		Batu Sangkar		1		3
	2	Buo			1	2
	3	Tanjung Ampalox			1	2
	4	Singkarak			1	2
3		Bukittinggi		1		3
	5	Maninjau			1	2
	6	Sungai Puar			1	2
	7	Bonjol			1	2
4		Payakumbuh		1		3
	8	Suliki			1	2
	9	Halaban			1	2
5		Solok		1		3
	10	Supayang			1	2
	11	Alahan Panjang			1	2
15	16	Totals	1	5	11	40

Source: Kielstra, "Koffiecultuur," p. 1485.

There were of course numerous opportunities for corruption, extortion, and graft available for warehouse personnel. According to Michiels' original regulations, for example, the individual grower had to deliver his coffee himself in order to be paid. This had been intended to minimize the chances for extortion by the various local chiefs,[83] but often resulted in a grower having to wait several days at the warehouse center because the warehousemaster was visiting some other warehouse for which he was responsible. This could be expensive for the grower, both in terms of time lost and in money used to pay for food and lodging.[84] If the warehousemaster were willing to overlook the irregularity, arrangements could be made with a broker and the peasant could go home, or perhaps avoid coming at all. For a small sum, the warehousemaster was almost always willing.

The coffee which continued to leak from the system into the private sector probably did so with the knowledge and doubtless also the assistance of the warehousemaster. Records had to be altered to explain why the deliveries were not as high as the estimates had been earlier, when the controleur visited the fields. It would be an easy matter, however, for the books to show that several hundred piculs of "rotten beans" had had to be "destroyed." The warehousemaster received f. 20 per month which put him on the same level with the nagarihoofd in most areas, but considering the amount of his responsibility and training and the numerous opportunities available for graft, this salary was too low.[85] Being a warehousemaster or even one of the other, lesser warehouse personnel was a lucrative position, and families were very eager to have one of their number on the payroll. The warehousemaster held an important patronage-dispensing position, each coffee-delivery area needed numerous assistants, clerks, secretaries, day laborers, and others to staff and service the local warehouses. A single warehousemaster could thus provide many jobs for relatives and friends.

Unlike the laras- or nagarihoofd, the warehousemaster need not be a native of the district where he worked. In fact, many of them, especially in the early period, came from a small area of Agam, an area in which there had developed a large pool of men literate in Malay. Moreover, many men from Agam already held positions in the civil service and could influence selections for the opening coffee bureaucracy jobs.

In addition to the positions associated with the warehouses,

---

83 General Michiels, Decision on Coffee Deliveries, October 11, 1847, in Kielstra, "Koffiecultuur," p. 1485.
84 Van Vollenhoven, *Padang en het Gouvernement*, pp. 6-8.
85 Verkerk Pistorius, *Inlandsche Huishouding*, p. 102; *Verbaal*, August 23, 1870, No. 6.

Minangkabau could also get related jobs as crop inspectors. These positions, called *koffee mantri*, had existed before on a kind of ad hoc basis arranged by the local controleur, but they became more numerous beginning in the 1870s. The creation of a systematic and organized corps of inspector-overseers was in response to prevailing government views that constant malingering on the part of both grower and chief was contributing to a perceived decline in coffee production. It was believed, in government circles, that more uniform supervision and pressure from officials was needed. The Dutch administrative official in charge of cultivation, the controleur, was the obvious person, but he was often responsible for a geographic area so large that he could devote but little attention to the details of coffee production in any one part. Moreover, numerous administrative tasks usually tied him to his headquarters, leaving him few opportunities to visit the villages and make Dutch presence felt directly.[86]

Padang rejected suggestions for creation of a corps of European overseers, which, it believed, would greatly increase administrative costs in salaries without the assurance of any corresponding revenue increase. Some Dutch officials suggested also that European interference in local affairs tended to offend the local people. If Minangkabau personnel were used, however, they would not only be more familiar with local customs, but would also receive a lower payscale than Europeans of the same rank. The inspectors would not be assigned to villages in their home districts, and this would remove them from the pressure of family ties and adat obligations which often made the nagarihoofd and penghulu ineffective guardians of the government's interests. A system of Minangkabau inspectors was thus established in 1874; seventy-nine men were initially appointed, divided into three classes. The new local inspectorate was fully Minangkabau-staffed and served directly under Dutch control—in no way subordinate to any Minangkabau chief whether government- or adat-appointed. Their direct connection with the Dutch officials gave the inspectors a great deal of authority in coercing peasants and village leaders.[87]

---

86 Chief Inspector Ples, March 12, 1878, *Verbaal*, August 13, 1878, No. 1.
87 Report of Governor Netscher, *Verbaal*, October 14, 1874, No. 31.

There were still problems in supervising village cultivators more closely, for the coffee groves were sometimes scattered over many plots, and often located outside the villages entirely. Many more officials had eventually to be appointed than had been anticipated.[88] The inspectors were chosen mainly from among the students at the secular elementary schools. Training at these institutions, however, stressed bureaucratic skills, such as writing and simple arithmetic, with no attention given to agricultural techniques. As a result, the coffee inspector often knew a great deal less about the cultivation he was supervising than the peasant, which naturally undermined local respect for the new officials. In turn, this tended to decrease their credibility as government overseers organizing village coffee production efficiently.[89]

Subsequently, similar supervisors were appointed to check on other export crops such as cinchona, tobacco, cloves, and cinnamon. They also became increasingly involved in regulating rice planting and other aspects of village agricultural activity. Because of their ties to the controleur and their knowledge of the individual villages in which they worked, they began acting as general agents of the government—reporting on local opinion and attitudes. In some places they exercised more authority and commanded more popular respect than the larashoofd himself.[90] They were moving from mere agricultural "experts" to administrators; this trend became more pronounced as the government bureaucracy became more complicated and the administration began to rely more and more on the literate civil servants rather than the illiterate chiefs. The chiefs, despite pressure from the government, rarely bothered to acquire more than a smattering of education, and many not even that. It is understandable therefore that, by the end of the nineteenth century, the Dutch placed more trust and more authority in the hands of the growing Minangkabau civil service than in the old adat-oriented administration.

---

88 Resident of the Padang Highlands, Canné, to the Governor, December 5, 1877, *Verbaal*, August 13, 1878, No. 1.
89 Governor Netscher, January 10, 1878, *Verbaal*, August 13, 1878, No. 1.
90 Governor Heckler, June 23, 1906, *Verbaal*, September 12, 1912, No. 66.

CHAPTER FIVE
SECULAR EDUCATION IN THE 1840s TO 1860s: THE ERA OF LOCAL INITIATIVE

Both political administration and the coffee cultivation program opened opportunities for Minangkabau literate in Malay to advance within the colonial system. Typically, those who responded most enthusiastically were the social and geographic groups traditionally associated with the merantau process—that is, middle-level socioeconomic groups, particularly from hill-country villages. Geographically, the villages tended also to be located in areas important for coffee cultivation. The intensity of Minangkabau interest in bureaucratic jobs increased as it became more obvious that here was another important means to power, prestige, and wealth. Compared with many other archipelago groups, the Minangkabau had an additional advantage in that their own language was almost identical with the so-called Bazaar Malay which had become the lingua franca of Dutch diplomacy, administration, and commerce in the Indies since the days of the VOC.

Before about the 1870s, the Minangkabau element in the colonial bureaucracy was small and, with the exception of the warehousemaster, jaksa, and, perhaps, the so-called "indigenous secretary," the jobs did not attract more than lower-middle level groups. Established, well-to-do merchant or artisan families usually preferred to follow their traditional vocations, though recognizing the advantages which the new, colonial situation presented. Specifically, such families found that a smattering of secular education could often be useful to their own pursuits; once children had acquired enough skill to keep the books or copy correspondence, they withdrew from school to enter the family business. The Minangkabau chiefs, both government-appointed and adat, rarely displayed more than a perfunctory interest in education, because their own positions were generally guaranteed by the colonial government regardless of individual qualifications.

Conflicting Dutch and Minangkabau perceptions about the role of school training often caused irritation between them. The Dutch liked to idealize secular education as a general civilizing force which would produce enlightened chiefs and reliable bureaucrats, while the Minangkabau approach was more practical. Families were reluctant to invest scarce resources in sending a child to the secular school unless the probable financial return was better than that already available from apprenticeship in a traditionally recognized occupation.

Nevertheless, a certain number of Minangkabau did display an early interest in secular education, studying at first privately as apprentices in government commercial or administrative offices. Beginning in the mid-1840s, and largely on the personal initiative of a single Dutch official, secular schools were established in various nagari in the highlands. The first of these was located in the regional administrative centers of the upland plains and in the coffee-producing centers in the hill areas. Supervised and financed by the nagari themselves, the only Dutch involvement was the occasional guidance offered by an interested controleur. That individual schools might seem "inadequate" by Dutch pedagogic standards and that many disappeared entirely after operating only a year is not surprising; what is, is that so many survived and even expanded. Those that did, did so because they filled a particular local need; they provided another, increasingly recognized, avenue for advancement outside the ever more static village social and political system.

The first indication of the quiet success of secular education came in 1852 in a report which Governor van Swieten submitted about the expanded bureaucracy needed by the forced coffee-delivery system. The new network of warehouses established in 1847 had to be staffed by literate Minangkabau skilled in bookkeeping, and to van Swieten's amazement, rather than being hard-pressed to find such people, all the positions were filled immediately. He was doubly impressed because there had been no government policy directed toward educating the Minangkabau for the civil service,[1] and their training had taken place in spite of colonial policy rather than because of it.

---

1 Report of Governor van Swieten, February 12, 1852, *Verbaal*, June 15, 1852, No. 3.

Local Interest vs. Government Policy: The Case of Padang

The importance of Minangkabau initiative in the rise of secular education in West Sumatra is illustrated by the fate of the first totally government-supported school, founded in Padang in 1825 by General de Stuers. As part of his general program for controlling Minangkabau, de Stuers wanted the heirs of the coastal nobility to attend a secular, Dutch-run Malay-language school. He hoped thereby to produce a literate and "civilized" class of chiefs who would better appreciate and, therefore, better uphold the Dutch government. To placate fears of the local people that their unsuspecting children would be kidnapped into Dutch culture, de Stuers appointed the Islamic advisor to the Padang judicial council (a Minangkabau) to supervise the school.[2]

The Dutch regime in Padang financed the new school's entire operations, providing f. 50 per month in 1824 and increasing this to f. 60 in 1825. Some 80 pupils enrolled, but it soon became clear that their families sent them out of deference to the government, not because they believed the education was necessary or even useful. The teacher, a Christian missionary named Evans, soon clashed with the chiefs because he refused to allow pupils to read the Quran in class. The chiefs withdrew their children, and, in 1828, rather than force the issue, the government decided simply to close the school.[3]

As the headquarters of Dutch operations from before the nineteenth century, Padang, by 1825, was already developing into a relatively cosmopolitan and urban center. But its permanent residents were, to a large degree, untouched by these developments, remaining among the most tradition bound and aristocratic minded of the West Coast people.

The government school, then, had been directed at exactly the segment of the population with the least need or desire for literacy, arithmetic skill, or the other attributes associated by the Dutch with "civilized

---

2 General de Stuers, Instructions of March 16, 1825, *Exhibitum*, August 24, 1826, No. 41.
3 Report of Governor van Swieten, February 12, 1852, *Verbaal*, June 15, 1852, No. 3. Padang had had a government-subsidized mission school dating from 1819, but its concern had been directed at the local Christian population. Pupils were mostly army children (non-Minangkabau), local Chinese, and pagan people from the nearby offshore islands such as Mentawei. *Algemeen Verslag van den Staat van het Schoolwezen in Nederlandsch-Indië 1827-1833* (Batavia: Hoofd-Kommissie van Onderwijs, n.d.), p. 49.

behavior." The coastal chiefs were concerned only that the Dutch honor the traditional lines of chieftaincy in appointing new rulers. The chief could hire some petty functionary to write letters and keep records if that were needed, and, at this early stage of administrative development, it probably was not. It soon became apparent that the Dutch would not alter established patterns of succession just because a prospective heir could not read. In this general atmosphere, it is not surprising that the school soon closed. The clash with the teacher only provided the justification for withdrawing the children from what the chiefs already considered a useless and time-wasting institution. Secular education obviously was not merely a matter of providing schools but one of appealing to particular local interests and needs.

First Success: The Highlands in the 1840s

The first and most successful of the Minangkabau secular schools, known popularly as the nagari schools, were founded in the Padang Highlands in the 1840s, initially at the instigation of a particularly energetic and concerned Dutch official, C. P. C. Steinmetz, Resident of the Padang Highlands from 1837 to 1848. Steinmetz believed that Minangkabau youth should be exposed to the values of education, which included, in his view, not just reading, writing, and arithmetic, but "civilized behavior," "good hygiene," and other aspects of a "European style of life and culture." His original intent in beginning the schools was as much to create good citizens as to fill any particular jobs in government or private life.[4] Residents had a great deal of independence in local policy making, and, thus, Steinmetz could carry out his program without prior approval from the Governor. In fact, he informed Governor Michiels only after the project was well underway, and then only because Michiels had inquired about it.

The initial nagari schools were established in such small and unlikely hill villages as Puar Datar, Rau, and Matur, as well as in market and administrative centers of the upland plains, such as Bukittinggi, Batu

---

4 The major source of information on Steinmetz's plans and their success comes from a collection of his papers published in: H. E. Steinmetz, "Inlands Onderwijs van Overheidswege in de Padangsche Bovenlanden voor 1850: De Grondlegger, Zijn Invloed and Zijn Persoonlijke Bemoeienissen op dit Gebied," *TBG*, 64 (1924), pp. 303-20.

Sangkar, and Solok. In either setting, however, the pupils most interested in the schools came from middle-level families who wanted the skills as stepping stones to new or better jobs, jobs which they hoped would improve the whole family's socioeconomic position in the village.

The Dutch role in the nagari school operation was minimal, consisting at most of occasional visits by the controleur, if he were personally interested in the operation of the school. In West Sumatra, however, Dutch officials were few, and most of them were strategically placed to facilitate supervision and control of the coffee harvest. Often their offices were located in small hill villages, isolated from neighboring districts by rugged hills and narrow passes. Even to supervise the coffee crop was difficult under such circumstances, and though the controleur might instigate the establishment of a nagari school, afterwards the villagers were on their own.

The nagari school idea devised by Steinmetz served as the model for most subsequent schools in the region until the early 1870s, when the central government finally decided to assert its control over education in Sumatra's West Coast. During the early period, the chiefs, both government and adat, acting through the nagari council, would first find a building with enough extra space, usually the nagari council hall or the local coffee warehouse, and the villagers would make the tables, chairs, and any other furniture needed.[5] A literate villager, usually the warehousemaster or a secretary in the local government bureau, acted as the first teacher, and was generally paid from the nagari treasury. In most cases, no tuition was charged, but pupils usually had to buy all their own school supplies and whatever food or clothing they might need.[6] Many parents, especially in the early years, believed this burden was too great for the perceived benefits, and in some areas, were able to pressure the nagari council into buying the school supplies and, sometimes, into providing a clothing allowance as well.[7]

The basic curriculum was divided into four levels: pupils began with reading in the fourth (lowest) class; added writing in the third; simple

---

5 Regulations of Resident Steinmetz concerning Indigenous Education, November 24, 1843, in Steinmetz, "Inlands Onderwijs," pp. 206-9.
6 Ibid.
7 Letter of Steinmetz to the Governor, April 16, 1844, in ibid., pp. 310-11.

arithmetic in the second; and copying essays, bookkeeping, geography, and advanced arithmetic in the first. All instruction was given in the Malay language beginning in the lowest grade. This differed from the usual practice on Java, and it was possible because Minangkabau and Malay are essentially the same language.[8] Religion as a subject was specifically excluded. Pupils were also explicitly forbidden to wear European clothing. Steinmetz was very sensitive to the often-expressed fear among Minangkabau villagers that the secular schools were meant to convert pupils to Christianity and draft them into the Indies army. Suspicions lingered, however, though such religious and cultural qualms about the secular schools tended to be expressed most often by members of the village establishment, people who had no interest in the education offered anyway.[9]

Unlike the abortive Padang government school, the highlands nagari schools were open to whoever wished to attend, regardless of status or position.[10] Though the curriculum had been designed to provide basic skills which would contribute to the overall progress of the villagers and make them better "citizens,"[11] bureaucratic needs and opportunities heavily influenced its subsequent development. The subjects which received the most attention were those needed by aspiring bureaucrats, particularly such skills as copying documents and keeping books. In practice, overwhelming attention was given to copyist techniques, to the detriment of comprehension of the documents being copied.

Many villagers had apparently already recognized that opportunities existed with the colonial bureaucracy. By 1846, only three years after the first schools opened, seventy-five pupils had already graduated and been placed as clerks in government bureaus and in the offices of larashoofd or had become supervisors over cultivation activities.[12] Most had probably

---

8 Steinmetz Regulations, in ibid., pp. 206-9. It is also possible that the "Malay" language referred to by Steinmetz was actually Minangkabau Malay rather than the Bazaar Malay used in Java. The Dutch tended to apply the term "Malay" when referring to the Minangkabau people during the early period of their occupation, and they may have called the local language that as well.
9 Interviews: Batu Sangkar, August 26-30, 1967; Payakumbuh, November 21-24, 1967; Solok, November 2-6, 1967; Padang, August 1967.
10 Report of Resident of the Padang Highlands Steinmetz, in Steinmetz, "Inlands Onderwijs," pp. 311-12.
11 Steinmetz Regulations, in ibid., pp. 205-9.
12 Report of Resident Steinmetz to the Governor, April 16, 1844, in ibid., p. 311.

already received some education before they entered the nagari school. The Arabic script taught at some surau, for instance, could be used for Malay-language texts as well as for the Arabic-language Islamic texts. Many government documents meant for dissemination among village level officials in Sumatra in this early period were transliterated in Arabic rather than Roman script.

Many nagari school pupils withdrew after only a year or two. Often these were from chiefly families and did not need to be literate, while others entered trade and needed only a smattering of bookkeeping techniques or literacy. Nor was a diploma necessarily required for a job in the colonial bureaucracy; influence, luck, and other intangible factors continued to be important. It was a financial burden to keep a child in school, despite the free tuition, and there was no guarantee that a diploma would be worth more in the long run than four years as an apprentice to, say, a textile dealer. And in the latter instance, one had the additional advantage of earning money while learning the trade. For whatever reasons, many pupils left before completing the four year course, although the number varied from time to time and place to place. Statistics are either incomplete or nonexistent, but in 1846, for example, 106 of the 416 pupils enrolled in the highlands schools had left "before completing the prescribed course of study."[13]

By 1846, there were eleven of these autonomous nagari schools. Five were located in regional headquarters towns in the upland plains—Bukittinggi, Batu Sangkar, Payakumbuh, Sijunjung, and Solok. The other six were in the main towns of important hill-country coffee districts—Bonjol, Maninjau, Sungai Puar, Buo, Singkarak, and Puar Datar.[14] Survival was difficult because members of nagari councils were rarely the people with the most to gain from a secular education, and thus schools often were starved for funds. Their fortunes often depended on the amount of pressure that could be exerted on nagari councils. This in turn depended on the vagaries of family politics, whether those who wanted secular schools were in a position to pressure their penghulu and through them the laras- and nagarihoofd.

---

13 Ibid.
14 Ibid., p. 311.

Although Steinmetz had argued that Batavia should pay the costs of educating the people to staff its civil service, all attempts to gain government funding failed.[15] In 1848, a Royal Decision authorized the Governor General to spend f. 25,000 a year to train Javanese notables as civil servants, but the ruling Council of the Indies rejected efforts to apply this to Sumatra's West Coast, as this was outside the scope of the original decree.[16] From the purely economic point of view, Batavia could undoubtedly see that Padang did not lack trained Minangkabau under the existing education arrangements, so why spend money when it was not necessary? Developments in the nagari school, especially in the highlands, were thus left almost completely to local initiatives.

---

15 Report of Resident Steinmetz, in ibid., pp. 311-12.
16 *Verbaal*, June 2, 1852, No. 4 and June 15, 1852, No. 3.

MAP 4: NAGARI SCHOOLS

Expansion in the 1850s: A Teachers' Training Institute

In the early 1850s, schools were founded in towns in the Lowlands Residency, including the territorial administrative centers of Painan (school opened c. 1855), Pariaman (c. 1854), Padang (c. 1853), and Air Bangis (c. 1854). At the same time, schools were opened in the northern interior at the regional center of Lubuk Sikaping and the villages of Panti and Talu in the northern rim of hills. Though geographically part of the highlands, these three villages were administered from the lowlands center at Air Bangis until late in the nineteenth century, and the founding of the schools was probably part of developments taking place in the Lowlands Residency. In the late 1850s, schools opened at two other coastal villages, Asam Kumbang (c. 1859) and Pelangi (c. 1858).[17]

The Batavia government, though it still refused requests for financial support to the nagari schools, did agree, in the 1850s, to establish a state-supported Normal School in West Sumatra to provide more uniform and intensive training for prospective teachers. Batavia, however, was not yet prepared to invest more than a token amount in educating the Minangkabau, and opposed on financial grounds proposals for a full-fledged Dutch-run Normal School like that in Surakarta, on Java. It would agree only to an experimental school with ten pupils and a Minangkabau headmaster.[18]

The school would be established in Bukittinggi, the most dynamic commercial and administrative center in the highlands and the one which was considered the most removed from the jealousies and petty rivalries which supposedly characterized life in other highlands centers.[19] Bukittinggi was also the center of the coffee-delivery network for the important northern producing areas, as well as the headquarters for the Dutch administration of the Highlands Residency and the Agam Assistant Residency. As such, it provided an eminently suitable atmosphere for aspiring civil servants. Although Padang would also have

---

17 The date in parentheses indicates the first year the school was recorded in the colonial educational reports; one assumes that this represents the first full year of operations for that school.
18 *Verslag van het Inlandsch Onderwijs in Nederlandsch-Indië, 1866* (Batavia: Landsdrukkerij, 1867), pp. 2-4. Hereafter cited as *VIO*.
19 Letter of C. A. Buddingh, April 26, 1855, *Verbaal*, July 14, 1856, No. 7.

been suitable, Dutch officials expressed fears that its cultural atmosphere was not sufficiently Minangkabau,[20] though their real misgivings might have been that, once drawn into the commercial life of Padang, the pupils would no longer be interested in returning to the highlands as school teachers.

Batavia had at first suggested that pupils from Sumatra should just be sent to the Surakarta Normal School, but the Resident in Bukittinggi contended that "no qualified youth with a proper upbringing" would be willing to leave home for two years to go there.[21] A more important drawback of the Surakarta institution was that its curriculum was arranged for Javanese language speakers and Javanese culture areas, and would be ill-suited to Sumatra-oriented teachers or their needs. The Resident, who was evidently an admirer of Rousseau, feared, moreover, that the unspoiled Sumatrans would be contaminated by the unfamiliar and, he implied, decadent customs of Javanese culture which they would encounter in Surakarta.[22] Dutch officials also worried that the teacher trainees might very well use their expensive education for non-teaching careers, and they wished to remove as many temptations as possible.

The Bukittinggi Normal School (in Dutch called the Kweekschool Bukittinggi) was officially founded by government decree on April 1, 1856. Assistant Resident van Ophuijzen from Solok was transferred to Bukittinggi to act as general supervisor over the institute and its curriculum. He was chosen because, according to the Governor, he had displayed special interests and ability in Malay education, which meant in essence that he spoke Malay fluently and could easily read and write it in Arabic characters, the alphabet commonly used in Minangkabau.[23] The actual day-to-day operations of the Normal School were under a Minangkabau headmaster, Abdul Latif. Brother of the Head Jaksa for the Highlands Residency, Latif owed his appointment more to political influence than proven pedagogic ability.[24]

---

20 *VIO*, 7866, pp. 1-3.
21 Resident of the Padang Highlands to the Governor of Sumatra's West Coast, November 17, 1855, *Verbaal*, July 14, 1856, No. 7.
22 Ibid.
23 Ibid.; *VIO*, 1866, pp. 2-4.
24 Interviews in Kota Gedang (Latif's home village), October 1967; Herman, "Het Onderwijs in Nederlandsch-Indië (Historisch Overzicht Sedert 1816)," *TNI*, 1 (1868), p. 477.

The decision to leave most school operations up to the Minangkabau headmaster meant that the Normal School was quickly domesticated to serve local interests and abilities rather than Dutch plans. Van Ophuijzen, perhaps, had sufficient interest and ability to take the time to direct the institute very closely, but succeeding Residents did not.

As first formulated, the Normal School had a very extensive and ambitious curriculum patterned after the more affluent Surakarta institute. Entering students need not have graduated from a nagari school, but they had to be at least fourteen years old and already possess some ability to read and write in Malay and to do elementary arithmetic. The three-year curriculum included reading and writing in Malay (in both the Arabic and the Roman alphabets), geography, surveying, bookkeeping, letter writing, and the proper format for official reports. These subjects would prepare students to teach in a nagari school and there to train children to become "proper and competent chiefs and civil servants." The Dutch government would pay the teacher's salary, buy the school furniture, and provide an allowance for each pupil. The teacher's duties not only included classroom instruction but also supervision of the pupils' daily behavior, dress, and hygiene out of class. It was envisioned as a rigorous and all-encompassing training, and the Assistant Resident was instructed to supervise it carefully, checking that the teacher followed his prescribed duties to the letter.[25]

The largest single group of students came from neighboring Agam, although a few were from Tanah Datar, Solok, and even Padang. A significant number came from families of chiefs, but these were not always the majority; a large number of merchant families were also represented—the rest being artisans, clerks, and others. Children who were in line to succeed to lineage penghuluships could not enroll on the grounds that they would be unable to serve full terms as teachers.

By 1863, teachers at nine highland nagari schools had received at least some education at the Normal School. Two others were teachers in Benkulen,[26] and Minangkabau teachers later spread to other parts of Sumatra in the wake of newly established Dutch administrations. (One

---

25 *Verbaal*, July 14, 1856, No. 7; *VIO, 1856*, pp. 73-78.
26 *VIO, 1863*, pp. 196-236 and 249.

exception was the Batak areas, which needed people who could teach in the local language.) The Governor in Padang initially limited the Normal School quota of ten pupils to people from the highlands, on the grounds that the institute had been established specifically to train teachers for the schools there. He thus denied admission to pupils from Benkulen, Lampong, Palembang, and even the Lowlands Residency, unless there was an unfilled vacancy,[27] but under pressure from other Sumatran officials, he eventually had to assign quotas to nonhighlands areas. In 1866, of the ten pupils enrolled five came from the highlands, two from Tapanuli, one from Padang, one from Pariaman, and one from Air Bangis/Rau. Nonetheless, most students still came from the highlands area, and, indeed, from the immediate Bukittinggi vicinity. According to one report, this was because the chief secretary to the highlands Resident, a man from nearby Kota Gedang, used his position to assure entry for members of his own lineage.[28]

The great attraction of a Normal School education, Dutch plans to the contrary, did not stem from any desire by Minangkabau to become school teachers. During the first decade of its operation, the institute enrolled some forty-nine pupils, but of the twenty-eight graduates, only twelve actually took up teaching positions. Families soon discovered that the controleur and other officials gave preference to Normal School pupils when hiring civil servants, especially for jobs as cultivation supervisors, secretaries, and top warehouse personnel. A Dutch education inspector, J. A. van der Chijs, bitterly concluded from the state of affairs that the government believed that any more or less literate Minangkabau was good enough to serve as a teacher, but better educated Minangkabau should be reserved as officials or assistants to Dutch administrators.[29]

Considering the rudimentary level of education offered in the nagari school, it is not surprising that students from the teachers' institute had an important advantage in competing for jobs as warehousemasters, jaksa, and other important civil service positions.[30] Nor, considering the

---

27 *Verbaal*, November 16, 1865, No. 45.
28 *VIO, 1866*, p. 10. By the 1860s, the former Kota Gedang headmaster of the school had apparently retired.
29 Report of van der Chijs, in *VIO, 1866*, pp. 6-8.
30 *VIO,* 1856, p. 72; *VIO,* 1863, p. 195.

value of administrative jobs both in terms of money and opportunities for patronage, is it surprising that graduates preferred these jobs to teaching.

An additional appeal of the Normal School, from the Minangkabau viewpoint, was that the government actually paid pupils to attend, so that families need invest nothing of their own in order to participate in the new experiment. Pressure for admittance was especially strong from families in nearby Agam. Here the merantau drive was also strongest traditionally, and any proven means of advancement was eagerly sought. Power and influence in Dutch government circles were important factors in facilitating admission. Many of the pupils, as a result, came from Kota Gedang, near Bukittinggi—the home of the Head Jaksa, the Resident's private secretary, and the former headmaster of the Normal School itself.[31] The nagari school in Bukittinggi was also one of the best in the highlands, so that children from the area received a preparation for advanced education that was objectively better than their competitors from other highlands schools.

In fact, however, the education at the Normal School was probably not all that "advanced," in many respects differing little from what pupils could get in a good nagari school. The Minangkabau headmaster himself certainly had no particular training in pedagogy and only a superficial knowledge, at best, of many of the other subjects in the broad curriculum he was supposed to teach. He himself had never received any advanced training,[32] and his teaching staff consisted of advanced pupils and former graduates, none of whom had received any extra training elsewhere. At most, the teacher at the European elementary school in Bukittinggi would occasionally tutor the Normal School staff and students.[33] Teacher training was, as a result, more a process of shared ignorance among instructors and pupils. Dutch Assistant Inspector for Native Education, J. J. van Limburg Brouwer, visited in 1872 to report on education in West Sumatra, and he professed himself "shocked" by the condition of the Normal School. He believed that an important reason for the school not meeting the standards of other Indies Normal Schools was its lack

---

31 *VIO, 1866*, p. 10; interviews, October 1967, in Kota Gedang.
32 Report of Inspector van der Chijs, in *VIO, 1866*, pp. 6-8.
33 *VIO, 1870*, p. 58.

of materials, such as maps, textbooks, etc. But he also discovered that no one, neither Dutch nor Minangkabau, cared enough about the school even to provide a permanent building for it; classes were still being held in the anteroom of the local adat council hall.[34] There were no regular exams, although occasionally a local Dutch official might hear the students' lessons, and students spent most of their time learning to read and write by rote.[35]

Nevertheless, however deficient the content of its education, mere attendance at the Normal School qualified its graduates for better jobs than those available to a nagari school graduate.

Nagari Schools in the 1860s: Problems of Record Keeping

The best (and often the only) detailed information on individual nagari schools appears in the colonial records for the years 1863 to 1869. During those years, detailed statistics on student enrollment, family backgrounds, schoolteachers, and financial arrangements were apparently solicited from the various controleur in West Sumatra. Not all complied with the request in the same way or even consistently every year, but incomplete returns are better than none, and they are the only statistical evidence of any kind about education in West Sumatra during the nineteenth century. The results of the controleur's reports were sent to Batavia where they were published in a yearly compendium on indigenous education in the Indies, the *Verslag van het Inlandsch Onderwijs in Nederlandsch-Indië*. The published report was the only information on indigenous education forwarded on to the Minister of Colonies, except for occasional documents needed to support particular debates.

The education reports are deficient in many respects. If they record the number of pupils who "left school" in a given year (and often they do not), they rarely indicate how long these pupils had attended or if they were considered "educated" on leaving. Though often the family background is provided for those enrolled, it is not indicated for those who left so that it is difficult to tell which families kept pupils in school to

---

34 Report of Assistant Inspector for Indigenous Education J. J. von Limburg Brouwer, March 26, 1872, *Verbaal*, November 23, 1872, No. 30.
35 Ibid.

completion and which did not. It is never clearly stated whether

Table 7. Total Pupil Enrollment in Nagari Schools

School Location	1855	1856	1857	1858	1859	1860	1861	1862	1863	1864	1865	1866	1867	1868	1869
Padang Highlands															
Batu Sangkar	13	16	28	24	30	30	24	32	38		61	59	46	31	60
Bonjol												17	17	20	24
Buo												19	29	32	26
Bukittinggi	10	36	40	38	34	24	26	33	45		63	54	56	80	81
Halaban								20	20		36	40	50	40	43
Lolo												27	11	15	9
Lubuk Sikaping		12	13	9	29	37	32	26	26		22	20	14	15	17
Payakumbuh	16	9	36	53	38	57	56	43	100		97	97	51	57	40
Palembayan														35	31
Panti		4	4	4	4	4	4	4	13					Data unavailable	
Puar Datar							20	42			44	50	64	52	51
Rau		18	16	17	17	8	21	21	40		38	22	15	15	17
Solok	37	37	36	36	37	50	56	48	54		67	52	46	53	32
Talu		13	25	25	25	25	23	17	27		29	18	9	10	18
Padang Lowlands															
Air Bangis	17	20	31	36	21	31	32	21	16		18	12	4	9	4
Asam Kumbang				27	32	32	20	18	20		18	17	9	9	
Batang Kapas				38	40	40	38	52	61		58	53	38	31	5

Secular Education in the 1840s to 1860s: The Era of Local Initiative

School Location	1855	1856	1857	1858	1859	1860	1861	1862	1863	1864	1865	1866	1867	1868	1869
Padang Lowlands															
Indrapura						12	14	12	13	2					
Padang	110	113	110	122	124	111	135	124	134	237		132	101	Data unavailable	191
Painan			16	23	27	24	33	34	34	39	39	26	28	Data unavailable	37
Pariaman	30	25	32	57	75	82	57	49	55	70	35			Data unavailable	
Pelangi				46	33	33	34	35	38	39	38			Data unavailable	
Sungai Limau									45	80	45			Data unavailable	
Tiku									38	44	38			Data unavailable	
Trusan			46	49	41	55	69	61		55	51	30	28	Data unavailable	31
Total	233	303	287	601	615	629	658	680	919	1128	805	647	661		717

Source: *Algemeen Onderwijs Verslag; Verslag van het Inlandsch Onderwijs*.

the person whose occupation is being given is the "father" or the "mamak," an important distinction in determining the actual position of the child in society. One must assume that it was probably the mamak simply because the reports often indicate that the "sons" of chiefs usually became chiefs upon the death of their "fathers." This clearly must refer to a kemanakan-mamak relationship, not a son-father one. Sons of chiefs did not succeed their fathers; a chief was succeeded by his nephew. One assumes then that the records indicate the occupation of the pupils' "father" in the sense of his "guardian," that is mamak, rather than his actual blood father. Within the reports themselves, terminology is not consistent; whereas one official may report in great detail about the actual occupations (listing carpenters, merchants, goldsmiths), another (or even the same one the following year) may say only that a certain number were in business for themselves (*particulier*) as opposed to working for the government or "farming." The occupation of "farmer" is itself misleading since the other information given makes it quite clear that these families were "farmers" only in that they made their living from agriculture rather than trade or artisanry. The same carelessness of terminology occurs in dealing with students who left school. Sometimes what happened to them is spelled out but more often the record indicates merely that they entered trade, went home, etc.

The reasons for inclusion or exclusion of certain items are never clarified, nor is there any mention of why the reports were being sent at all. As mysteriously as they began, in 1869, local statistics ceased to be included in the colonial education reports. Moreover, the published reports began to cover three-year periods rather than being issued annually, as before. Apart from an occasional mention, the individual schools of West Sumatra again drop from view. But, for the brief period of the 1860s, one has enough information to draw individual portraits of most of the schools and relate them to the different geographical and cultural spheres of Minangkabau.

The Hills: Schools in Coffee Country (the 1860s)

From the 1840s, the nagari schools in the hills had tended to coincide with the areas of important coffee establishments. In purely practical terms, such areas had jobs for graduates and also a literate person (the coffee warehousemaster) to serve as a teacher. Because penghulu and government chiefs received commissions on the coffee delivered by their constituents, the coffee country chiefs tended to be more affluent than their colleagues elsewhere. They could contribute to schools, or at least allow their portion of nagari council funds to be spent to this end, without great financial hardship. Moreover, social structure in the hill villages was less rigid. Less distance separated penghulu from dependent, and he was consequently more susceptible to pressure from below. In the hill villages, many penghulu families also participated in the merantau tradition, and, as a result, they had a greater community of interests with other families of their lineage. All these factors contributed to the success of the nagari schools located in otherwise unremarkable little hillside villages, a success which is the more remarkable when one discovers that the only comparable schools elsewhere in Sumatra were those in the few relatively "urban" administrative and market centers of the highlands.

The first four hill country schools were established in Buo, Puar Datar, Rau, and Bonjol, in the early 1840s. All four villages were formerly centers for the Padri movement. Buo (sometimes referred to as Lintau Buo), Bonjol, and Rau had each harbored a famous leader of the Padri. Puar

Datar is located over a small mountain spine from Bonjol and was the site of an important fort constructed by Imam Bonjol. Each village was the warehouse center for an important coffee-producing region. Warehouses were located in Bonjol and Buo in 1847. Rau and Puar Datar each had one by the late 1850s, though in the case of Puar Datar, there had been one in nearby Suliki since 1847.

The village of Rau is located far on the northern fringes of the Minangkabau world, where Minangkabau melds into the sphere of the Mandailing Batak. Here on a small intermontane rice plain, Padri leader Tuanku Rau had established a fortified surau from which he carried his brand of militant Islam north into the pagan Batak country and west to the commercial centers of the coast near Air Bangis. The dense Panti jungle tended to isolate Rau from the rest of the highlands and focus its communications to the north and west. The Dutch accentuated this by building a road between Rau and Air Bangis in the 1850s. The area (known as Pasaman or Ophir) was administratively part of the Lowlands Residency until 1891, when it was integrated into the Highlands administration and its headquarters established at Lubuk Sikaping.

The Rau area was extensive but underpopulated: only 15,000 people were recorded in 1852.[36] Rau had an established school by 1845. In this case, the connection with coffee production was clear, for in 1844 the Resident had reported to the governor in Padang that more Minangkabau personnel would be needed to supervise local cultivators before the government could expect any important harvests from the Rau districts.[37] The inhabitants responded enthusiastically both to education and to coffee. In 1847, the closest government coffee area was at Bonjol, some 80 kilometers to the south, but by 1860, Rau itself had become one of the major producing centers of the highlands.[38]

The school at Rau was small but effective. In the early 1850s, it averaged about sixteen pupils divided among three levels.[39] The villagers built a separate building to serve as a schoolhouse in 1858 and soon afterward hired a graduate of the Bukittinggi Normal School to serve as its teacher.

---

36 *Verbaal*, July 13, 1858, No. 35.
37 Ibid.
38 *Verbaal*, May 14, 1860, No. 42.
39 *Verbaal*, July 14, 1856, No. 7.

The school was financed by levies on the nagari treasuries of surrounding villages, and these funds were used to pay the teacher and provide all the school supplies.[40]

The Rau school must have transformed the local community. The largest single group of pupils, some 20 percent, came from agricultural backgrounds, but upon leaving school, an overwhelming number became traders. No one returned to the land. One suspects that the Dutch road to Air Bangis had opened new commercial opportunities to the interior districts near Rau. Many "graduates" of the school also found jobs as clerks, coffee supervisors, and petty government functionaries, such as "vaccinators." The children of traders and small businessmen provided another 5 percent of the pupils and those from religious families a relatively large 7 percent. An interesting fact about the composition of the student body was the wide variety of family backgrounds from which the pupils came. No one group had an obvious monopoly over entry to the school; this was true of other hill villages also.

Table 8. Parents' Backgrounds—Highlands Schools 1860s (in percent of total enrollment)

School Locale	Merchant/Private Business	Artisan	Maritime	Agriculture/Landlord	Wage Earner	Penghulu	Lesser Adat Functionary	Religious	Government Chief	High Government official	Clerical Official	Supervisory Official
Normal School												
Bukittinggi	32	3				12	17	2	31	3		
Hill Villages												
Rau	5			20	3	1	2	7	3			
Bonjol	7			2		17	2	2	5			

---

40 Unless otherwise noted, the information, statistics, and judgments on the schools for the period of the 1860s have been compiled from the volumes of the *Verslag van het Inlandsch Onderwijs*. Individual citations will not be made unless they concern a particular point found in specific reports.

School Locale	Merchant/Private Business	Artisan	Maritime	Agriculture/Landlord	Wage Earner	Penghulu	Lesser Adat Functionary	Religious	Government Chief	High Government official	Clerical Official	Supervisory Official
Puar Datar	6	5		11		25			39	8	3	2
Buo				11					79		5	5
Lubuk Sikaping		4		18		34		25	15			6
Panti	8			15		8		8	38			
Talu				15		23	7	8	1			
Halaban		1		22		44	5	12	16			
Administrative Centers												
Bukittinggi	15	13		7		16	7	4	18	7	1	2
Payakumbuh	8	5		26	2	23	2	1	26	3	1	2
Batu Sangkar						29			31			
Solok		2		56	5	14			16	1	2	5

Source: *VIO, 1863-1869*.

The recorded statistics for Rau demonstrate some of the general problems in the school records for the period. Of the forty pupils listed as having attended the school, twenty-two said that their guardians' occupation was "deceased." Another problem is the vagueness of the statistics about the fate of students who left school. Although the reports, as noted, record that most graduates went into trade or government service, the actual statistics presented are almost meaningless. Of the fifty-one students mentioned as having left school between 1863 and 1869, it is said only that eight were "educated." Another ten were expelled for lack of interest, and two died.

Unlike the case with many plains or coastal villages, in the Rau area several chiefs had attended the school. At least four of the larashoofd and one nagarihoofd had received a smattering of education, sufficient to be worth noting in the official record as local literati. Though few in absolute numbers, the five semieducated government chiefs of Rau nonetheless represent one more than reported for the populous plains area surrounding the urban center of Payakumbuh. Seen in this context, the number assumes more significance and helps explain why the nagari councils in the Rau area villages were more willing to assume the burden of educating the area's children. The chiefs kept close watch over the school and its teacher. They were particularly irritated because the teacher kept his class hours rather irregularly and had to be pressured to spend time teaching.

South of Rau, beyond the thick jungle and on the other side of a narrow and rugged mountain pass is the village of Bonjol. A thin, mountain plain next to a shallow broad river provided the base upon which Imam Bonjol had built his religious movement and for a decade resisted Dutch incursions against his mountaintop fort. Unlike the families at Rau, the people of Bonjol were less interested in secular education. The school established in the 1840s later closed unnoticed, to be reopened in 1863. It was supported by levies on the inidividual laras- and nagarihoofd, f. 4 and f. 1.50 per month respectively. This may account for the fact that the greatest single group of pupils (some 17 percent) came from penghulu and government chiefs' families. This in turn helps explain the singular lack of "successful" alumni. Most pupils returned home, after having attended for some time. A few took jobs as clerks for local chiefs, but none entered the Dutch bureaus. It is possible, though there is no specific reference to it, that the adat types who dominated the school enrollment had frozen other, perhaps more interested, groups out of the school. In villages elsewhere, one sometimes finds that adat dignitaries came to regard school attendance as a prerogative of their class—despite the fact that they never used the training they got and had no intention of doing so when they enrolled. In any event, the records about Bonjol are too scanty to provide any real evidence.

Puar Datar, in the 1860s, was probably a much smaller village than Bonjol, but its inhabitants displayed more interest in the local school. Their land is almost entirely steep hillsides where mainly dryfield agriculture, particularly coffee cultivation, is practiced. A steep and winding valley trail connects the village to Suliki farther down country and eventually to Payakumbuh on the plain. But standing in the ruins of Imam Bonjol's Puar Datar fort, on a small rise at the edge of the village, one looks off into a vast distance of rugged hills and inaccessible little valleys. Puar Datar had an ideal geography and climate for coffee. But in terms of its school, the important characteristic of the village society was not coffee cultivation so much as the large group of perantau merchants who traditionally left the village each year. The success of the school established in the early 1840s is attested to by the large group of bureaucrats who sent their children there in the 1860s. These men had joined the bureaucracy after their training at the Puar Datar school a decade or so earlier. Some 13 percent of the pupils came from bureaucratic families, and another 11 percent from artisan and commercial backgrounds. Though in a relatively sparsely populated area, the Puar Datar school had an enrollment which rivaled that of more populous areas, such as Solok. The villagers had built the school of wood, with glass windows and a thatched, *ijuk roof*, and it was one of the most magnificent in all the highlands. Puar Datar's essential character as a perantau village is further reflected in the wide cross-section of the community which sent pupils to its schools. In 1865, the controleur suggested that he might consider literacy a factor in ratifying future appointments for penghulu; twenty-three heirs to such titles signed up the following year. But in general the penghulu had not otherwise been an overwhelming segment of the school pupils.

Of the four villages, Buo is located in the most agriculturally rich area, on a broad plain surrounded by hills situated roughly midway between the major highland plains of the Lima Puluh Kota and Tanah Datar. It had a school in 1846, but this had apparently closed down shortly afterward, to reopen in 1865. It was not a particularly successful operation partly because well-to-do families were charged tuition for their children, which tended to discourage enrollment from among merchant or other affluent groups. Almost all pupils came from families of chiefs, either government or adat. Attendance was irregular because few families could see any return on their investment. During the five years when records were kept, only one pupil was placed in government service, one went on to the Normal School, and two went to the medical institute in Batavia—not an especially outstanding record for a total enrollment of 106. The others, upon leaving school, entered "no determinable employment"; in other words, they returned home.

From the beginning Buo had been an important coffee area, but in other respects it differed from such northern regions as Puar Datar and even Rau. It had served as the headquarters of one of the top adat figures in the old Pagarruyung administration, and thus it had had close ties to the traditional aristocratic life of the Minangkabau court. During the Padri movement, the local Muslim leader, Tuanku Lintau, though a follower of Imam Bonjol, had generally directed his own appeal more toward winning over the "royalist" faction than toward destroying "infidel" adat practices. People from the Lintau/Buo area have always been associated with the perantau merchant tradition and the area has historically had contact with the outside through the east coast rantau. In the 1860s, however, the "adat aristocratic elements" apparently controlled the school. Partly, it seems, this occurred because the perantau merchants and artisans who were interested in education sent their children to the school in Payakumbuh where many families had relatives.[41]

Three new schools were established in the northwestern coffee regions in the 1850s—at Lubuk Sikaping, Panti, and Talu. Of the three, the one at Lubuk Sikaping seemed to attract the most local interest. Its pupils came from a wide variety of backgrounds, though heavily concentrated in penghulu, lesser adat functionary, religious, and agricultural families. The chiefs collected funds for the school by making levies on the population, which created some resentment, and finally led to government intervention to stop it. Of the twenty students who left school during the six years covered by the reports, nine were termed "educated" and the rest "disinterested." None apparently entered either government service or trade, though one went on to the medical institute in Batavia. In 1869, the chiefs decided that the teacher, a former Normal School student, was unqualified (after six years of service in the school), and they discharged him. They also discontinued their own financial contributions. The school closed.

The school at Panti had existed since at least 1854, but, until 1864, had only twice had more than ten students. The teacher had studied at

---

[41] Interviews, Lintau/Buo, November 1967; Taufik Abdullah, *Schools and Politics: The Kaum Muda Movement in West Sumatra (1927-1933)* (Ithaca: Cornell Modern Indonesia Project, 1971).

the nagari school in Rau but was not considered especially well-educated himself. The bulk of the student body came from chiefly or agricultural families. In 1864, the last year the school was mentioned, the educational report recorded "no report received" from Panti.

Talu differs from the other centers under discussion because it apparently never became an important coffee-collection center, though geographically located in the heart of northern coffee country. Situated on a large fertile rice plain, its population preferred sedentary agriculture to the merantau, and Talu children were not encouraged to seek nonagricultural livelihoods. Geographically, Talu belongs with the hill-country region, but its mentality and aristocratic life-style had more in common with distant Lima Kaum, a satellite of Batu Sangkar, than with hill villages, such as Rau or Puar Datar. Most of the Talu students came from agricultural, religious, and penghulu families. But unlike Rau, where pupils used the school as a training center for future employment as officials or traders, in Talu pupils tended to return home to their families. Because they did not use their newly acquired knowledge, they quickly forgot it. Enrollment at the school suddenly increased when the local controleur pressured the chiefs to send their own dependents. Such pupils, however, did not regard school training as a condition for success in life and made only indifferent progress in their studies. The only education which had any positive value in local eyes was that given in the village surau; other education was an unnecessary and sometimes expensive frill.[42] There were government jobs available, but they were filled more often by the teachers at the Talu school than by the pupils, with a resulting constant turnover in the school's staff. In the six years reported, 48 of the 111 pupils enrolled left school—47 returned home and one went to Mecca. None was considered to be "educated" upon leaving. They had attended out of deference or fear that the Dutch wanted to see at least token enthusiasm for education; the chiefs did not want to upset their cordial relations with the new regime. Personally, however, they had no regard for school.

The school at Halaban, though only opened in 1862, had been established in a more receptive environment than some others which

---

42 *VIO, 1863*, pp. 212-14.

had been in operation longer. The village is near the Lintau/Buo area, and, in fact, Tuanku Lintau had fled to Halaban when the Dutch attacked his headquarters in Lintau during the Padri period. Less rich in land than Lintau/Buo villagers, Halaban natives could see the possibilities which secular education could offer. Most pupils came from agricultural, chiefly, and religious families, but they came, not out of a sense of obligation (as at Buo), but because they wanted to leave the village. The school grew rapidly, and many of its graduates entered the government service or continued their education elsewhere. Those enrolled tended to stay on for several years, perfecting their penmanship and recitation. From 1863 to 1869, 235 pupils were enrolled but only eighteen left—five joined the government service, two went on for advanced education, three were removed, two fled, and one died. The local people had pride in their school and built a separate schoolhouse in the grand manner with glass windows and a tile roof. Pupils had to buy their own school supplies but, unlike the case with Talu, this did not significantly discourage enrollment.

The last of the schools to be opened in the coffee areas was that in Palembayan, north of Lake Maninjau; it began operations in 1867. Enrollment was high, averaging about thirty-three. This is especially impressive considering that, unlike many other schools, in Palembayan pupils had to pay tuition, f. 1 per month. The teacher was a local warehouse official who had studied at the Padang nagari school.

These nine schools may seem frail foundations on which to build a new "enlightened" society, but not if seen in the perspective of developments elsewhere in West Sumatra. Most of the Minangkabau people lived, not in the hill villages but in the large rice plains, and yet not one of the rice-plains villages had even established its own school much less kept it in operation. The achievement of the hill villages was truly noteworthy, and it demonstrates the importance of a local merantau tradition to the success of secular education.

The villages with long-established traditions of perantau merchants, artisans, or even religious men made the earliest and most efficient use of the secular schools, absorbing them into existing patterns of nonagricultural activity. The wealth which coffee provided for the nagari treasuries enabled such hill villages to finance schools and teachers. Coffee money alone was not enough to assure success. The extensive coffee areas to the south of Lake Singkarak, for example, did not display a similar push toward secular education. The southern areas differed in social structure from those of the north which probably explains their record in education. In the south, the village leaders were often called raja, indicative of their role as paramount chiefs who could exercise quasi-autocratic authority over their dependents. These chiefs were less in step with the interests of their subordinates, probably because the distance between them in the social hierarchy was significant. Schools appear in these areas only at the end of the century and even then they are few and are the results of Dutch government planning rather than local initiative.

The Highland Plains: Schools in Administrative Centers (the 1860s)

The only schools located in the major rice plains areas of the highlands were established at the Assistant Residency seats—Batu Sangkar, Bukittinggi, Payakumbuh, and Solok. These schools dated from the 1840s. Though settlements had existed in these areas before Dutch arrival, their development as "urban" commercial and administrative centers occurred during the colonial era as a result of connections with the Dutch regime. Many Minangkabau from surrounding areas, especially perantau artisans, merchants, and speculators, crowded to these rapidly growing towns. As a result, the original families, though often still recognized as the pro forma ruling elite, had in fact lost control over local affairs.

Batu Sangkar, Bukittinggi, Payakumbuh, and Solok each served as the headquarters for regional Dutch bureaus. They were as such more cosmopolitan and dynamic, and their inhabitants had more immediate contact with Dutch influence and colonial opportunity than was true in most other parts of West Sumatra. A combination of various factors, therefore, caused the four towns to develop rapidly in the nineteenth century as commercial and governmental centers, attracting large transient populations, many of whom provided services to the new European establishment. Among such people, there was probably a much greater sensitivity to the kinds of opportunities available beyond the usual life of the village. They had already left their home village once in search of a new livelihood, and this made subsequent moves that much easier. Moreover, the concept of extra training as a means to extra income was well-established in perantau families such as these.

Bukittinggi, the seat of the Assistant Residency of Agam also served as the headquarters for the Padang Highlands Residency and had, therefore, that much more importance and activity as compared to other regional centers. The nagari had expanded greatly after its selection as the center for Dutch military operations against the Padri in the 1820s. The building of Fort de Kock, and its use as the garrison fort for Agam and the whole northern region, attracted immigrants from the rest of the area who hoped to prosper by provisioning first the military and later the civilian establishment. The original village and its inhabitants were soon overshadowed and often brushed aside. This created a continuing irritation which hindered relations among the various residents of the town, especially as the original villlagers withdrew ever deeper into crusty traditionalism.

Blessed with a cool, dry, upland climate and located on the edge of a major rice plain, Bukittinggi was an ideal location for the Dutch headquarters. A market center from pre-Dutch times, under the Dutch Bukittinggi became the most important communications and transportation focus in the highlands, the hub for the road network and later the railroad as well. Not only were people attracted to work directly for Dutch bureaus, but also artisans, food dealers, and other service-industry people flocked to the town. The varied and essentially urban nature of the population was reflected by the student body of the local nagari school. They came from a wide variety of families fairly evenly distributed among government chiefs, penghulu, bureaucrats of all levels, merchants, and artisans, with a sprinkling of agricultural and religious families. Bukittinggi's role as a perantau center is shown in the relatively large proportion of merchant (15 percent) and artisan (13 percent) families represented among the student body of the nagari school.

Founded in the early 1840s, the Bukittinggi nagari school had immediately attracted local interest. Of all the highlands schools in the 1840s, Steinmetz had found the Bukittinggi one had the best students in terms both of devotion to their studies and progress that they made.[43] Its enrollment showed a fairly steady rise between 1854 and 1869, beginning at twenty-one and reaching eighty-one by the end of the 1860s. Those

---

43 Steinmetz, "Inlandsch Onderwijs," p. 311.

who came generally attended regularly and, on leaving, they entered government service; only a few became traders and, reportedly, no one simply returned home or was discharged for lack of interest. These early education reports provide the first indication of Bukittinggi's future development as the focus for those interested in the new civil service and secular education generally. The area north and west of Bukittinggi had long been important for perantau traders and artisans, and, by the end of the nineteenth century, it would be known for its teachers, doctors, and civil servants as well. Few students in the Bukittinggi school came from the rice villages of the nearby Agam plain (or even from families of the original Bukittinggi village itself); rather they were from villages in the foothill areas nearby—Koto Tuo, Balingka, Kota Gedang, Sianok. Such villages had only small areas for growing wet rice because they were hemmed in by the rugged hills stretching from Lake Maninjau to Mount Singgalang. Their inhabitants had long and often famous traditions as perantau goldsmiths, merchants, carpenters, and weavers. Prospective students from these villages usually had perantau relatives in Bukittinggi with whom they could live while attending school.

The Bukittinggi area's wealth also came from its being the major collection center for one of the largest coffee-producing regions of the 1860s. Chiefs in the nearby foothills had high incomes from the coffee commissions.[44] Large merchant families had developed through servicing the coffee transport system and dealing in other export materials produced or collected in the area. Most of the civil servants and professional people among the Bukittinggi elite came from these villages and had attended the nagari school. Some, as children, had walked daily from their village to Bukittinggi to attend school; they left home before dawn and returned late in the afternoon. In the process, they might cover ten or twenty miles a day. As a result, they would be unable to assist at home, in the fields or with other family enterprises. This made their education a double burden on the family—first the direct expense and second the lost labor.

A large proportion of the commuting students came from the relatively nearby village of Kota Gedang, located opposite Bukittinggi across the vast, deep canyon called the Ngarai. This canyon borders Bukittinggi on

---

44 *Verbaal*, January 3, 1872, No. 10.

the south and west, separating it from the foothills of Mount Singgalang. Proximity was not the only advantage of the Kota Gedang students. Several nagari school teachers of the 1860s were also Kota Gedang natives, and they eased the way as well as provided a constant stimulus, encouraging village families to send children to the school.

The Bukittinggi school had a good reputation among the Minangkabau because its students were so successful at getting good jobs or gaining admittance to advanced educational institutions, specifically the Normal School. As a result, the school attracted many students from elsewhere in the highlands.[45] Because Bukittinggi was the center of a large colonial bureaucracy and the location of the Normal School, its nagari school was strategically placed to display to prospective pupils the wide variety of colonial opportunities. Students could see in their daily surroundings how secular education could serve as a stepping stone to advancement through government or private service. Not only that, but when they "graduated," they had more easy access to these jobs because they often had been in contact with prospective employers for some time.

Payakumbuh, the Assistant Residency seat of Lima Puluh Kota, has a different character from that of Bukittinggi, in large part reflecting the different geographic character of its immediate surroundings. Whereas Bukittinggi is physically close to the hill country, home of the dynamic perantau elements, Payakumbuh is more in the center of its large rice plain, the Lima Puluh Kota. Socially, the adat traditions of the Lima Puluh Kota plain have tended to emphasize chiefly privilege, and most villages in the area follow rigid hierarchies of chiefs exercising aristocratic prerogatives and firmly controlling their followers. The villages in the immediate area of Payakumbuh, in contrast to those near Bukittinggi, did not have well-developed merchant and artisan family traditions, but rather depended on rice cultivation for which ample good land was immediately available. The chiefs apparently enrolled their children in the Payakumbuh school in large numbers, but not from any interest in education as such. They regarded school as part of the perquisites and privileges of their exalted station. Their enthusiasm was generally minimal and their attendance a sometime thing. In 1863, the Assistant

---

45 *VIO, 1863*, p. 222.

Resident for Lima Puluh Kota suggested in a public speech that, because the government paid its representatives (that is the various village chiefs) well, it had the right to expect them to take advantage of the nagari school and get the kind of education which the government believed they needed to fulfill their duties. At the same time, they should assure that their heirs did likewise.[46] As a result, nagari school enrollment suddenly rose to 100, but attendance continued to be irregular, and, by 1866, the total enrollment had dropped back to about fifty. The chiefs had decided that the government would not or could not enforce the Assistant Resident's threat.[47] The chiefs themselves disagreed with the Dutch opinion that they needed to be literate. From their point of view, they could always hire a secretary to do such menial tasks as writing reports and keeping records.[48]

Payakumbuh was less important as a trading center than Bukittinggi. Though the town is located on the main route to the east coast, a major Dutch aim of the nineteenth century was to divert all trade from the eastern ports to Padang. Insofar as they were successful in this effort, Payakumbuh lost significance as a commercial center. Nonetheless, it still formed the hub for activities in the Lima Puluh Kota. The pupils in the nagari school came from a wide variety of backgrounds, though the heaviest concentration were from penghulu (23 percent) and government chief (26 percent) families. Payakumbuh's administration and commercial sectors contributed small but significant numbers of pupils—merchants (8 percent), artisans (5 percent), and bureaucrats (6 percent). Another 26 percent of the pupils came from neighboring agricultural families.

Unlike most highlands areas, in which school financing came from nagari treasuries or levies on chiefs, in Payakumbuh, the parents of the pupils had to contribute to the cost of the teacher's salary.[49] An important reason for this was that Payakumbuh chiefs did not have as much extra income from coffee commissions as those in parts of Agam

---

46 Ibid., p. 224.
47 *VIO, 1869*, p. 267.
48 Viewing it all in retrospect, the present-day penghulu have argued that their ancestors thought that attendance at the nagari school implied collaboration with a kafir government. Interviews, Payakumbuh, November 21, 1967. (Apparently working as a nagarihoofd and accepting coffee commissions does not in their view constitute "collaboration.")
49 *VIO, 1877*, p. 182.

and other areas. Although located in an important population center, the Payakumbuh warehouse collected, for example, only 3,773 piculs of coffee in 1867, as compared to the 14,205 and 20,513 collected in the same year in Bukittinggi and Batu Sangkar respectively. Solok, which in many respects resembled Payakumbuh in its general social and economic configurations, likewise collected only small amounts of coffee—7,796 piculs in 1867.[50]

Enrolling children at school meant a greater expense for Payakumbuh families and required a correspondingly greater interest in Western training. As shown by the reports, local chiefs had little motivation and most middle-level families in the villages could do well from rice cultivation. The semiagricultural villages of the foothills were located rather far away, which would have imposed the additional costs of room and board on pupils' families, though many from the village of Halaban did come to the school. One such village, Puar Datar, already had its own school anyway and others, such as Suliki, soon established them. Payakumbuh had traditionally been a strong center for religious education. After the harvest, boys and young men from the neighboring villages usually went to spend time training in tarekat lore at one of the many local centers. For people living and working in a traditional, village agricultural environment, such education had more meaning than learning how to add numbers or copy government documents. From its beginning in the 1840s, the nagari school had not attracted many dedicated pupils. Most made only indifferent progress and showed little interest. Education was not a valued commodity in the community, and it made no difference in one's position in village society. Boys often left school to marry wealthy women, and turned their backs on secular training.[51]

When pressed about their disinterest, parents pleaded poverty, but the social and economic structure in the area around Payakumbuh were probably more likely factors. Those who were interested in the new opportunities open to the secular "educated" person did apply themselves to their studies. Upon leaving school, they could find jobs in the coffee warehouses and other government enterprises. The vast majority, however,

---

50 See Table 3 in Chapter IV.
51 Steinmetz, "Inlands Onderwijs," p. 311.

merely withdrew. From 1863 to 1869, of the sixty-eight students who left the school—seven entered government enterprises, two became traders, two went on for advanced education, six were withdrawn by their families, three were dropped for absenteeism, forty were expelled for "laziness," and seven "ran away." For families in Lima Puluh Kota rice villages, secular education had no relevance. At a time when the chiefs complained that their villages were too poor to send children to school, the local tarekat centers were building large impressive mosques, surau, classrooms, and dormitories. Families were donating lands for the perpetual upkeep of the religious foundations.[52] Religious training, especially that available in the closed company of the local tarekat community, had more meaning for their future lives and needs than arithmetic.

Batu Sangkar owed most of its development as an important town to the Dutch occupation. The traditional center of the Tanah Datar plain had been at nearby Pagarruyung, site of the Raja's court. As the heart of the former Minangkabau kingdom, Tanah Datar also had other locations with traditional importance—among them Buo, Lima Kaum, and Sungai Tarab, each the site of an important royal minister or advisor. In military terms, however, the Dutch found the small kampung of Batu Sangkar a better place for their fort, Fort van der Capellen, the first major Dutch garrison in the interior. A market and commercial center of fair size grew around the settlement, especially as the coffee trade took on increased importance in the 1840s and 1850s. The decline of Pagarruyung as a center after the Dutch occupation undoubtedly contributed to the rise of the new town around Batu Sangkar. Many Minangkabau who would have been found around the court now transferred their operations to the center of the new regime. The hills near Batu Sangkar favored large coffee crops and nearby towns produced handicrafts which were important trade items.

Compared with Payakumbuh and Bukittinggi, however, Batu Sangkar remained a smaller, less "cosmopolitan" place. Many of its inhabitants did see the nagari school as a new opportunity, however. Over half of the students belonged to families of government chiefs or penghulu, and, unlike the Payakumbuh students, those in Batu Sangkar used the school

---

52 Interviews, Syekh of two tarekat centers near Payakumbuh, November 21 and 23, 1967.

as a training ground, often for jobs in the government service. Enrollment climbed steadily, and those who came tended to attend regularly. On completing their education, the students entered trade or joined the civil service, particularly the staffs of the coffee warehouses. Not everyone had a favorable view of secular education, however. As elsewhere, many of the traditional aristocracy found it an unnecessary expense. This was especially the case with those from surrounding rice villages (such as Lima Kaum), for whom attending school meant either commuting or else taking lodging in town. Since such villages were not historically homes for perantau merchants, artisans, etc., village families only rarely had relatives living in the town of Batu Sangkar, and thus children would have to board with strangers—both expensive and undesirable. Education imposed unnecessary burdens and financial hardships for such families who had no plan to use the training which their children might receive.[53]

Solok, south of Lake Singkarak, is traditionally considered the home of the most conceited and arrogantly aristocratic of all the Minangkabau. This quality proved the bane of many a schoolteacher's career. The first teacher complained that his pupils were so surly, they did not learn their lessons.[54] During van Ophuijzen's tenure as Assistant Resident for Solok in the early 1850s, the school offered an extensive and high-quality curriculum, made possible by his own special tutoring of students.[55]

The overwhelming proportion of the students (some 56 percent) came from agricultural families, with another large segment from penghulu (14 percent) and government chiefs' (16 percent) families. There were also several from bureaucratic backgrounds (8 percent) and even from wage earners' (5 percent) families. Whatever their backgrounds, however, few pupils showed a real interest in applying their education. In 1867, for example, twenty-six children left school; one became a clerk and the other twenty-five returned home where they "soon forgot that little they had learned."[56] The school was financed by general donations administered through the nagari treasury. But the chiefs belittled education as an effort unworthy of their status. Even when the Assistant Resident proclaimed

---

53 *Verbaal*, July 14, 1856, No. 7.
54 Steinmetz, "Inlands Onderwijs," p. 311.
55 *Verbaal*, July 14, 1856, No. 7.
56 *VIO*, 1867, p. 185.

it a duty of every chief to encourage local parents to send their children to school, the effort had only small results. The chiefs themselves had no education and they could not believe it had any intrinsic value. Merchants and traders, who displayed an increasing interest, were hindered by the great distances between their villages and Solok.

Solok itself had probably less commercial importance than Payakumbuh; it was an area with deeply entrenched and wealthy landholding families. A broad rich sawah plain which surrounds the town on all sides provided sufficient livelihood and gave little impetus toward trade or other nonagricultural pursuits. For these families, aristocratic privilege was a keenly appreciated and jealously guarded possession. The prevailing attitude apparently dictated that Western education, because of its connection to the colonial rulers, conferred a certain amount of prestige, and hence school should be reserved to those with "noble" blood. At the same time, however, there was no interest in spending a great deal of time at school or attaining any particular proficiency in the skills which it provided.[57] Enrollment rose at a steady rate, but the futures of departing students varied little between 1863 and 1869—almost to a man they went home and picked up the threads of their former lives in the village elite.

The administrative centers on the plains were hybrid communities in which the most dynamic elements often were foreign—either ethnically so in the case of the Dutch or geographically so in the case of the perantau. Perantau Minangkabau from hill villages settled in these centers in increasing numbers, and they married local women here. The children of such unions were often the most interested and constant pupils at the local nagari school.[58] They were also often the kemanakan of merchants, since a perantau often married the sister of a business associate. In any event, the woman was not usually from a notable family because such families did not encourage their women to become second wives to middle-class, perantau merchants. The children were rarely heirs to a chieftaincy. They grew up in an atmosphere which stressed achievement—in commerce, artisanry, or service—rather than birth.

---

57 Interviews, Solok, November 1967.
58 Many of the educated people of Batu Sangkar, for example, had fathers from Kota Gedang in Agam. Interviews, Kota Gedang, October 1967.

The schools themselves were sometimes controlled by the native-born elites, the district and family chiefs, men who rarely recognized any value in secular education, though the more "enlightened" of them might be prepared to tolerate its presence. Given the social and economic structure of the plains villages, probably few of these local chiefs' client families were particularly interested in education either. Bukittinggi is an exception; many of its satellite villages were areas of marginal rice cultivation, and their people had therefore more interest in alternative means to a living. The nagari treasuries of the four centers were probably well endowed by virtue of the important regional markets which were held weekly in the four towns; where merchants and restauranteurs were assessed rent for the space they occupied. The relatively large Dutch establishment in each center could provide a constant pressure on the chiefs to demonstrate their commitment to the regime by maintaining the secular schools. But it is significant that no other schools were established in the plains. Plains villages unlike hill villages generated no independent desire to establish their own schools. Children whose futures were planned around the yearly cycle of wet-rice agriculture had no need for literacy, arithmetic, or "civilized behavior."

Schools on the Coast: The Administrative Centers (the 1860s)

The coastal port centers of Painan, Padang, Pariaman, and Air Bangis had had a longer history of foreign contact and interaction than the highlands villages and towns. Their autocratic princes had learned that accommodation to outside forces, whether from Aceh or Europe, was usually to their financial and political advantage. The Dutch pampered the coastal raja and played up to their pretensions, preserving the status quo and the air of aristocratic society which this entailed. As a result, the attitude among coastal rulers proved at the most hostile, and at the least ambivalent, toward the concept of the nagari school, especially if the raja were supposed to pay the costs. The coastal raja were even less susceptible to pressure from their constituents than the most "aristocratic" highlands penghulu. In the highlands villages, the groups most interested in the nagari schools were the middle-level artisans, merchants, and upwardly mobile families generally. On the coast, such groups were nonexistent among the permanent residents who formed the raja's own dependents.

The middle-level people (merchants, artisans, service people) were outsiders and were usually under Dutch jurisdiction. They were thus only peripherally the responsibility of the chiefs. This ambiguity in jurisdiction helps explain one of the major differences between coastal and highlands schools—more direct government influence and support was available for the coastal schools.

The success of the nagari schools in the highlands, especially in seemingly insignificant little villages, was an obvious embarrassment to the Dutch officials of Padang, the center for government operations and the largest town in West Sumatra. The chiefs, for their part, saw nothing of value in education and forthrightly refused to provide any funds so that others might attend. The Padang rulers argued that, unlike the highlands chiefs who had access to extra money from the coffee cultivation system, they had no extra funds available for such extravagances as Western education.[59] The fact that the Dutch governor found this complaint reasonable indicates that the coffee-cultivation system was (or, more

Table 9. Parents' Backgrounds—Lowlands Schools 1860s (in percent of total enrollment)

School Locale	Merchant/Private Business	Artisan	Maritime	Agriculture/Landlord	Wage Earner	Pengulu	Lesser Adat Functionary	Religious	Governemt Chief	High Government Official	Clerical Official	Supervisory Official
Port Centers												
Padang	1				2		2		1	5		
Painan	9	6	3	19	1	29	1	4	2	2	2	1
Pariaman	25	7	2	14	1	5		2	6	1	7	
Air Bangis	8			6		64			16			
Trusan	5	1		4		63		1	9	1	2	1
Coastal Villages												

---

59 Report of Governor van Swieten, February 12, 1852, *Verbaal*, June 15, 1852, No. 3.

School Locale	Merchant/Private Business	Artisan	Maritime	Agriculture/Landlord	Wage Earner	Pengulu	Lesser Adat Functionary	Religious	Government Chief	High Government Official	Clerical Official	Supervisory Official
Pelangi	3		1	17	66	3			6			
Batang Kapas	1	3	4	59	13			7	6		1	3
Asam Kumbang									53		8	
Sungai Limau	9	3		10		4	15	7	8			
Tiku			22	49		22			6			

Source: *VIO, 1863-1869.*

correctly, was thought to be) a very lucrative operation for the highlands nagari and their chiefs. The Padang administration agreed to help finance a school for local children if the chiefs would construct the building.[60] The rationale behind government financing was that qualified Minangkabau were needed in the expanding colonial bureaucracy. In Java, the government paid to educate prospective civil servants, and so the Governor General agreed to do so in West Sumatra—but only along the coast, not in the highlands.[61]

Though the chiefs did not care about education for their families, obviously many Padang residents did. Their children had apparently already received some training elsewhere because when the school opened in 1853, fifty-nine of those who enrolled were immediately placed in advanced classes.[62] Many of these were doubtless children who had studied in highlands schools earlier, and then come to live with relatives in Padang. Others had probably studied privately; merchants and government officials often ran private tutoring sessions for relatives or the children of friends. The advanced pupils were not children from local aristocratic families, in any event, because with rare exception none of

---

60 Ibid.
61 *Verbaal*, June 2, 1852, No. 4.
62 *VIO, 1854*, p. 227.

these had so much as looked at a book since the school fiasco of 1826.[63]

As with perantau elsewhere, men from the highlands villages whose careers had brought them to Padang almost always soon married a local woman. According to highlands adat, a woman could not leave her family's house—even to accompany her husband. If a man planned to spend any time at all in a new place, he would marry locally; this gave him a permanent and convenient base of operations. Many of the pupils in the Padang school (as had been the case in highlands market centers) were undoubtedly the children of such marriages. Many others were children who had been sent to Padang to live with relatives in order to attend the large school. As it became known in highlands villages that one could obtain high quality education in Padang, many more families sent their children. According to Dutch standards, the Padang school had the best teaching staff and equipment.[64] By the 1860s, the government was paying the salaries for two teachers and several teaching assistants. School enrollment reached 237 in 1864, but in 1865 the building burned and, for the next three years, education in Padang floundered. It recovered again by 1869. Almost all pupils from the school who "graduated" entered trade or the government service, especially the coffee warehouse bureaucracy.

Painan, the territorial center for the southern coast, had been the first point of Dutch commercial activity on the West Coast. Padang surpassed it already by the late eighteenth century because of its superior harbor and closeness to the main highlands sources for export goods. Painan, however, remained an important commercial center for its own area and had a significant perantau population, a population which quickly accepted the idea of secular education. The natives of Painan, particularly the raja, showed only nominal interest and refused to contribute to school upkeep. The teacher was paid by the Dutch administration, and, in 1869, the long unfinished schoolhouse was also finished with a government subsidy.[65]

---

63 Report of Governor van Swieten, February 12, 1852, *Verbaal*, June 15, 1852, No. 3. See also above pp. 78-79.
64 *Verbaal*, July 14, 1856, No. 7.
65 *VIO, 1869*, p. 146.

Pupils at the Painan school came from a wide variety of backgrounds, typical of a commercial center. Those who left school usually entered the public service as clerks and petty bureaucrats; several became teachers in nearby villages. For example, between 1863 and 1869, of the twenty pupils reported as leaving school, two became petty bureaucrats, one an assistant to the warehousemaster, one a teacher, three went home, two went to Padang with their families, and one died.

Pariaman, located north of Padang, is on the edge of a broad coastal rice plain, giving it a more agricultural orientation than either Padang or Painan. The hill country at the edge of this plain was potentially important coffee land but, by 1860, had remained undeveloped.[66] Pupils at the Pariaman school came from a wide variety of backgrounds, the largest single group being agricultural (14 percent) and commercial (25 percent), representing a fairly strong interest in both the town and the surrounding rural areas. Despite the rather aristocratic organization of local society, the raja barely went through the motions of enrolling their children. They did use the school in their own particular way, however, extorting money from local hamlets whose families wanted to send their children to the school.[67]

Air Bangis, the northernmost port town in West Sumatra is on the very fringes of Minangkabau culture. Pupils in the local school came overwhelmingly from chiefs' families—both penghulu (64 percent) and government chiefs (16 percent). Nine of the twenty-two pupils who left school between 1863 and 1869, were considered "qualified," but, reportedly, none took government jobs or did anything else that required the education they had presumably received. School enrollment meanwhile dropped steadily throughout the decade. The chiefs became increasingly disgruntled at the "useless burden" of supporting the nagari school and withdrew their own children as a measure of protest. In 1864, fourteen of the pupils were from chiefly families, and by 1866 it had dropped to just four.

Trusan, though no longer an important administrative center by the 1860s, resembled the other port towns in that its raja had been a former

---

66 *Verbaal*, May 14, 1860, No. 42.
67 VIO, 1863, p. 207.

ally of the VOC, and as a result, his family retained numerous perquisites, chiefly those of pomp and circumstance. Like Air Bangis, most (72 percent) of its school children came from chiefs' families, mainly those of penghulu (63 percent), the others being spread among a wide variety of occupational backgrounds. The teacher was a close relative of the Trusan raja, which seemed to be his major qualification for the job. The chiefs sent their children solely because they believed it a duty, not because it had any independent value. The sense of duty proved fleeting, and enrollment declined steadily after 1862.

The profiles of the port centers reinforce the notion that a "successful" school resulted from ambitious and interested middle-level families. In growing urban centers such as Padang, Painan, and Pariaman, which attracted many highlands merchants and other ambitious types, the schools served as the keys for opening new careers, in government service, and for improving old ones, by becoming more "modern" merchants. In declining port towns, like Trusan, Air Bangis and apparently also Indrapura (the records are scanty but indicative), the schools became the preserve of disinterested but status-conscious chiefs' families. The merchant element here was smaller and more quiescent, the more dynamic elements having already moved to the major and growing ports where the real activity was now taking place. The children of the aristocracy in either event attended only to gain whatever possible distinction could be acquired by attendance at a secular school. At this early date, however, Western education as such conveyed little independent prestige of its own. It was mainly a tool required for a very few specific jobs.

Coastal Villages: A Quasi-Maritime Environment

Several schools were opened in the late 1850s and early 1860s in small coastal villages. The people here were mainly in maritime occupations or rice cultivation. Generally, these villages provided infertile soil for the nagari school. The coastal villages were not particularly prosperous on the whole, and they were ruled by small cliques of aristocrats who claimed that their ancestors had been given the territory by the Raja of Pagarruyung. Such villages did not, as a rule, have well-developed middle-range families who contended for power with the penghulu (generally known as raja on the coast), and as a result there was an important gap between the chiefs on top and the peasants below. Of the five schools which appear in the records in the 1850s and 1860s, three—Pelangi, Batang Kapas, and Asam Kumbang—closed before 1869; the other two—Tiku and Sungai Limau—dropped from the record and one must assume that they too closed.

The Pelangi school drew mainly from agricultural (66 percent) and maritime (17 percent) families, but there is no indication that pupils used school training to find other livelihoods than those pursued already by their elders. Generally, no one really seemed to care about the school and few bothered to come regularly. In 1865, the building collapsed and was not rebuilt. No one apparently even noticed that it was gone.

The Batang Kapas school, farther up the coast, came to almost the same end; its building collapsed in 1867. Most pupils at the school (59 percent) came from agricultural families and another 19 percent came from chiefly backgrounds. With only the rare exception, those who left school did not do anything with whatever training they had received. The records mention that from 1863 to 1869, eighty-one pupils left school; one became an assistant warehousemaster and one a clerk; the rest went home. After the school collapsed, the only regular pupils were four Chinese children, and the Batang Kapas chiefs felt it an untoward burden to finance the education of these foreigners. The school was closed.

Asam Kumbang is located near the foothills behind Painan. The majority of pupils (53 percent) came from the families of government chiefs. But they attended classes only irregularly, and apparently they never did anything with what little training they managed to acquire. The school closed in 1867 because everyone concerned agreed it was a waste of time.

The pupils at the school in Sungai Limau, a coastal village north of Pariaman, came from a wide variety of backgrounds. Agriculture and traditional adat or religious positions, however, accounted for a large percentage (36 percent), with government chiefs another 8 percent. In 1865, the school disappeared from the records; no reason was given. The same happened with the Tiku school a few miles farther up the coast. Both schools had opened in 1863. Tiku was in a coffee-growing area and some 49 percent of its school children came from families engaged in growing coffee. The records, however, give no indication what, if anything, the pupils did with the training.

Unlike the small village schools in the highlands, those on the coast did not serve as a ladder for social or economic change. The coastal villages, by and large, did not have traditions of merantau. They were not pressed by excess populations seeking to enter trade and artisanry as an alternative to marginal rice cultivation. Along the coast, income was supplemented by maritime activities—fishing or shipping. Although a shipper operates much like a trader, in the sense that he provides a service, at the same time these men operated out of their home villages rather than moving to some other town and setting up a new residence.

The Nagari School and the Community

The record of the nagari schools appears poor at best if measured by outside, "objective" criteria such as attendance, textbook quality, or teachers' capabilities. If, as conventional wisdom tends to suggest, only those who "collaborate" can benefit from colonial society, then by that measure too the schools are also a failure, for the "tools of the regime" (the penghulu and government chiefs) rejected secular education. Despite the seeming odds of poor finances and official disinterest, however, families who wanted secular education were able to get it and were then able to use what they had gotten to good advantage. When set against the background of West Sumatran society at mid-century and given all the factors which militated against education, the nagari schools' accomplishments assume a greater significance.

To get an education under the outwardly adverse circumstances prevailing in village schools required determination and stamina. The issue of the nagari school often became involved in the more general problems of the relationship, and specifically the mutual obligations, between the chiefs and their dependents. Because the laras- and nagarihoofd were, in many ways, recent modifications and extensions of a traditional adat system of penghulu government, the resolution of the school problem in a particular village reflected the configurations or traditional lines of competition and conflict in that village. In hill villages, where social distances were small and movement between the middle and top layers of society correspondingly easier, pressure could be exerted on chiefs to provide schools for their followers. The needed funds were available through commissions from coffee harvests and levies on local markets.

But not all coffee villages or market towns followed the pattern. Villages where middle levels showed the most interest in secular education tended to be those where merantau, that is learning a trade in order to pursue it outside the village, was the most highly developed.

"Success" or "failure" when applied to the nagari schools thus depends on the perspective from which one wishes to view them. From the Dutch government viewpoint, one which emphasized attendance records, quality of instruction, beautiful buildings, and plentiful textbooks, almost all the nagari schools were "failures." But, to be fair, the Dutch had no right to condemn education in West Sumatra because it failed to measure up to their standards. The government had steadfastly refused to supply the funds which would have made such standards attainable. In 1857, for example, the Governor General had ruled that funds could not be used for local schools whose teacher had not been educated at a government institution.[68] By the 1860s, many nagari schools had teachers who had in fact been trained at the government operated Normal School in Bukittinggi. But, in 1864, the Governor General decided that, because the people of West Sumatra paid no direct taxes, government money could not be used to finance schools there.[69]

At the same time, however, schools in the Batak areas to the north of Minangkabau were receiving large measures of government aid—in addition to the money already provided by the Protestant Mission Society which operated the schools. The government's rationale for its subsidy was that secular education lessened the danger of Islamic conversions among the pagan Bataks, hence making administration of the area that much easier. This view was based on the conclusions drawn by Mission Society ministers in Tapanuli. In 1856, one of them had written to the Governor General that the spread of Islam from Minangkabau was threatening the political stability of Tapanuli. The Governor of Sumatra's West Coast, under whose jurisdiction Tapanuli fell at the time, immediately decided to neutralize the threat by providing alternative "social training" in the form of government-run secular schools. He proposed a total of f. 4,440 for ten village schools; this included a salary for the Christian missionary

---

68 Decision of the Governor General, October 8, 1857, *Verbaal*, April 24, 1858, No. 21.
69 Decision of the Governor General, March 1, 1864, No. 5, *Verbaal*, May 24, 1864, No. 38.

who would serve as the supervisor for education in Tapanuli. The state would also provide teachers' salaries and all school supplies.[70] By 1863, f. 6,795 was being spent each year by the government to maintain eleven schools in Tapanuli. On the other hand, in the Minangkabau area, of the twenty-eight schools in existence, money was available for only the Padang, Pariaman, and Trusan nagari schools and the Bukittinggi Normal School.[71] In Benkulen, Bangka, and Lampung, the government also paid teachers' salaries and provided educational materials to village schools during this period.[72]

The nagari school therefore developed as a domestic Minangkabau institution. Its operation in any given community reflected the political and social structure of that community. What pupils learned reflected the dominant local perception about what they needed for their future lives. Sometimes this attitude stressed arithmetic and literacy, sometimes Quranic recitation; the importance of the nagari school to the community varied accordingly.

Chiefs, whether penghulu, laras- or nagarihoofd, did not need education to become chiefs or carry out their duties as chiefs. Despite all Dutch efforts to the contrary, this remained the case. One governor in the 1850s, exasperated at the total illiteracy of the chiefs, thought to pressure them into sending their heirs to school. He decreed that, henceforth, population registers and other local records would have to be kept by the chiefs rather than the controleur. He believed that if a chief's work required literacy, then chiefs' families would have to take a more personal interest in education. In fact, though the chiefs briefly acquiesced to the implied threat to their position by enrolling their heirs in school, they hired private secretaries to deal with the matter of record keeping. And so did their successors.[73]

In merantau villages, almost always in or on the edge of the rugged hill country, chiefs often showed a more active interest in education—not because they were chiefs and believed it had value to their administration

---

70 *Verbaal*, August 3, 1857, no. 6.
71 *VIO*, 1866, pp. 17-18.
72 *VIO*, 1862, p. 215.
73 "Welk Middel Men ter Westkust van Sumatra te Baat Neemt om de Waarde van het Lager Onderwijs Beter te Doen Schatten," TNI, 2, 1 (1858), pp. 39-40.

of the village but because their families needed a means to supplement incomes derived from rice cultivation. Their interest was a function of the "minus" agricultural area in which they lived. In such villages even heirs to the penghulu's title often joined the migration to the rantau during their youth, earning a living as trader or artisan. Commercial families, whether or not they were also chiefs' families, were among those who first recognized the value of understanding the European business techniques—an understanding which could be at least partially gained at the nagari school. Knowledge of these matters was especially important for those whose businesses brought them in contact with the Dutch economic sphere; for the smaller, marginal trader such knowledge had correspondingly less value. The petty trader needed education neither to aid his own affairs nor to assist him in dealing with Dutch contacts (he had none).

For the lower middle-level families, however, secular education could represent an alternative to their traditional occupation, rather than a means for improving it. As the Dutch bureaucracy expanded, Minangkabau families could see that being a clerk in a minor office might lead to becoming a secretary to the controleur or warehousemaster. Moreover, it became apparent that having a relative inside the civil service would be an advantage when dealing with the Dutch and could provide an important source of position and income. Having a relative with a government bureau also gave a family an advantage over others when new jobs became available. The high position held by Kota Gedang families in civil service posts and in the professions in the late nineteenth and early twentieth centuries stemmed from their early recognition of the value of government service. They used their acquired influence carefully in order to assure that their heirs and followers would continue to gain admittance to the best schools and jobs. They began early and it paid off handsomely.

Because the nagari schools were operated locally and served local interests, it is not surprising that the style and content of instruction followed Minangkabau rather than Dutch ideas of pedagogy. Dutch inspectors complained that pupils learned by rote and that promotion was based on various subjective considerations rather than objective exams. One inspector condemned nagari school education as being focused on the "mindless copying of official documents" and the perfection of penmanship. Pupils memorized texts but could not comprehend the subject matter.[74] It would be fair to ask this inspector in turn how many Dutch officials to his knowledge ever needed or wanted their secretaries' opinions about the subject matter of a letter. One could even argue that many Dutch officials probably preferred that their transactions remain confidential; few clerks would be able to discuss documents they had transcribed if they couldn't understand the content. Most clerical jobs did not require comprehension of documents; scribes and secretaries in Dutch bureaus were nineteenth-century equivalents of today's typewriters and photocopy machines.

Nagari school education followed the same pattern as traditional education available in the village surau. In the surau, boys learned to recite the Quran and to write out passages in beautiful Arabic characters. They memorized but never understood. Even the most learned ulama rarely knew the Arabic language (in which most Islamic religious texts were written) well enough to read and understand an unfamiliar book, or sometimes even the Quran itself. He was considered learned by virtue of his long years spent memorizing lectures given by other ulama who themselves often only barely understood what they taught (having learned it in turn from yet other semiliterate ulama). The same techniques were admirably suited for the nagari school. One need only substitute the Malay language and official reports for Arabic and the Quran. Moreover, since Malay was written in Arabic characters, the transition was not even all that great. Steinmetz had found in 1846, for example, that pupils who had had some prior study with a village Islamic teacher could skip the first grade of the secular school.[75]

As the surau served different purposes depending on the interests of the pupils, so too did the nagari schools.[76] Few boys who went to the surau intended to become ulama, nor would they remember for very

---

74 J. J. van Limburg Brouwer, "Het Gouvenemental Inlandsch Onderwijs op Sumatra," *TNI*, 5, 2 (1876), pp. 6-10.
75 Report of Resident Steinmetz to the Governor, March 4, 1846, in Steinmetz, "Inlandsch Onderwijs," p. 311.
76 This comparison of the surau and the nagari school should not be taken to mean that they represented two mutually exclusive alternatives. Pupils who attended the secular schools still went to the surau classes, which were usually conducted in the late afternoon or early evening. The subsequent decline of the traditional surau in the twentieth century occurred more from the new developments in the Islamic community as a whole than from secular school competition.

long what they had learned. It was part of the process by which one became a proper citizen, an enlightened member of the community. One attended more or less according to individual interest, did what work one wanted, and left whenever one felt sufficiently "educated." Nagari school pupils and their families, not surprisingly, saw secular education in the same terms. The chiefs, if they showed any interest in it at all, saw it as part of the "finishing process," nominal attendance being one of the things an aristocrat in colonial society was expected to do. Like the surau training, it conveyed no tangible benefit, had no utilitarian function. The nagari school, in contrast to the surau, was divided into specific grades which were meant to represent levels of achievement. But, in fact, here too the comparison with the surau was not all that different. As with the surau, all students studied together in one room—each "grade" practicing more or less the same "assignments" with the only difference being their degree of competence in executing them. Advanced students helped tutor their juniors, exactly as in the surau. If a student believed he had learned all that a particular teacher could convey, he might move on to another school, particularly one in a large center such as Bukittinggi or Padang. The tradition of the wandering student was already a well-established one in Minangkabau; religious scholars had always traveled from one ulama to another learning the speciality of each. Like the religious scholar, the secular school pupil left school, establishing himself as a teacher or taking a government or trade position, when he believed he had learned enough or when there was a suitable opening available. "Graduation" from either type of school was a personal and subjective decision made by pupil and teacher, not the result of passing some comprehensive exam.

Unlike the surau, however, the secular school had meaning for only a limited sector of society. All Minangkabau were Muslims and all respected the skills and training of the ulama. But secular education was like learning a trade; it was important for earning a livelihood but had almost no meaning in terms of general personal development as a Minangkabau. Prestige came from other factors—the chiefs already had it by virtue of their birth, the high official or large merchant by vir-tue of his achieved position. Literacy might be the tool for achieving prestige but it was not particularly praiseworthy in and of itself.

The nagari school performed a function in Minangkabau society, but that function was determined not by Dutch administrative notions but rather by Minangkabau desires. Various elements in society used education or ignored it in accordance with their own evaluation of its usefulness to them.

CHAPTER SIX
EDUCATIONAL REORGANIZATION IN THE 1870s: THE GOVERNMENT ELEMENTARY SCHOOLS AND ADVANCED EDUCATION

The nagari schools had been "successful" in their own terms, that is, they had provided new skills for groups in Minangkabau which, whether because of their geographic location or their social position, found traditional routes to success insufficient. But the nagari schools had not generated great enthusiasm from all or even most parts of the population. They provided no sure guarantee of access to top-level bureaucratic jobs, for such positions were few and influence was still an important factor; nor did the nagari schools have any independent prestige which could stimulate interest in attendance for its own sake. The closest proximity to a prestigious institution was the Normal School in Bukittinggi, whose "graduates" often achieved high-level bureaucratic jobs as warehousemasters and jaksa. Upper middle level ambitious families showed more interest in formal education after the establishment of the Normal School.

From the Dutch point of view, the nagari school should have been regarded as "successful" in the sense that administrators did not have trouble finding suitable secretaries, clerks, and other petty officials to handle the lower bureaucratic jobs which required literacy. Only a few important positions in the administration were open to Minangkabau, and the Dutch administrators still preferred to appoint literate men from families with connections to the colonial regime. Not all of these had studied at the nagari school or even at the Normal School.

The appearance of the nagari schools had not resulted in a rigid structuring of education in West Sumatra. Pupils did not have to complete a specific curriculum to qualify for specific jobs. The criteria for obtaining these were fairly subjective, and family influence remained important. Warehousemasters, in the early years, for example, were often related closely to the penghulu families or village hierarchy. Their appointment may have been the result of influence, in recognition of high status or a means of neutralizing a potential threat to village stability.

By the 1870s, colonial administration itself was beginning to change, to become more "modern" and less "traditional." Objective criteria and competent training were becoming more important for both Dutch and Minangkabau officials. At the same time, the Dutch regime was being intensified in Riau, Bangka, Kalimantan, East Sumatra, and other western archipelago areas recently absorbed into the colonial administration. Geographic expansion alone opened many new jobs, for example as opium office administrators, cultivation inspectors, tax officials, warehouse personnel, clerks, secretaries, and teachers. Teachers became especially important as the Dutch government began to regard education as the means for integrating local elites into the colonial order. The Liberal philosophy, rampant in Holland and the Indies by the 1870s, emphasized the role of private enterprise and education's place in providing the climate for such enterprise to flourish. Businesses were being reorganized and expanded to operate on more "modern," rational lines. This undoubtedly stimulated Minangkabau to organize their own activities in accord with the new, modern Dutch models. Written records, bookkeeping, reports, and correspondence were becoming more important in business, whether run by Dutch or Minangkabau entrepreneurs, and the nagari schools were seen as inadequate in providing the necessary training.

Most nagari schools were in a poor financial condition. Teachers were poor and preferred to take jobs in the government service, whenever possible, rather than continue teaching. Textbooks and other materials were practically unavailable. Standards varied widely from place to place, and there was no way to enrich the curriculum because the Normal School itself operated on much the same educational level as a nagari school. The new government interest in education, which began in the 1870s, to a certain extent solved the purely institutional problems by making government funds available to the nagari schools and by reorganizing the Normal School into a major center offering education on a par with the best normal school anywhere in the Indies. The Minangkabau, especially townspeople, began to look with new interest at the schools. They could see that education had more purpose and content, and they realized that it was becoming a real entree into colonial officialdom and society.

The new government elementary schools of the 1870s and afterwards had a standardized curriculum. They had new Malay language textbooks, which had recently been published in the Indies and were designed for local elementary school systems. The schools acquired more prestige in large measure because they began providing an "education" rather than merely "training." The Dutch government began expressing more official interest in education generally. This in itself conferred a great deal of prestige on the schools in the eyes of ambitious families, and to a certain extent in the eyes of village notables as well. More and better advanced education was also available. The Indies Medical School which had formerly trained only *doktor djawa* (a sort of combination medical corpsman and sanitation inspector) was slowly reorganized into a regular institute for training doctors. Teachers were given the chance to take advanced training in Holland. A wide variety of advanced educational opportunities in Batavia were opening to Minangkabau who did well at local schools, including the chance to attend European schools in which the medium of instruction was Dutch. Ability in Dutch conveyed a great deal of prestige in local eyes, but not until well into the twentieth century did it become an important criterion for the civil service. Education was becoming a respectable alternative path, on a par with being a rich merchant in terms of its economic prospects, and with being a learned ulama in terms of its prestige. By the late nineteenth century, according to Minangkabau villagers, three occupations had overwhelming status: *angku doktor, angku laras, angku guru* (lord doctor, lord larashoofd, lord teacher). The appearance of doctors and teachers on such a list was a new and significant development.

The increased interest in education reflected a general change in attitude among Minangkabau in middle- and upper-level families. Education no longer represented the mere acquisition of useful tools of the trade; it was becoming one of the requirements for participation in the Dutch-Indies society. To the extent that a given family had decided that the most important sector of society was the Western (or "modern") sector, to that extent did members of the family press to enter schools and acquire an education. In the course of the late nineteenth century, Minangkabau who accepted this ideal were continuously increasing in numbers.

Changing Currents in Indies Society

The changing nature of education in West Sumatra is attested to in the transformation from the nagari school, run by and for the Minangkabau without much concern or interference from the Dutch, to the government elementary school, in whichDutch attitudes, and physical presence as well, were greatly felt. The government elementary school itself was part of the Indies-wide standard educational system; it no longer represented a local answer to local needs. These changes in turn were part of more general currents and attitudes present in the Indies in the last quarter of the nineteenth century. In the 1870s, West Sumatra, as the other so-called Outer Possessions (meaning everything but Java and Madura), was being increasingly integrated into one systematic colonial administration—an administration which also displayed more interest in all aspects of local society and its organization.

During the 1870s, the administration which had previously been developed from Java was extended to the rest of the archipelago. The so-called Liberal Era, in which private enterprise and its needs were extolled at the expense of the former state economic system, had new demands and needs. Planters expected the state to provide them with a well-developed economic infrastructure in the form of roads, railroads, police organizations, medical facilities, and post offices and to handle the administrative tasks competently so that business' own essentially commercial job would be smooth and easy. As business rationalized its own operations, the colonial regime likewise rationalized and unified its administration. Direct Dutch rule was gradually extended to all areas of the Indies, organizing them as a part of one system. During this period, for example, the numerous treaties with the independent coastal Minangkabau raja and the assorted individual accommodations which had been made with interior rulers (as for example Sungai Pagu) were transformed into the same style of larashoofd government prevailing elsewhere in West Sumatra. All areas were now absorbed under the same judicial and legal regulations which had been in force in most of the highlands since at least mid-century.

The development of a full-blown and modern administrative structure required many more Minangkabau officials with better skills—and semiliterate men for the numerous middle and lower echelon posts upon which the weight of such a structure rested. Systematic taxation, an increased scope for the state monopolies of opium and salt, and innovations in population registry and supervision all required more personnel. The railroads being built in West Sumatra, and in the rest of the Indies, needed clerks and conductors. The newly organized regions of northern and eastern Sumatra needed indigenous officials. Minangkabau perantau civil servants, who had a relative head start in education, came along in the baggage of the Dutch colonial officers and took positions in the indigenous ranks of the new administrations. Because of the nagari schools, the Minangkabau had gained at least a generation head start over most of the rest of Sumatra's peoples in the competition to provide officials for the bureaucracy. During the late nineteenth century, the most important resource which Minangkabau provided to the newly integrated archipelago-wide colonial system was a corps of civil servants, doctors, and professional men. Education combined with the tradition of merantau aided the Minangkabau in the competition with other ethnic groups for positions with the government.

The quickening interest in secular education benefitted from another important aspect of the changing colonial world of the 1870s. Not only did the new Dutch regime have a genuine need for trained civil servants, but, at the same time, the Liberals, who exercised increasing control over colonial policy, gave the regime a philosophic bent which favored spreading education not just to meet specific bureaucratic vacancies but as part of a greater civilizing program. In 1867, for example, an Education Office was established as part of the new Department of Education, Religion, and Industry. This indicates not only the interest in education per se but demonstrates a more general Liberal inclination to merge education and religion as part of more general economic development.

Having created an office, one of whose jobs was indigenous education, the Indies administration now had a bureaucratic interest in fostering education among Indonesians. In 1872, an Inspector of Education was appointed for the first time for the Sumatra/Borneo Territories, including West Sumatra. Much of his attention was in fact devoted to Minangkabau, and his headquarters were located in Padang. The first appointed inspector, J. J. van Limburg Brouwer, was determined to transform the nagari schools into models of educational theory and practice. An English observer, J. S. Furnivall, commented somewhat cynically that the whole development of indigenous education in the Indies was the result of creating a group of Dutch bureaucrats, who had an "almost irresistable inclination to justify their position and magnify their own importance, [and therefore] were impelled to foster the establishment of schools and increase the number of pupils..."[1] Though perhaps overstated, certainly the importance of bureaucratic advocacy should not be forgotten when examining the educational developments of the 1870s and after.

As education became a growing subject for bureaucratic interest, it naturally assumed a new importance and prestige among colonial administrators. Such feelings were quickly transmitted to Minangkabau officials and villagers, and in turn were reinforced by the obvious availability of more opportunities based on secular education. The new government elementary school acquired an importance as part of a large Indies system, something which the locally oriented nagari school had never had. The Minangkabau graduate of one of the new West Sumatra elementary schools could, in the nature of things, expect to serve in Medan, Pontianak, or Jakarta, not just in Palembayan, Rau, or Bukittinggi. More important, he could enroll at an advanced institute and become a well-paid schoolmaster, a medical doctor, a lawyer, or a high-level bureaucrat with a certain amount of administrative responsibility. In short, school graduates could now reasonably expect a better-paying job with more responsibility than that of a clerk to the local larashoofd, as had often been the fate of nagari school graduates before. Upper middle level families that had formerly stuck to their pre-established merchant traditions became increasingly interested in education and government service. Being a doctor in Bukittinggi or the director of the opium monopoly for Riau, for example, presented economic and prestige possibilities which rivaled those available to either a gold dealer or a coffee transport contractor.

Education came to be viewed with new eyes because of its increased benefits. Whereas, in the period before the 1870s, education in Minangkabau had been almost wholly an indigenous development, thereafter it became more and more a product of currents flowing throughout the whole Indies world. But at the same time, though the

---

1 J. S. Furnivall, *Netherlands India: A Study of Plural Economy* (Cambridge: University Press, 1967), p. 220.

opportunities offered the Minangkabau were increasingly tied to Indies-wide conditions, the response which they displayed to these opportunities were ever the consequence of local interests and initiatives and local evaluations of the opportunities. The educational zeal of the Minangkabau continued to derive from internal factors not external pressures.

The Government Reorganizes the Institutional Structure

Prior to the 1870s, the Dutch administration had not taken an important part in the operation of the nagari schools particularly in the highlands. Its major contribution to education had been the establishment and financing of the Normal School in Bukittinggi (1856). But even that institution had eventually become domesticated into Minangkabau society, serving essentially Minangkabau ends and being run to suit Minangkabau interests. Individual Dutch officials had on occasion tried to "reform" particular nagari schools, feeling perhaps that proper pedagogy and sufficient textbooks were the means to an "enlightened" and "educated" citizenry. But in the village world of most of West Sumatra, Dutch presence was felt only on occasion and then only briefly. If the local constituency did not exert pressure for improved teachers or schoolbuildings, the chiefs could usually avoid the issue with an outsider like the controleur. The Padang administration, reflecting a general disinterest in indigenous education which emanated from Batavia, had not been disposed to force the issue. Nor had it provided any general guidelines which the controleur would be expected to enforce. Government interest was concentrated on the cultivation system and the economic and political situation generally. The establishment of the Office of Education and the 1872 appointment of van Limburg Brouwer as inspector for Sumatra greatly altered the situation. Over the course of the 1870s, the individual nagari schools were reorganized as government elementary schools.

A Royal Decree, issued in March 1871, publicly placed responsibility for indigenous education in the hands of the Dutch regime. Government-sponsored Normal Schools would be established in all areas of the Indies in order to provide sufficient teachers to man a comprehensive network of elementary schools. The schools would be organized according to a standard curriculum, and pupils would have to pass standard tests. Individual schools would no longer, as in Minangkabau, be administered by local chiefs according to local interests and abilities. Each government elementary school would be controlled by a school commission consisting of a European (either a local official or where there were none, a private entrepreneur) and several of the "foremost natives of the area,"[2] which would oversee the daily operations of the school according to standards set by the newly formed Office of Education. Although the Minangkabau chiefs remained the most numerous element of the board, the European member would obviously be the most important because he represented the power of the purse.

The government would now set standards and demand that they be met. Under the new organization, the state treasury would pay all school costs both for the village elementary schools and for the Normal School.[3] This was a radical new departure, for only six years previously, Batavia had dismissed a recommendation that the government finance schools in the various Minangkabau districts as being completely unjustifiable.[4] Under the new system, the government still did not agree to anything grandiose. It would subsidize the existing nagari schools, but only those which qualified. As the schools improved, they would be integrated into the Indies-wide public school system. How many (if any) new schools would be founded at state expense, the government was not prepared to say.

This is not to imply that all local differentiation and initiative were now gone or that all areas of the Indies would have exactly the same schools, as determined by Batavia. The character of a given village was retained in the local school commission. As finally established in West Sumatra, the school commission usually consisted of three people: the chairman was the head of the Minangkabau administration (larashoofd or nagarihoofd); the secretary was the local European official (usually a controleur), or a private individual if there were no official; the third member was a penghulu of the village, representing the nagari council. The school board members need not themselves be literate and, with the exception of the European official, apparently they rarely were.[5] As a

---

2 Royal Decision of March 22, 1871, *Verbaal*, March 31, 1873, No. 43.
3 Ibid.
4 *VIO, 1866,* **p. 25.**
5 J. J. van Limburg Brouwer, "Het Gouvernemental Inlandsch Onderwijs op Sumatra," *TNI*, 5, 2

result, many of the same local political factors which had affected the nagari schools continued also to influence the operation of the government elementary schools.

In order for a nagari school to qualify as a government school, it had to have a graduate of the Normal School as its teacher.[6] Since government inspectors disapproved of the quality of education being offered at the current Bukittinggi Normal School, this was to be reorganized along the lines of other government operated teachers' training institutes in the Indies. New regulations, issued in Batavia in December 1872, provided for a Dutch headmaster and assistant headmaster, with a Minangkabau serving as the second assistant headmaster, and additional Minangkabau teaching staff. The former head of the Normal School, Chatib Labeh, was unceremoniously demoted to an elementary school teacher—not even receiving one of the lesser Normal School staff positions.[7]

The Normal School, already the most prestigious of the various educational institutions in West Sumatra, was made even more desirable. Its students received increased perquisites and allowances under the new system, despite the fact that, at the same time, enrollment was increased from ten to fifty. There was now free room and board at the school plus a monthly allowance—f. 15 for seniors and f. 12 for underclassmen.[8] That this allowance was more than generous in local terms can be understood when it is compared to that of the nagarihoofd in most nearby villages; they received only f. 20 per month in 1872.[9]

The Normal School became known popularly as the Sekolah Radja, or Pririce's School; this is a useful way to distinguish it from the pre-1872 Normal School. The nickname may have derived, as some assert, from the Acehnese princelings sent there, in later years, to gain a bit of European polish, but it is more likely that the comportment of its Minangkabau pupils first gave rise to the label. Sekolah Radja students clearly did not regard themselves lightly. They dressed in fine clothing of European style. Each had an individual room in the long dormitory building attached

---

(1876), pp. 19-20.
6   Director of Education, January 17, 1873, *Verbaal*, June 5, 1873, No. 30.
7   Director of Education to the Governor General, October 29, 1873, *Verbaal*, February 4, 1874, No. 9.
8   *VIO, 1872*, pp. 1-3.
9   Governor of Sumatra's West Coast, December 17, 1872, *Verbaal*, January 28, 1876, No. 20.

to the school complex, and there were servants assigned to look after their needs. The school had been built as a showcase for Dutch efforts to improve local "civilization," and, according to one account, it compared favorably with any secondary school in the Netherlands itself.[10] In their free hours, the students walked proudly through the streets of Bukittinggi; one old man related nostalgically that street vendors and other lesser beings would give way before the strolling students, proof positive of the latter's lofty status.[11] Moreover, they studied a wide variety of subjects designed to produce "cultivated" and "well-versed" teachers who could serve as fitting examples to all the residents of the town to whose school they would later be assigned. One European observer commented that the effect of all this privilege was sure to produce "dandified" Minangkabau who fashioned themselves after the outward aspects of European culture with very little understanding of its inner values.[12]

The curriculum at the new school encompassed all manner of learning—Dutch, Malay, penmanship, arithmetic, geometry, Indies geography and history, Dutch history, natural science, surveying, drawing, draftsmanship, agricultural techniques, pedagogy, singing, and physical education.[13] It is small wonder that the pupils thought themselves magnificent beings when compared to the "simple" village trader or farmer. Competition for entrance was exceedingly intense, and one had to have a sponsor, generally a parent or mamak, who was connected to the Dutch establishment in some way in order to get in. A merchant could usually gain entrance for his family members by virtue of his wealth and his consequent informal ties to the establishment. The early nagari schools, and to a limited extent the old teachers' institute, could not have matched this new school as a conveyer of status and prestige. Even a few chiefs began to reconsider their earlier derogatory feelings about sending their dependents to school. But, by and large, students had to have a certain amount of prior education at a local school and those who did (mainly middle-level families) were still in the majority at the Sekolah Radja.

---

10   M. Buys, *Twee Jaren op Sumatra's Westkust* (Amsterdam: Akkeringa, 1886), p. 50.
11   Interview, Sekolah Radja graduate, Bukittinggi, October 1967.
12   Buys, *Twee Jaren*, p. 55.
13   *VIO, 1878-1882*, **p. 35.**

The advantages open to the Western educated still rarely outweighed those already conveyed by virtue of high birth and wealth to the notables in the important plains villages. The families who in traditional practice had scorned the merantau ideal continued to scorn outside employment even if in the relatively more prestigious locale of the government office. But the Sekolah Radja, and later the other advanced education institutions, did begin to attract more upper middle-level families, often families which had formerly relied on trade. Even penghulu families from semi-merantau villages (such as Kota Gedang near Bukittinggi) became more interested in the possibilities of high-ranking civil service jobs and professional positions (such as doctors). Penghulu families were to a certain extent handicapped because of their relatively late entry into education, and those who showed the most interest were often families which had already indicated a vague willingness to attend the nagari school.

Admission to the Sekolah Radja was heavily weighted in favor of families which had already achieved rank in the civil service—as jaksa, warehousemasters, administrative aides. Such families had long since pioneered the way to educate their children in order to assure their admittance to Dutch-organized institutions. These families were already operating in a semi-European environment; much more so than the penghulu families whose greatest interest continued to be in the traditional village scene.

Pupils from West Sumatra were eligible for advanced teachers' training not only at the Bukittinggi Sekolah Radja but also at institutes being established elsewhere. A colony-wide Normal School, which would bring together advanced students from all parts of the archipelago, was established in Batavia, in an effort to standardize the education being offered in Indies elementary schools. This may have been part of a Dutch desire to standardize the Malay language taught in the village schools. The government wanted to increase use of Riau-Malay, a well-developed language, and end reliance on Bazaar Malay, an uneducated polyglot which varied widely from region to region.[14] The total quota for the Outer Islands at the Batavia Normal School was to average some 100 per year, of which Minangkabau and the people from the Moluccas received the

---

14 *Encyclopaedië van Nederlandsch-Indië*, 2, p. 655.

largest portion—20 pupils each.[15] The only area to rival West Sumatra, then, in numbers of pupils was the heavily Christian Moluccas, a place

Table 10. Geographic Origin of Sekolah Radja Pupils

Area of Origin	Fixed Quota	Present Dec. 1877	Came 1877-82	Total	Died	Expelled	Promoted	Total who Left	Present Dec. 1882	Present Dec. 1887	Came 1877-92	Total	Died	Expelled	Promoted	Total who Left	Present Dec. 1892
Sumatra's West Coast /Nias	25	35	59	94	1	21	34	56	37	43	40	83	2	6	35	43	40
Benkulen	5	9	8	17	1	6	5	12	5	5	11	16	1	6	5	12	4
Lampung	5	1	4	5	-	1	1	2	3	-	2	2	-	2	-	2	-
Palembang	5	2	-	2	-	2	-	2	-	-	9	9	1	2	2	5	4
Riau/Sumatra's East Coast	5	1	5	6	-	2	-	2	4	-	2	2	-	-	-	-	2
Bangka	3	-	-	-	-	-	-	-	-	-	-	-	-	-	-	-	-
Billiton	2	-	-	-	-	-	-	-	-	1	3	4	1	3	-	4	-
Aceh	*	-	1	1	-	1	-	-	-	-	-	-	-	-	-	-	-
Totals	50	48	77	125	2	33	41	74	49	49	67	116	5	19	42	66	60

* No quota. Acehnese were admitted above and beyond quota limit for total enrollment.
Source: *Verslag van het Inlandsch Onderwijs 1877-1882*, pp.78-79, and *1888-1892*, p. 57.

where missionaries had been working for generations to assimilate the indigenous population to Western civilization by means of education.

Students from the Bukittinggi Sekolah Radja were also eligible to continue their education in Holland. Each year a Dutch teacher in Amsterdam, D. Hekker, would take several Indonesian students into his home to drill them in Dutch and European customs. Such students were being trained to qualify in the exams for European headmaster, that is,

---

15 *Verbaal*, January 31, 1871, No. 30.

to teach in a school where Dutch was the language of instruction rather than in the common Malay village school. The first student from the Bukittinggi school went to Holland in 1877.[16]

Even though only a small-scale operation, this chance to study in Holland, like that for advanced education in Batavia, was important because it represented a new opportunity for Minangkabau children. In the same way that the road system and the civil service in West Sumatra had opened more possibilities for the inhabitants of the highlands to travel to other areas in Minangkabau or nearby Sumatra, now the new educational system was providing a colony-wide scope of operations. At the same time, the new opportunities for teachers helped set them apart, at a higher level from the rest of the society by virtue of their now-unique training; particularly their formal training in Dutch. In the 1840s to 1860s, the nagari school teacher had really hoped to get out of teaching and become an administrative official, and, at the first opportunity, he did so. After the 1870s, however, teaching had more prestige and teachers received better salaries, both of which helped make teaching a desirable career in itself, not just as a stepping stone into jobs with the civil administration.

Under the reorganized educational system in West Sumatra, then, the government elementary schools had less trouble finding qualified teachers. Government support assured teachers of adequate salaries regardless of where they taught. Before the 1870s, teachers' salaries at the nagari schools in the highlands had averaged about f. 20 per month, many places paying much less, depending upon local interest and generosity. Low salaries had been an important deterrent to teaching, and the Dutch had been unable to pressure nagari councils into raising them even in the few instances when they had tried to do so. The chiefs usually insisted that education was an obligation of the *Kompeni,* that is, the Dutch government, and not of the local people.[17]

The Government Elementary Schools

The nagari schools had been renamed government elementary schools,

---

16   *Verbaal,* June 9, 1879, No. 9.
17   Director of Education, January 17, 1873, *Verbaal,* June 5, 1873, No. 30.

an indication of new government interest in their development. In theory, the post-1871 elementary schools offered more intensive and standardized education. Guaranteed financial support and continuous government supervision were designed to insure high quality education. The visible changes were probably not all that rapid or indeed all that extensive. In the first place, the school commissions still represented the Dutch idea of the community's leaders—Dutch-appointed larashoofd or nagarihoofd, the controleur, and the local aristocracy, the penghulu. The board membership was obviously weighted completely toward the "aristocratic" status quo. As noted earlier, the Dutch administration continued to believe that adat government was the best government for Minangkabau, that changes in penghulu-ships represented extralegal activities, and that birth was the most important criterion for selecting district leaders. The Royal Decision of 1871, which had placed the burden of education on the colonial government rather than local initiative, had

Table 11. Elementary Schools in Sumatra

Location	1878	1888	1898	1908	1909 (subsidized)
Government Elementary Schools					
Padang Lowlands	10	14	11	13	
Padang Highlands	14	18	21	27	
Tapanuli	14	20	19	20	
Benkulen	7	9	9	12	
Location	1878	1888	1898	1908	1909 (subsidized)
Lampung	1	3	3	7	
Palembang	2	5	5	14	
Jambi	-	-	-	2	
Sumatra's East Coast	-	1	1	11	
Aceh	-	2	1	14	
Riau	1	1	3	5	
Bangka	1	2	2	4	

Total	50	75	75	129		
Private Indigeneous Schools						
Padang Lowlands	6	3	11	33	40	(11)
Padang Highlands	2	-	6	38	62	(52)
Tapanuli (Missionary)	9	64	152	390	470	(399)
Benkulen	-	-	1	1	2	(1)
Lampung	1	-	-	-	-	
Palembang	-	1	3	19	36	(33)
Jambi	-	-	-	6	6	(2)
Sumatra's East Coast	-	-	-	-	29	(26)
Aceh	-	-	1	9	10	(3)
Riau	-	-	-	-	-	
Bangka	-	-	-	-	-	
Total	18	68	174	486	655	(527)

Source: Report of Inspector Grivel, *Verbaal*, September 7, 1910, No. 32.

specifically stated that education was needed for the "children of the indigenous chiefs," although others were not specifically forbidden to enroll.[18]

But the fact of government financial support, at the same time, helped counteract chiefly dominance over the schools' operations. Before the 1870s, the nagari council had often had to finance the school from what the members considered to be their own earnings, but this was no longer true. Although chiefs might have no more inclination to accept education for themselves, they now had less reason to obstruct the progress of others. Unfortunately the records in the education reports for the 1870s

---

18 Royal Decision, March 22, 1871, *Verbaal*, March 31, 1873, No. 43.

to 1890s and beyond do not give in great detail the composition of the student body nor what became of them upon graduation, or departure, from school. The occasional notation in a specific report does tend to confirm, however, that there had been little change from the previous period in the types of families most actively seeking education for their children. A notable exception to this is that many of the pupils represented the second and third generation of civil service families. In the era of the nagari school, trading and agricultural families often sent children because they wanted to break into the civil service; once having joined the government succeeding generations continued the tradition. Though the records do not indicate the occupations of parents, corroborating evidence is available from family histories, and it tends to show that once one member had joined the civil service, his children and nephews usually followed the pattern. This was not a new pattern, for merchants and artisans who specialized in particular items, for example cloth or gold, usually all belonged to one family in the village. If several such families existed they usually intermarried, thus establishing large dynasties in their particular calling within the village. Sometimes these family groups had branches linked by marriage in other villages. The goldsmith in Kota Gedang married a girl from a goldsmith's family in Kota Gedang; when he went to the rantau in Padang, Medan, or Batavia, he married another woman, again usually one from a goldsmith's family. This is only natural, of course, because his most important contacts would be within his professional community. The rising civil service dynasties, if such they may be called, followed the time-honored pattern, substituting only a new occupation.

In the process whereby the government took over operation of the nagari school, the Minangkabau clearly were the victors. They had for years been demanding government assistance in running their schools, but Batavia had always refused. Now, when Batavia decided that tuition would have to be charged at the new schools to help defray the costs of education, the Minangkabau demurred. They upheld their objection, because the 1871 regulations stated that, in places where free education had formerly been offered, government schools could not now charge tuition. Since levies on either the chiefs, the population, or the nagari council, rather than tuition, had previously supported the nagari schools, the villagers how argued successfully that the new government elementary schools fell under the provisions of the decree and should not charge tuition.[19]

The government announced that schools qualifying to become government elementary schools would be completely funded from the state treasury. Teachers would receive f. 30 per month, with raises at ten and twenty years service to f. 40 and f. 50 respectively. An assistant teacher would be appointed for every thirty students enrolled at the school; he would receive a salary of f. 25 per month.

---

19 Royal Decision of May 3, 1871, *Verbaal,* May 26, 1871, No. 19.

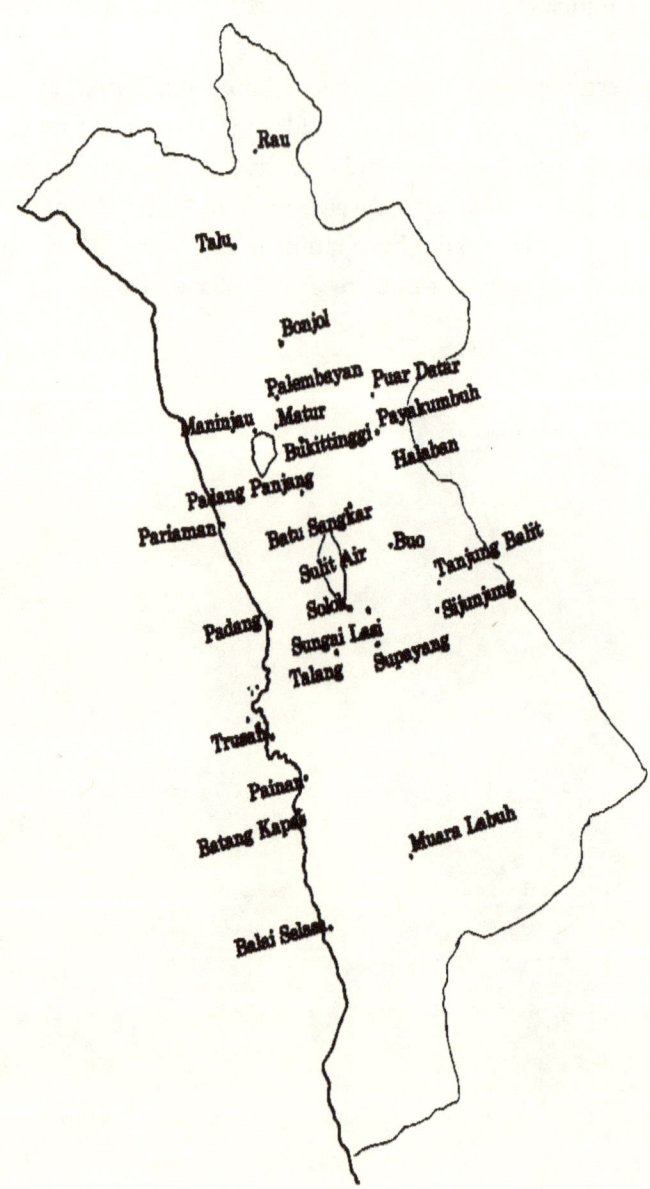

MAP 5: GOVERNMENT ELEMENTARY SCHOOLS 1880

Teacher trainees could be hired at f. 15 per month to assist at particularly crowded schools.[20]

The knowledge that the government would assume the cost of operating the local schools resulted in a wave of new ones being opened all over the highlands and, to a lesser degree, along the coast as well, where they tended to be schools which had been closed earlier. Nine schools appeared between 1871 and 1877, five in the vicinity of Solok. This area had shown very little interest in education previously, apparently because the chiefs maintained firm control over village affairs and showed no particular inclination to organize education. Probably few villagers in the area would have used the schools in any case; most people earned a substantial living from wet-rice cultivation already. The new schools were not all in rice villages, however; one was at Sulit Air, which had previously had a nagari school, and the others were at Tanjong Balik, Supayang, Talang, and Sungai Lasi. One was opened at Padang Panjang, the important military and communications center at the upper entrance of the Anai Pass, and another at Matur, a small trading community near Lake Maninjau. Along the coast, a new school opened at Balai Selasa, an agricultural and export center south of Painan. After operating on its own for about a year, each school then applied for a subsidy from the government, leading to eventual incorporation into the government system.

The government, however, was selective, taking only those schools with qualified teachers. In 1873, for example, only seven nagari schools were recognized as the first government elementary schools: Talu, Rau, Bukittinggi, Batu Sangkar, Solok, Payakumbuh, and Pariaman.[21] This was twelve less than the Assistant Inspector of Indigenous Education in Padang had recommended. The Governor General had decided that the teachers at the twelve rejected schools—Painan, Trusan, Maninjau, Matur, Palembayan, Bonjol, Singkarak, Buo, Sijunjung, Halaban, Puar Datar, and Muara Labuh—were not qualified Normal School graduates. Therefore, the government could not legally pay their salaries, and the schools did

---

20 Report of Assistant Inspector for Indigenous Education van Limburg Brouwer to the Director of Education in Batavia, June 30, 1872, *Verbaal,* June 5, 1873, No. 30.
21 Decision of the Governor General, March 14, 1873, *Verbaal,* June 5, 1873, No. 30.

not become government elementary schools.²² By 1882, however, all the remaining schools had been accepted as public schools, although in many cases they had apparently not changed teachers.²³

The fact of government subsidy had caused a slight geographic shift in the pattern of school placement. Prior to the 1870s, most schools had been concentrated in the hills to the north of Bukittinggi and the hilly areas east of Lake Singkarak. Now they appeared in the most "aristocratic" areas south of Solok and along the coast. The social backgrounds of the pupils themselves are difficult to establish. The records give only the totals rather than individual schools and then only in three major divisions: civil servants/ aristocrats; private enterprise/traders; and agriculturalists. The figures are only available for the 1870s, so one cannot even determine if the ratio between the three groups was changing.

The few general discussions and reports on education do indicate that the socioeconomic backgrounds of the pupils had not changed that much. Van Limburg Brouwer, the Inspector of Education, said that, although in the highlands the children were those of village notables and respected members of the village (apparently in the sense of "successful," that is to say wealthy), along the coast the pupils were almost entirely from the trading families in the towns.²⁴ Since such trading families were usually perantau from the highlands or their descendants, obviously the local notable element had not changed its mind about the value of secular education. Small highlands villages in the hills, although without European officials, continued to establish successful schools on their own initiative, a fact which amazed some Dutch officials who believed that the "educational development of a people is a question of centuries."²⁵

An important clue to the general nature and progress of education in West Sumatra during the latter nineteenth century appeared when the government proposed in 1892 to divide elementary education into two different categories of schools—First Class Schools for notables and

---

22 Report of the Assistant Inspector of Indigenous Education, Padang, June 30, 1872, *Verbaal,* June 5, 1873, No. 30.
23 *VIO, 1878-1882,* p. 21.
24 Van Limburg Brouwer, "Gouvernemental Inlandsch Onderwijs," p. 3.
25 N. Graafland, "De Reorganisatie van het Inlandsch Onderwijs," *Verslagen van het Indisch Genootschap* (1889), p. 100.

wealthy men, and Second Class Schools for the general public.[26] Though it might seem to represent a step forward for education, in Minangkabau it actually had the opposite effect. The regulation stipulated that Second Class Schools could have only three grades and should teach subjects useful in daily life in the village. The existing elementary schools in Minangkabau had five fully developed grades and were geared toward helping students from non-notable families escape from the daily life of the village. For an education suited only to the village milieu one went to the village surau not the elementary school. According to one Dutch education inspector, in other areas of the Indies pupils rarely continued beyond the lowest classes, and thus the institution of a Second Class School would probably improve education for them. In West Sumatra, he said, not only was this not the case, but the idea of the First Class School was clearly unworkable. Children of the local chiefs rarely attended school at all, and, if they did, they went to the village elementary schools, taught in Malay. This differed from Java where notables' children sometimes attended the European elementary schools.[27]

The debates over reorganizing education in West Sumatra provide strong support for the assumption that, even after 1870, it was not the chiefs or notables that sought education. The belief lingered in notable circles that education was meant for those families needing outside help to survive—a kind of reverse snobbery by which illiteracy indicated aristocracy and economic self-sufficiency. The Dutch, however, clung to the idea of a literate class of Minangkabau aristocrats. In 1909, the Director of Education wanted to establish Second Class Schools in West Sumatra just for the sons of chiefs and other village notables. The local Inspector of Education reported that he could not find enough notable families who were willing to send their children to be able to fill even one schoolroom. If high status schools were established, he said, they would be filled with the children of the middle families who continued to put pressure on the education system to expand.[28]

---

26 Royal Decision on Indigenous Education, 1892, *Verbaal,* September 23, 1892, No. 13.
27 Inspector of Education van Ophuijzen to the Director of Education, December 23, 1901, *Verbaal,* March 24, 1902, No. 19.
28 Inspector of Education Grival to Director of Education, November 30, 1909, *Verbaal,* September 7, 1910, No. 32.

New Opportunities for Advanced Education

The growing commitment of the Dutch to education led to new opportunities for Indonesians to obtain advanced training in certain fields in addition to teaching. A significant feature of such training was the opportunity (and indeed the necessity) to learn Dutch. The government elementary schools like their predecessors, the nagari schools, had only offered Malay-language instruction. For many Minangkabau, the most important advanced institute was that created by the reform of the Indies Medical Institute, the STOVIA (School tot Opleiding van Indische Artsen). Originally established in Batavia in 1851 in order to provide medical corpsmen for the various rural areas, the institute's graduates *(see* above p. 110) were basically public health technicians; they were not even government officials of any standing. By training, they represented little more than an indigenous herbalist with a European veneer. The only real medical technique they learned was vaccination and perhaps some pharmaceutical skill. Though upon graduation they were called "doktor djawa," the "doktor" was an honorary title only; they were not really physicians.[29]

Some Minangkabau had attended the institute from the very beginning (two arrived in 1856, for example),[30] but graduation from there apparently did not assure them of any better job in the West Sumatra health service than that already available to the student from the nagari school. The records of the 1860s indicate that many of the nagari school graduates entered the health service as "vaccinators," apparently acquiring whatever "medical" training they needed on the job. Study at the STOVIA did have certain advantages; students' expenses were paid by the government, including the cost of traveling to Batavia. After 1864, the school was reorganized, and students subsequently received a living allowance during their studies. Graduates could now become independent medical practitioners rather than merely assistants, but they remained a part of the government service. The only difference was that now they served directly under the head of the regional government in the area in which

---

29 *Ontwikkeling von het Geneeskundig Onderwijs te Weltevreden, 1851-1926* (Wel-tevreden: Kolff, 1926), pp. 1-5.
30 Ibid., p. 4.

they worked.[31] Even so, the doktor djawa continued to occupy a relatively low position in the civil service; the title and job carried little prestige and were not the object of much competition among West Sumatran families.[32]

In 1898, another reorganization of the STOVIA took place, expanding its size and scope. Students now had to have a good knowledge of Dutch before being accepted, and the curriculum was expanded to include advanced medical and physical sciences. Before graduation, students had to serve as interns in the military hospital (to which the school had long been an adjunct).[33] The STOVIA now graduated "doctors" not "medics." Of the 183 students who had enrolled in the STOVIA between 1874 and 1900 only some seven had been from West Sumatra, but in the period from 1900 to 1914, at least 36 of the 200 pupils enrolled were Minangkabau.[34] The doktor djawa had become Angku Doktor. Professional medicine was now open to Indonesians, and many Minangkabau soon perceived that it would be a prosperous and prestigious career. Families that had already been literate for one or two generations, in many instances now turned to medicine. This included both families that had joined the civil service as well as those continuing in more traditional occupations such as merchants. At the same time, some very wealthy, and even notable, families that had shown no prior interest in education began to consider the STOVIA a worthwhile venture.

Another form of advanced education which attracted the Minangkabau were the new courses designed specifically to train indigenous officials (called *ambtenaar* to distinguish them from clerks). These aspiring officials learned some Dutch as well as Malay. After the turn of the twentieth century, special schools were established called OSVIA (Opleiding School Voor Inlandsche Ambtenaaren), but before then, Minangkabau were trained as ambtenaar at the Sekolah Radja in Bukittinggi. Batavia then

---

31 Ibid., p. 5.
32 Ibid., p. 6.
33 Ibid., pp. 26-30.
34 Ibid., pp. 349-59. There is a certain amount of difficulty determining which students were in fact Minangkabau since the only indication given in the enrollment list is birthplace. Many village names were not listed in the available gazetteers so it was impossible to determine where they were located. Also many Minangkabau were born outside West Sumatra, the children of perantau fathers. The actual number of Minangkabau may have been much higher than the figures given indicate.

decided to admit an extra ten pupils to the school each year specifically for training as ambtenaar, and special courses were added to the curriculum for their benefit. For the most part they took the same courses as the future teachers but they omitted the last year—in which the teachers practice teaching in the attached elementary school.[35]

The government had hoped that the larashoofd would send their nephews to the school for training as district leaders, but in fact most of the pupils in the ambtenaar courses were the children of merchants, teachers, and civil servants. Not one was the kemanakan of a larashoofd—although four were sons of larashoofd. The chiefs continued to rely on the knowledge that their nephews would succeed to the chieftaincy regardless of prior training. It is a measure of their recognition of the value of education, however, that they now often sent their sons to school, most commonly, sons whose mothers were not related to important families, and thus who had no independent future already assured to them.[36]

Promising Minangkabau students could also continue their education on Java at the OSVIA school there. The prospects for such aspiring civil servants improved greatly after 1914, when the West Coast administration was reorganized to a government based on a merit civil service rather than notable families. The larashoofd and nagarihoofd were replaced by *demang* and assistant demang, men who, theoretically at least, owed their positions to their training. These men could serve anywhere in the Minangkabau area, and also in the other Malay speaking territories, such as East Sumatra, Riau, and Kalimantan. The position of demang was administratively no higher than that of larashoofd had been. But unlike the larashoofd, the demang had been chosen for his objective qualifications and therefore he commanded more prestige than a local aristocrat. He was truly a member of the Dutch administrative circle and participated in the Dutch-Indies Society.

Already, by the turn of the century, the West Sumatra schools were beginning to produce more educated people than the current administrative system could absorb. More children sought admittance than could be accommodated in the government schools. This contributed

---

35 Decision of the Governor General, January 25, 1901, *Verbaal,* March 4, 1901, No. 54.
36 Governor Heckler to the Governor General, October 17, 1907, *Verbaal,* October 21, 1908, No. 44.

to the growth of numerous private secular schools, which were opened by graduates of the secular schools who could not find other jobs. By 1910, for example, the number of such private schools located in West Sumatra was already half of the total for all Java,[37] and they were so successful, that one Governor suggested closing the government schools and subsidizing the private schools instead because more private schools could be financed for the same amount of money.[38] The number of Minangkabau interested in Western education was expanding geometrically following the lines of the extended family clusters. One educated man would stimulate his children and his nephews to attend school and they in turn their own children and nephews. What started as a small trickle in the 1840s and 1850s had developed into a modest flood by the 1900s.

Socioeconomic Backgrounds of Students

For the period of the 1870s and after, information about pupils' family backgrounds is scarce, for those attending elementary school it is all but nonexistent. But through interviews with village elders, it is often possible to compensate for this lack of statistical data and, at least, to determine what kinds of local families had children who received advanced training at, for example, the STOVIA or Sekolah Radja. This limits the survey to only those who stand out by virtue of their later status as successful teachers, doctors, or high officials, and often shows more about the village itself than about its intellectual families. In villages where there is an aristocratic distaste among the upper ranks for leaving village life (whether as merchant or doctor) one can find out very little about the educated elite, sometimes not even if there was one. The very nature of the secular educated elite, moreover, means that it cannot be found in the village because its members have spread out over Indonesia. The people who know best about the education of the villagers are most likely the very ones who are no longer there. But despite all the limitations, interviews do bring to light information on the background of the secular educated elite and, in most cases, the profiles differ little from those established for the 1860s.

---

37 XY, "Het Inlandsch Onderwijs ter Sumatra's Westkust," *Koloniaal Tijdschrift*, 2, 1 (1913), p. 396.
38 Governor Heckler, Letter, June 23, 1906, No. 2874, *Verbaal*, September 12, 1912, No. 66.

Pariaman, a wealthy but aristocratically oriented coastal community, had at least three students who graduated from the Sekolah Radja in the early years. One was the nephew of a penghulu (his son in turn became a trained economist and was governor of West Sumatra between 1966 and 1978). The second was nephew of the larashoofd of Pariaman and the third the nephew of a rich man but the son of an ordinary villager *(orang biasa)*. The village notables of Pariaman, however, could not really remember details concerning any of these families, which tells something about the low importance attached to education and also that these particular families were apparently not especially well known. The notables could remember much better the aristocratic prerogatives of families in the district, which were the original settlers, and where they had come from. They also knew about the large local copra merchants, copra being the leading export and mainstay of the area since the late nineteenth century. Pariaman has an acquired reputation as the home of many school teachers, but the local establishment could not explain why this should be so or even verify that it was so. Education proved to be a subject to which they devoted little thought.[39]

Table 12. Family Background of Pupils: 1872

Schools	Notable/ Civil Servant	Trade/ Private Business	Agriculture	Total
Government Elementary Schools				
Total Minangkabau	241	405	316	956
Total Java	2758	2780	3535	9051
Municipal Elementary Schools (Subsidized and Unsubsidized)				
Padang Lowlands	84	87	133	304
Padang Highlands	368	178	345	891
Total Minangkabau	452	265	478	1195
Total Java	1825	453	2560	4861

Source: *Verslag van het Inlandsch Onderwijs*, 1872, pp. 47 and 84.

---

39 Interview, elders of Pariaman, November 15, 1967.

Table 13. Family Background of Pupils: 1873 and 1877

Schools	Notable/Civil Servant	Lower Classes	Chinese	Arab
Government Elementary Schools				
Padang Lowlands, 1873	98	477	93	2
Padang Highlands, 1873	306	1227	1	11
Padang Lowlands, 1877	158	1134	75	
Padang Highlands, 1877	411	1227		30
Nonsubsidized Nagari Schools				
Padang Lowlands, 1873	48	78		34
Padang Highlands, 1873	86	53		17
Padang Lowlands, 1877	20	72		17
Padang Highlands, 1877	52	94		17

Source: *Verslag van het Inlandsch Onderwijs, 1873-1877*, pp. 58 and 114.

In Sulit Air, a small merantau village high in the hills overlooking Lake Singkarak, the first Normal School graduate was the son of a tailor and the nephew of a surau instructor. He was able to get into school through the good offices of his father-in-law who was a very rich man of the area. Although in theory the Normal School was for children of high parentage, in fact, so long as someone would be "responsible" and so long as the prospective student could pass the required entrance exams, it was possible for anyone to get in. The Iarashoofd family of Sulit Air did not display any particular interest in education until well into the 1930s. And even then it was only in a modest way and family members rose no higher than as lesser civil servants. The most famous man from Sulit Air was H. Zainal Abidin Achmad, onetime chairman of Parliament in the postindependence period, who graduated from a religious school and came from a long line of merchant-haji families on both sides. The people of Sulit Air continued to hold to their tradition as perantau merchants throughout the nineteenth and early twentieth century, and even now live abroad some ten months out of every year, returning home in a great noisy, wealthy caravan each Puasa.[40]

In Matur, which did not open a school until about 1876, education caught on rapidly. Matur is located high above Lake Maninjau in hilly country where the sawah must be terraced and irrigated with the water from small swift mountain streams. Though Matur did not have a school before the 1870s, once established it grew in enrollment almost immediately. Matur pupils had a special interest in becoming teachers; first one and then another child gained admittance to the Sekolah Radja, each then smoothing the way for the others to follow. The success of the first few also provided a model for others to emulate. For a relatively crowded area like Matur, becoming a teacher soon proved to be a better livelihood than remaining in agriculture. According to villagers today, by the 1920s every family had at least one teacher, and this provided an important educational resource for young children in the families. The quick success of the Matur school was in large part due to the fact that the first teacher was the larashoofd of Matur. He himself was self-taught, but he believed that for a village like Matur, the land squeeze could only be overcome by education, which would allow village men to leave and join the government service. Almost no one had enough land in Matur, and even the penghulu pushed their dependents to enter the school, one for example having four sons who graduated from the Sekolah Radja. After the mid-1920s, the villagers of Matur became less interested in the Normal School, which probably reflected the increasing scarcity of all kinds of government jobs at that time; new teachers had only the alternative of setting up a private school. Although families in other villages began to switch to careers as doctors and lawyers about this time, this was apparently not true of Matur, though no one could think why.[41]

In Painan, a port town on the southern coast, the families that had traditionally worked for Dutch merchants tended to display the most continuing interest in education, especially the advanced education available at the Sekolah Radja. Other than by their long-time Dutch ties, these families were not particularly distinguished, that is, they had no "aristocratic" bloodlines. The most impressive civil service dynasty

---

40 Interview, village leaders of Sulit Air, November 3, 1967.
41 Interview, retired teachers, Matur, November 16, 1967.

originated on one side from a jaksa and the other a warehousemaster. Another series of three families all began as ordinary agriculturalists, in the sense of substantial "farmers" rather than peasants.[42]

The main center for the secular educated elite continued to be the small villages in the hills surrounding Bukittinggi. These villages still had not established schools of their own—although in 1908, one of them, Kota Gedang, did set up its own scholarship fund to train teachers for a proposed village school. Generally pupils walked over to Bukittinggi or else boarded with family members there. Since these villages were by and large merchant or artisan centers, most families had relatives in Bukittinggi with whom children could stay while attending the large government elementary school there. Koto Tuo, in the foothills of Mount Singgalang, is renowned for its merchant families, and it is from the wealthy merchant dynasties that the first Koto Tuo people with advanced education come. Civil service dynasties sprang up suddenly. In one generation, the men were merchants and the women married merchants; in the next, all the men were teachers or government employees. In one Koto Tuo merchant family, for example, there were four sons of whom two were teachers, one an assistant demang, and one the foreman for the coal mine at Sawah Lunto. The next generation maintained the tradition, becoming teachers, engineers, etc. The first doctor from Koto Tuo was also the son of a rich merchant family. One of his brothers was a civil servant and another carried on the family merchant tradition. The daughter married the man who later became the demang of Sulit Air. The doctor had two daughters (by different wives) both of whom entered medical school and each of whom married a professional man (one a lawyer and the other a doctor).[43]

The village of Sianok, next to Kota Gedang and across the Ngarai from Bukittinggi, was another rich merchant community. The first doctor in the village came from a long line of merchants; his son also became a doctor. The other two early doctors also came from merchant families. None of them had any apparent connections with local penghulu or nagarihoofd families.[44]

---

42 Interview, village leaders of Painan, December 4 and 6, 1967.
43 Interview, nagari council IV Kota, September 1967.
44 Ibid.

The information on backgrounds for all the villages is very sketchy at best, but the essential patterns of education emerge even so, and they differ little from those established by the 1860s. Areas which had a press of population on the land tended to show more interest in secular education. For example, the village of Maninjau on Lake Maninjau was thickly populated, and by the late nineteenth century it had used all its available land. Pupils had to be turned away from the school, and if a pupil were expelled, his relatives came immediately and protested vehemently. But only six miles away, a village which still had much good sawah land did not have enough pupils to fill a classroom regularly.[45] The highlands hill villages with their traditional interest in merantau and their more open society continued to show a correspondingly greater interest in education than the plains and coastal areas. The highlands itself showed a relatively greater interest in secular education than the coast. By the early twentieth century, the ratio of the population of the coast to that of the highlands was 4 to 9, but the pupil ratio was 1 to 9.[46] Along the coast, the prejudice against learning a "trade" (any trade) remained. In the novel *Sitti Nurbaja,* one of the characters, a penghulu of Padang, wants to send his son to the STOVIA. His sister remonstrates with him. There is no need to learn Dutch, she says, if one can attain rank without it.

---

45 H. W. Stap, "Een Statistiek in de Onder-Afdeeling Oud-Agam, Afdeeling Agam, Sumatra's Westkust," *TBB,* 52 (1917), pp. 151-52.
46 H. Colijn, Advisor on Administration for the Outer Islands, April 24, 1909, *Verbaal,* September 7, 1910, No. 32.

CHAPTER SEVEN
THE GENEALOGY OF THE NEW ELITE: A CASE STUDY

As mentioned earlier, a major problem in determining the course of secular education in the nineteenth century and its impact on the villages and people of Minangkabau is the lack of data. The available evidence suggests that middle-level merchant and artisan families, that is to say, those groups with an already developed merantau tradition, were the ones who took advantage of secular education, and that, conversely, the families of penghulu and government chiefs showed less interest. But it is difficult to document this.

One way to overcome the lack of documentation is to examine genealogies of the families that became successful in the civil service and the professions in the twentieth century and then work back along the path by which they achieved those positions. This is difficult because many families apparently do not keep a written genealogy and even if they do only the women's children are listed, because only they belong to the matrilineage. Constructing a genealogy which takes into account the occupations of the men, whether brothers or husbands, uncles or fathers, is thus no easy task. But gather the family women around the kitchen fire or the men around a table over a cup of coffee, and one can eventually pull out of their collective consciousnesses an almost complete background of the various village families, for at least several generations back.

Tracing Minangkabau genealogies is interesting not just for the light it sheds upon the rise of particular bureaucratic or professional families, but, at the same time, for what it tells about Minangkabau society itself. One can see through the genealogies, for instance, how the matrilineal organization could be as easily manipulated to multiply the options of a given youth as to check his progress (the implication in many twentieth-century novels). The system is not as rigid as is often portrayed, and once a few rules of the game are learned, a youth can play upon the family situation, often to his great advantage.

An interesting insight that comes out of the genealogies, one which might not otherwise be suspected, is the importance society actually attaches to a child's father. This is not with regard to his role as "father" necessarily, but rather in the wider terms of the advantages which liaison with his family brings to the mother's family (which is, of course, the future child's own family). Descriptions of Minangkabau and its matrilineal society often give the impression that the father is only a shadowy figure who sneaks into the house at night and is gone by daybreak. This is patently not the case. The father apparently has always had an important position, as an advisor in the councils of his wife's family as well as with regard to the future of his children. The marriage tie in some respects was contracted with the man's family because of a belief that it would most likely benefit the expected children. The maternal uncle is important, of course, especially in negotiating and arranging major rites concerning the child's future, as for example his marriage. But the child in Minangkabau does have two sets of equally important "parents" either of which can help him in his future life and both of which are members of larger families which also recognize a certain obligation toward him.

The genealogies also show the extent to which families tend to cluster into groups based on marriage ties. Ideally, a young man marries the daughter of his maternal uncle; her lineage is often the same as that of his own father, which keeps everything in the family. Certain families as a result tend to intermarry frequently from one generation to the next, and most of their principal relationships are with each other rather than with branches within their respective lineages. This makes it difficult to compile the genealogy of a whole matrilineage, because each subunit knows mostly about the members of its own immediate circle and those of the group with which it intermarries; but it may not know exactly where the common link is between its own branch and the others in the matrilineage. Members know they are related to other branches directly because they have the same penghulu (and indeed quarrel constantly over the position), but often they cannot document the connection with names or even the generation in which the direct link existed. Since villages tended to require that each man marry a girl from his own village, almost everyone is distantly related to everyone else, especially in the smaller villages. They refer to themselves as "cousins."

The families that are actually tied by marriage bonds usually cluster into similar socioeconomic groups—merchants, religious scholars, adat notables, etc. Two families of cloth merchants, for example, will tend to intermarry, and this virtually predetermines that children and nephews will become cloth merchants also, serving the useful purpose of keeping the business and its trade secrets within the family. Because certain family groups become so tightly intermarried, the lines between matrilineal and patrilineal relatives become cloudy, making obligations to children that much more inclusive. Whatever way one wants to figure a relationship, most members of either family have some responsibility for the child. Such clustering proved very important when the value of secular education and opportunities of the civil service were first recognized. After someone in a family cluster decided that secular education was important, whether because it was useful in wholesale commerce or in becoming a jaksa, the ideas were quickly disseminated through the whole family cluster. Children were reoriented toward school training rather than, or in addition to, the traditional apprenticeship in the family business. When one family member broke into the civil service, he used the opportunity to share his good fortune with a clutch of his immediate relatives.

The success of the first families in education and the government service, stimulated other village families to emulate them, and also to seek marriage relationships with them. In this way, the scope of educational interest and opportunity for jobs spread in waves out from the original cluster through its related families and into the village as a whole. The more tightly interlocked village families were by mutual marriage relationships, the easier the new idea would spread. In addition to the traditional clusters of merchants, some villages now developed clusters of bureaucrats, doctors, or school teachers. Such families often specialized in a particular kind of "intellectual profession" in the same way as other families specialized in a particular trade.

The penghulu had their own mutually supportive and interlocking clusters based on other notable families, which doubtless helped reinforce aristocratic prejudices, and may explain why an enthusiasm for secular education did not get started in such clusters. With few links to these clusters becoming imbued with an interest in secular education, the penghulu had few direct contacts with its successes. Within notable clusters, position was conferred by right, and education was at best a rite of passage on the road to becoming a village notable. In the 1920s, when secular, Dutch-language education became an important criterion of elite status, many laras- and nagarihoofd families began to place more emphasis on school attendance. But their essential attitude toward it remained unchanged.

By taking as a case study one village which developed an overwhelming interest in secular education in the nineteenth century, one can see how the various factors mentioned above operated in practice. The genealogies of village families which moved into the civil service or the professions diagram how the stimulus reached out along family lines in an almost geometric progression, spreading through the village.

Introducing Kota Gedang

The various elements which coincided to produce a drive for secular education among the highlands Minangkabau were nowhere more strongly concentrated than in the village of Kota Gedang, located across the Ngarai canyon from Bukittinggi (capital of the Assistant Residency of Agam and the Residency of the Highlands).[1] An eighteenth-century center of perantau goldsmiths, by the early 1900s, Kota Gedang had a territory-wide reputation as the home village of many indigenous colonial bureaucrats—villagers served as jaksa, warehousemasters, tax officials, etc., throughout Sumatra and Kalimantan, and some held posts in Batavia as well.

A 1915 report estimated that 165 men from Kota Gedang were then serving as officials with the civil service, seventy-nine of them outside Minangkabau. It is also noteworthy that seventy-two of the 165 were listed as fluent in Dutch, indicative of a fairly advanced education.[2] By 1940, the village had attained even greater fame as the birthplace for doctors, lawyers, and engineers,; men who constituted a large number of the small

---

1 Much of the following is based on information gained through field research conducted in Kota Gedang during September, October, and November 1967. For most of that period, I lived in the village with the family of a semi-retired doctor.
2 K. A. James, "De Nagari Kota Gedang," *TBB,* 49 (1915), p. 193.

preindependence contingent of professionally trained Indonesians. By 1942, for example, forty sons of Kota Gedang had graduated as doctors from the STOVIA. In the late 1960s, an observer reported that one out of every eleven natives of Kota Gedang was a *sarjana* (a general term for any graduate of an advanced educational institution, that is, beyond high school).[3] Advancement in the Dutch world did not mean collaboration with it; two of the most famous prewar nationalists also came from Kota Gedang families—Haji Agus Salim and Sutan Sjahrir. The first Indonesian woman educator and journalist, Rohanna Kudus, who predated the well-known Kartini by more than a decade, also hailed from Kota Gedang.

These accomplishments, remarkable by any measure, are the more amazing from a village that in 1852 had a population of only 2,500, many of whom were family retainers or servants.[4] Kota Gedang was a village so small and agriculturally insignificant in Dutch terms, that no controleur was ever posted there. Moreover, despite its intellectual achievements, the first school located in the village itself was founded only in the early twentieth century, long after similarly small villages, such as Puar Datar or Sulit Air, had their own schools. Prior to that time, the youth of Kota Gedang walked to Bukittinggi each day to attend the nagari school and the Normal School. The trip required stamina. Though a distance of only a few kilometers measured in a straight line, the path is rugged and crosses the deep Ngarai canyon, into whose sheer chalk cliffsides are cut steep steps and tortuous trails. Only those with the desire created by intense interest or necessity could be expected to continue this trip day after day and year after year until graduation. Those with relatives living in Bukittinggi could arrange to board there, but these were only the lucky few. Most civil servants and merchants from Kota Gedang who worked in Bukittinggi also made the daily trip.

The Perantau Tradition

The village of Kota Gedang is a ghost town today, serving mainly as a retirement home for pensioned officials and a nursery for the few remaining grandchildren. Only some 900 people are year-round

---

3   *Aman Makmur* [Padang], September 17, 1967.
4   Report of the Resident of the Padang Highlands, 1852, *Verbaal,* July 13, 1858, No. 35.

residents. Most of the large family houses are permanently shuttered and barred. Kota Gedang died, a victim of its own success, an ironic twist to the questing spirit of its historic perantau artisan and intellectual ancestors. The twentieth-century concept of a supraethnic society in which a Minangkabau can live happily in Jakarta, Medan, or Makasar, never returning to his home village, created a new generation of perantau, who took their families abroad with them and rarely returned for so much as a visit to the ancestral home. Previously, only the most "adventurous" Minangkabau woman ever left her family's house, even to accompany her husband abroad. Thus men must always return to visit their families, and the village was always their permanent home. Since about the 1920s, however, young people have been growing up on the rantau in Java proudly asserting their Kota Gedang heritage and yet never having seen the village itself. By the 1960s, such young people are the second generation born on the rantau. The perantau ideal is not new for Kota Gedang, but, as with many other Minangkabau villages, it no longer serves as a means for sustaining family life in the marginally agricultural Kota Gedang. Now it has become a way to avoid the village entirely and usually forever—except for the romantic few who come home again to die and be buried with their forebears.

Before Kota Gedang withered away, it had traditional significance in its own small, and perhaps a trifle self-important, way. Along with neighboring Sianok, it was considered the parent village of the IV Kota confederation—encompassing the main villages of Sianok, Kota Gedang, Tabek Surajo, and Guguk, plus their numerous satellite hamlets. Federation leadership had historically alternated between Kota Gedang and Sianok. When the Dutch arrived, however, they conferred permanent paramountcy on Kota Gedang and named it the seat for the IV Kota laras district. Thus, whether by accident or clever manipulation, Kota Gedang was assured continuous access to any opportunities which might derive from association with the new order.

None of the villages of the IV Kota had sufficient rice land to sustain a desirable living standard. Almost all families had to pursue other trades: in Kota Gedang, the most common was as a gold or silver smith,[5] and

---

5 Ibid.

in neighboring villages it was mainly as merchants or peddlers. The whole IV Kota area had a highly developed perantau tradition before the Europeans came. In Kota Gedang, the perantau life was pursued by almost all males. Village families had numerous slaves and retainers who tended to daily agricultural tasks, and the women provided whatever general supervision was needed over the fieldwork. Men were free to practice their perantau occupations unburdened by domestic obligations. Their habit of traveling throughout the region served them in good stead later when the colonial regime required those serving the foreign bureaucracy to be willing to accept jobs in the newly acquired territories—Aceh, Riau, or Kalimantan.[6] Such an open-minded approach to geographic mobility contrasted sharply with the natives of other villages and towns, such as Padang. Though cajoled and threatened by turn, the natives of Padang refused to let their sons leave home, deeming it a tragedy beyond recall for a man to die elsewhere than in his mother's house, not to mention the shame attached to leaving home to earn a living.

In Kota Gedang, and indeed much of the IV Kota area, yearly harvests could barely support even the immediate relatives of the richest penghulu. Perantau life was idealized and a stigma was often attached to a youth, even the heir to a penghulu-ship, who stayed home. A perantau was usually expected to succeed on his own without family capital.[7] The impressive and new Indies-style homes which still stand in Kota Gedang provide mute testimony to the perantau's successes. And even today, successful sons of Kota Gedang continue sending money home to build ever more modern family houses, though they may never come to see them, nor will anyone else ever live in them. Yet the testimony is apparently necessary, for it proves one's success on the rantau and acknowledges one's ties and, by implication, one's obligation to the home village.

The people of Kota Gedang claim they are unsuited by temperament to the kind of interpersonal dealings required of good merchants; rather, they say, they incline more to the individual life of the skilled craftsman—or latterly, the intellectual. Though genealogical evidence contradicts their contention of a traditional indifference to trade, the fact that such a belief

---

6   D. Gerth van Wijk, "Een Menangkabausche Heilige," *TBG*, 24 (1877), pp. 224-25.
7   Personal interview with the penghulu's councils of the IV Koto, in Koto Tuo, September 28, 1967.

is now part of village conventional wisdom is an interesting commentary on the extent to which the inhabitants have divorced themselves from past values. Whereas artisanry is still regarded as a noble profession, villagers tend to regard merchants with a bit of disdain.

Kota Gedang and the Dutch

The experience of Kota Gedang residents at the hands of the Padri just prior to the Dutch arrival probably preconditioned them to value a stable colonial order. The nearby village of Koto Tuo, reputedly an historic offshoot of Kota Gedang and hence subordinate to it, became a Padri center fairly early. The first major Dutch military establishment in Agam was Fort de Kock, established in 1825, on the outskirts of Bukittinggi. Kota Gedang was caught geographically between the two opposing forces. It was also the holy center for a tarekat brotherhood, precisely the kind of eclectic Islam most hated by the Padri. The village had a shrine to an early eighteenth-century syekh supposedly born miraculously from a village virgin.[8] Obviously, it was a ready target for the religious puritans of Koto Tuo, supported by ambitious adat leaders, who no doubt were long resentful of their subordination to Kota Gedang penghulu in ritual and prestige matters.

It is charged by outsiders, and accepted by some Kota Gedang villagers themselves, that the village opted for the Dutch side early in the hostilities of the 1820s. Detractors assert that the Dutch promised that henceforth Kota Gedang would receive favored treatment, and that this explains its subsequent success in the civil service. Even if the charges of calculated collaboration are true, however, they do not explain fully the subsequent developments. The Dutch provided other villages equal and perhaps greater opportunities for both education and public service, but these villages did not display the same interest.

Kota Gedang villagers had a preexisting predilection for looking outside the village. While other villagers of the IV Kota continued as merchants and often used the Dutch coffee system as the springboard for developing large merchandising enterprises, many families in Kota

---

8   Van Wijk, "Menangkabausche Heilige," contains a full account of the syekh and his life.

Gedang gradually gave up their traditional vocations as craftsmen or merchants and began new ones as government servants. This does not seem to have been solely on economic grounds, that is, because gold working or trade had become significantly less profitable after the advent of the Dutch. In many other parts of the region Minangkabau in similar occupations were able to profit from the new internal and external markets being opened up, especially through coffee. Although Kota Gedang itself was not a major coffee-producing village because it lacked land, the surrounding area was ideal coffee country—in the foothills near Mount Singgalang and on the uplands around Lake Maninjau. In villages such as Koto Tuo and Balingka, large and prosperous merchant families developed. These villagers only really turned to secular education as an alternative path beginning in the 1920s and 1930s, perhaps as a reflection of the generally depressed economic situation of that time.

Kota Gedang, as the administrative center for the IV Kota nonetheless benefitted from the new money being generated by the coffee system. The foremost local example of this was Radjo Mangkuto, who had charge of transport arrangements for coffee produced in the whole IV Kota area and much of the surrounding region. He became so wealthy as a result that he chartered a ship to make the pilgrimage to Mecca, and afterward he continued to Holland where he presented King William III with several gold objects crafted in Kota Gedang. Radjo Mangkuto's brother, Abdul Rahman, was the Koto lineage penghulu (the Datuk Dinagari), but, more important, he was the first jaksa of Bukittinggi (1833-68). Another brother, Haji Abdul Latief, became head of the first Bukittinggi Normal School when it opened in 1856. The combination of an entree to the Dutch regime and easy access to education, all supported by great family wealth, was carefully used. From this nucleus, there developed one of the major clusters of civil servants and professional men in Kota Gedang.

As has been noted before, in the early era of secular education, families viewed school training as another skill like smithing; something to be learned but used to pursue essentially traditional goals. Attending school did not fundamentally change one's views or one's value system. Education was not, as it were, an "experience" it was equivalent to an "apprenticeship." The family of the Datuk Dinagari in Kota Gedang was no exception to this. They used their education and the positions it brought them in the Dutch regime as part of a power play within village politics. The village was still the major arena of activity for all families whether they were high colonial officials or wealthy landed notables. By the turn of the twentieth century, this had changed. The second generation of Western-educated officials and intellectuals began looking outward to Sumatra and the Indies as a whole. Their sphere of action enlarged and village affairs assumed lesser importance. Though still concerned about their prestige vis-à-vis other villagers, the new elite had less interest in running village affairs, except perhaps after retirement.

In the 1860s and 1870s, however, families still competed on an essentially village level. The cluster of families which surrounded and supported the Datuk Dinagari used their associations with the Dutch, their prestige as people who know their way around the new order, and the massive wealth they had gained from coffee deals, to engineer the election of one of their kemanakan, the new Datuk Dinagari (Djunaid) as the larashoofd of the IV Kota in 1872. They wrested the position from the lineage which had held it since the Dutch arrival in the 1820s.

The incumbent lineage, that of Piliang/Datuk Kajo, had apparently suffered a financial crisis after the preceding Datuk Kajo had squandered the family's resources on gambling and high living.[9] Nonetheless, the change in larashoofd to a new lineage created a great deal of turmoil and Djunaid eventually resigned. The Datuk Kajo family regained its former position. The Datuk Dinagari family continued among the most important of the village's families, but its significance was in terms of high civil service positions and, later, importance in the professions, especially medicine and law. Its sole reminder of the brief whirl in local adat politics is an ostentatious two-story European-style mansion built to house larashoofd Djunaid. The house is filled with overstuffed European furniture, mementoes of European acquaintanceships, and other tokens of high office—curiously symbolic that the family was more adept and at home in the Dutch sphere of the civil service than in the adat sphere of village politics, and perhaps more accepted in the former as well.

---

9   *Verbaal*, January 22, 1875, No. 19.

The Civil Service Dynasties[10]

The story of Djunaid represents an early stage in the development of the new Kota Gedang elite. Increasingly, attention was directed not at the adat competitions of the village but at the colonial politics of the supravillage world. Genealogies of these families provide specific examples of how the interest in education accelerated from one generation to the next. The first man who gained a position in the bureaucracy, typically a jaksa or warehousemaster, was often trained on the job because, in the early years, there was as yet no nagari. school in Bukittinggi. Why a particular individual was selected for a post is unclear, but obviously he had had contact with some Dutch official and had impressed that person with his competence. Jaksa and warehousemasters were important positions requiring competence and a sense of responsibility. The jaksa served as the controleur's or Assistant Resident's right hand man in local decisions, and functioned as an objective commentator on local problems. He had to be an outsider, unconnected with the village adat establishment and hence not subject to it. The warehousemaster was responsible for coffee collection, the core of the cultivation system, in his district, and often worked with only little supervision from the nearby controleur.

One of the major families of civil servants and later professional men were members of the Datuk Dinagari branch of the Suku Koto. They were the descendants of the previously mentioned Abdul Rahman, jaksa of Bukittinggi. He married a Kota Gedang girl and had two sons, both of whom were jaksa—one at Palembayan and one at Riau (the future father of Haji Agus Salim). Abdul Rahman's daughter married a Kota Gedang man who was warehousemaster at Batu Sangkar. Abdul Rahman also married a Padang girl, from whom he had two sons: a teacher and the first stationmaster of the rail depot in Padang. His kemanakan included five boys, none of whom excelled in government or private life with the exception of Djunaid, the future larashoofd. Of his nieces, however,

---

10 In the course of my field research in Kota Gedang, I compiled bilateral genealogies of about a dozen important lineages. Most are complete for four or five generations, in other words, back to the arrival of the Dutch in Kota Gedang. The information on the civil service dynasties and the comparative comments on the artisan, penghulu, and other families have been drawn from these genealogies. Because the charts themselves are very bulky, they have not been included in this monograph.

three married jaksa from Kota Gedang, one married a warehousemaster, and one an official in the comptroller's bureau. The only son of Abdul Rahman's brother Abdul Gani, the coffee contractor, was also a jaksa, in Padang. Abdul Rahman's brother Haji Abdul Latief, the head of the Normal School, had one son who held no position. Among Abdul Rahman's grandchildren and grand-nephews were a teacher, an engineer, three doctors, two medical technicians, two district officers, three jaksa, and eleven lesser government officials. But of these, it was as much the father as the mamak who determined their futures. For example, one niece married a man who was jaksa in Bukittinggi and, of their five sons, three were also jaksa (two of these were head jaksa), one was a district officer, and the fifth had a private business. Another niece, however, married a man of wealth but no vocation and, of her three sons, one taught school and one was a clerk.

This illustrates the point made earlier about the importance of the father in raising the children and influencing their careers, despite the apparent contradiction this raises with the matrilineal family structure. In practice, it seems, the role of mamak was traditionally more crucial in matters regarding marriage of female children, distribution of harta pusaka and other matters governing strictly lineage affairs. But he had less immediate interest or control over his sister's children than their own father. If the father could not help the children, or if he had died, or had divorced his wife, then the uncle would assume primary responsibility for the children.

The case history of a family in the Datuk Radjo Nando branch of the Sikumbang lineage illustrates also the role the father could play. Neither the matrilineal family nor its usual marriage partners represented important village literati until one member, Abdul Halim, was chosen nagarihoofd. He used his position to get three of his sons appointed as government officials and two others accepted by the STOVIA (only one graduated). Abdul Halim's sister married a man without government position but, by relying on her brother, three of her four sons became doctors. Another sister married a teacher and, of her six sons, one was a doctor and one a district official. But not all in the family group developed the same interest in secular education. A brother of Abdul Halim was a haji, an indication at least of wealth if not religious conviction, and none of the haji's sons went into any profession or worked for the government.

There is no information about the financial status of this family vis-à-vis other village families. Wealth, as indicated by the title of haji, might have tempered an interest in outside employment. Prior to Abdul Halim's generation, the women in the Datuk Radjo Nando branch had produced few children, and the lineage seemed in danger of dying out. This, among other things, meant that supplemental income would be less crucial. The rapid increase in family membership in Abdul Halim's generation suggests that economic necessity might account for the sudden interest in schools and government jobs.

The genealogy of the Datuk Bahano Kajo branch of the Piliang lineage contains two subbranches with different histories. Until just before World War II, the men of one remained exclusively goldsmiths and the women married goldsmiths. The members of the other branch, which retained the penghulu-ship, had no professions or vocations; all lived off family properties and, if they had any independent accomplishments, no one can remember them.

A striking change in family orientation could take place in one generation. The Datuk Palindih branch of the Sikumbang lineage went in one step from all goldsmiths to none. One of the men married the sister of the larashoofd Datuk Kajo, which gave the family a connection to the Dutch establishment, but this does not of itself explain why the overwhelming push toward secular education arose nor why it was so complete. In the family cluster, the first generation of nongoldsmiths included two jaksa, a demang, a treasury official, and a teacher. The next generation had eight doctors, many government officials, several engineers and lawyers. It was not until very late, however, that members of the larashoofd family itself exhibited any particular inclination toward advanced education. In the 1920s their children were attending the privileged Dutch-language schools as a matter of course. The last larashoofd (then demang) was the first to send his children to these schools, and, of his eleven sons who were educated before the war, one became a doctor, one a veterinarian, one a lawyer, and one a demang.

The case of the Datuk Maradjo branch of the Piliang lineage illustrates the fairly common combination of merchant and civil-service careers. The family which had the most success in the government were descended from a merchant father. Of his three sons, one became the warehousemaster in Batu Sangkar and another a merchant. The daughters married nonofficials and their children likewise held no position. The sons' children on the other hand included thirteen males, of whom there were three jaksa (two hoofdjaksa), two district officials, two teachers, and two officials in the opium office. Four others were successful merchants and one became a goldsmith. In the next generation, every male either held a government position or was a professional man. Two units of the family had close ties to Riau, holding at once the position of demang, head jaksa, and two posts in the opium office. This geographic concentration illustrates how one person could open the way for all his relatives. Many relatives also went to Riau as merchants.

Some Considerations

The brief discussion of some Kota Gedang families illustrates how the members of one village adapted to the colonial reality which existed after the 1830s and how they fit the new opportunities to traditional needs. Very early on, certain families perceived that the advent of Dutch rule could be advantageous, and discovered that power, prestige, and wealth could be gained in ways other than through the total collaboration of the adat rulers in coastal and plains villages. By using the traditional skills of intra- and interfamily politics to achieve new objectives, Kota Gedang families attained the same goals. Whether through force of necessity or shrewd evaluation, these families realized that the future lay in access to the growing native civil service rather than in the village adat structure. They pragmatically set about acquiring the necessary skills and contacts.

At first, some tried to use the new positions in traditional ways, that is to improve family chances in local politics and to acquire more village land. But by the early twentieth century, the new educated elite had opted out of the village entirely and had entered the greater world of the Indies society; village affairs were left to molder in the hands of the few who were too traditional to change, too comfortable in their accustomed molds, or too unenergetic to make the transition. In the words of wits on the rantau: the "Menang" (i.e., winners) have all left the village and only the "kerbau" (buffalos) remain.

Why Kota Gedang more than any other village identified the new trend and doggedly pursued it is a complex and not totally explicable phenomenon. Other villages had geographically better access to nagari schools. Kota Gedang children did get a crucial early entree into the Normal School, important less as a training ground for teachers than as a means to become high-level civil servants. Kota Gedang had early and close ties to the Dutch bureaucracy, but other villages also had ties. However, in Kota Gedang it was not the larashoofd family, the usual point of contact with Dutch officialdom, which had the most important relations with the Dutch but rather another lineage, which had direct ties in the form of jaksa and ware-housemasters. As elsewhere, the larashoofd family in Kota Gedang displayed little or no real interest in the alternatives provided by secular education. But this family held no monopoly on access to the Dutch, and hence did not discourage the chances of others who might want to join the colonial world. If in other villages, this was not the case, it could explain why, despite otherwise similar opportunities, these villages did not develop like Kota Gedang.

An important factor in Kota Gedang's rise was its entry into the upper levels of the civil service almost immediately. Families recognized that the positions of jaksa and warehousemaster were crucial ones and worked mightily to attain them. Appointments above the level of clerk required direct contacts as well as education in nagari school. The people of Kota Gedang early had a channel into the teachers' institute, whose graduates most easily became important civil servants, and Kota Gedang's geographical proximity to the center of Dutch administration in the highlands gave it an added advantage over the villages of the northern coffee regions. By 1900 advanced education required a knowledge of Dutch as well as formal academic subjects, and Kota Gedang children were pushed from an early age to acquire proficiency in Dutch and excel at elementary school so that they would be assured of a place in the roster of the advanced schools. Many families began sending their children to Jakarta in the 1920s, because competition for entry into schools there was less intense and the opportunities for advanced education and government jobs greater. Kota Gedang's merantau tradition meant that families usually had a relative in one of the larger cities with whom the prospective student could board.

Other highlands villages also developed civil service dynasties, though on a smaller scale. The pattern resembled that of Kota Gedang: families with good contacts could place educated members in the upper level of the civil service, but others had to be content with lesser posts and hope that talent and seniority would eventually be rewarded. None of these villages, however, can match Kota Gedang in the singleminded use of position in the government to pull others along with them. The major lineages of Kota Gedang developed an esprit de corps which included all the residents. Secular education and government service became accepted hallmarks of success. And, more importantly, individuals felt a communal not just a familial responsibility to help others reach the upper echelon. So long as anyone was left behind, it was an embarrassment to the rest.[11] As a result, anyone who wished to enroll in the nagari school or the Normal School could always find some "relative" who had a high position and was willing to serve as his "sponsor."[12] The Dutch, for their part, proved agreeable to a loose interpretation of "parentage" when quizzing prospective Sekolah Radja pupils about their family backgrounds. Family status was actually less important in the nineteenth century than it became after the "broadening" of the education base under the Ethical Policy of the twentieth century. By that time, however, sufficient numbers of Kota Gedang people had government posts to assure that, whatever conditions were imposed on admission, the village children would not be barred.

The close-knit feelings of Kota Gedang families reflect both the force of circumstance and historical tradition. A marginal agricultural village, Kota Gedang did not develop a deeply entrenched landed elite with aristocratic pretensions which might have separated them from society at large or lower-ranking members of their own lineage. Many heirs to the penghulu-ship in Kota Gedang spent their own youth on the rantau helping supplement family wealth. In some families, however, the process of Dutch rule did create a new, leisured class of penghulu, secure in their posts and less and less interested in outside chances, a class of idle rich derisively called the *Angku Senang* ("lords of pleasure," or playboys) by the other villagers of Kota Gedang.

The feeling of mutual self-interest was not wholly spiritual but also resulted from the extensive intermarriage among lineages in the village. Everyone was supposed to marry someone from the village. Although many perantau males married outsiders, they had an obligation to marry

---

11 Personal interview with Iljas St. Pamenan of Kota Gedang, in Jakarta, February 27, 1967.
12 These relationships were cast in kinship terms, even when there were no blood ties.

a girl from Kota Gedang as well. In 1920, a girl from Kota Gedang was formally disinherited by her family, and the nagari council, for eloping with a Javanese.[13] In fact children of a Kota Gedang father and alien mother would often return to Kota Gedang to marry. Thus the talent that was "lost" for one generation was "returned home" in the next.

A way to measure the growth of the secular education ideal is to follow the fortunes of the lineage penghulu-ships. During the nineteenth century, many artisan, merchant, and civil service families showed a great interest in marrying into a penghulu family, but after the turn of the twentieth century, this became less common. By about the 1920s, after families had begun leaving the village permanently and were no longer operating within the adat environment, the position of penghulu itself became less attractive. Many families never filled vacancies after a penghulu's death, or else they conferred the title on a noted doctor or government official in the hope that after his retirement he would return to Kota Gedang and look after family interests. Fewer and fewer people lived in Kota Gedang with passing generations. Because government was increasingly a matter for civil service officials, the penghulu became decorative but almost useless institutions. Even their prestige was gone, with doctors, demang, or professors considered of greater importance. As a result, the marriage pattern, to a certain extent, reversed itself. Whereas, formerly, families of goldsmiths sought to marry a daughter to a penghulu, now families of penghulu hoped to marry a daughter to a doctor. This illustrates the final resolution of nineteenth-century developments—the lineage penghulu, assured of their jobs by a Dutch-style adat, become obsolete when the adat administration ceases to have any meaning in practical terms. Penghulu families have often found it difficult to overcome this decline in position created because they chose to ignore the supravillage world and its opportunities in the nineteenth century. By the twentieth century the headstart gained by other families was often too great.

---

13 "Adatvonnissen (1920)," *Adatrechtbundels,* 20, pp. 143-46.

CHAPTER EIGHT
EPILOGUE: MINANGKABAU IN THE TWENTIETH CENTURY

By the turn of the century, the increasing numbers of Minangkabau desiring civil service or other government-related careers intensified the pressure on the Dutch administration to enlarge local schools and admit more pupils. Although formerly, reading and writing Malay plus good "references" had assured graduates of eventual appointment to higher positions, by the early twentieth century so many qualified applicants were available that literacy in Dutch was becoming a new standard for employment in the upper echelons. This resulted more from upgrading the requirements for existing jobs than opening new, higher-level jobs to Minangkabau. The Indies administration had not expanded enough to absorb all the elementary or even secondary school graduates.

The demand to learn Dutch became so great among the Minangkabau that anyone with the slightest knowledge of the language would establish a backyard school giving crash courses to aspiring civil servants and professionals. Those who had any influence with the Dutch government pressured to gain admittance for their children in the various European elementary schools in West Sumatra. In 1909, it was reported that over one-third of the total pupils at the European schools in West Sumatra were non-European, and without the stringent quota system governing admittance to these schools, the proportion would have been even higher.[1]

In an ironic twist of fate, the Dutch regime's growing recognition of the need for increased secular education for Indonesians adversely affected

---

1 Report of the Inspector of Education for Sumatra's West Coast, Grivel, March 22, 1909, *Verbaal*, October 18, 1910, No. 23.

the educational opportunities in Minangkabau. In 1892, the government had again decided to coordinate administrative responsibility and reorganize education in all parts of the Indies. Now teachers, assistants, and regional inspectors were to be established more systematically in the whole archipelago and more directly under the government's auspices, with indigenous schools divided into first- and second-class levels.[2] The result of this decree in West Sumatra, however, was to downgrade the existing schools, which were declared second-class schools, though in fact they offered better education than most schools of this level elsewhere. The new plan allowed only the children of chiefs and notables to attend the new "high quality," first-class schools, the reason being that there they would be groomed for rule. The projected number of second-class schools (called *volksschool,* or people's schools) was determined by the number of administrative districts in a given province, regardless of population density or the desire of the inhabitants for education. Thus, Jambi, which had about sixty-seven pupils per school and an absentee rate of 30 percent, was granted schools in the same proportion as Minangkabau, which averaged 150 pupils per school and an absentee rate of only 8 percent.[3]

The new "liberal" policy benefitted districts where education was relatively underdeveloped, while in areas such as Sumatra's West Coast, it tended to undercut the progress already achieved by denying any new schools until all other areas had received their quota. Pressure thus increased on the existing West Sumatra schools to such an extent that, in some places, only the upper civil service families could assure their children entry to even the government elementary schools.

In West Sumatra, part of the pressure was relieved by the numerous private schools which sprang up in response to increased interest in education—in 1912, in the city of Padang alone, there were twenty-three private schools (receiving no government subsidies) with a total of 1,200 pupils. This compares, for instance, to a total of fifty-three such schools for the whole of Java and Madura during the same period.[4] At the same time, religious schools were staging a massive comeback after decades

---

2   Royal Decree on Indigenous Education, 1892, *Verbaal,* September 23, 1892, No. 13.
3   Inspector of Education Grivel to the Director of Education, November 30, 1909, *Verbaal,* September 7, 1910, No. 32.
4   XY, "Het Inlandsch Onderwijs ter Sumatra's Westkust," *Koloniaal Tijdschrift,* 2, 1 (1913), p. 398.

of decay, because parents believed that any education which imparted literacy would enhance the prospects for employment. These schools had also enlarged their curricula, and pupils now learned to read and copy government documents in Malay, using both the Arabic and the Roman scripts. As the twentieth century wore on, some of these surau would be transformed into semisecular schools. Dutch officials feared that the resurgence of religious schools might lead to a more general revival of Islamic antigovernment activity.[5] In the event, these fears proved justified.

An important cause of antigovernment activity in Minangkabau, whether under religious or secular leaders, was the widespread unemployment among former pupils of the various schools. Not only did the government not have sufficient jobs in the West Sumatra administration but at the same time, increased education elsewhere was producing local recruits to fill jobs formerly open to perantau literati from Minangkabau. The unemployment problem was becoming apparent well before 1900. An ex-Governor of the West Coast, H. D. Canné, complained, in the 1880s, that the unemployed Minangkabau scholastics had begun to encourage villagers to agitate directly with the government for redress of any grievances. They suggested that villagers send complaining letters to government officials—letters which the unemployed scholars then wrote on the villagers' behalf, for a small fee.[6] The employment crisis later spread to graduates of the upper-level schools as well. In the 1920s, Governor Whitlau cautioned that a politically dangerous situation was building because, after overcoming great competition to enter school in the first place, pupils found that, on graduation, they "had achieved only an uncertain future."[7]

In such a situation, obviously, families which had already achieved a position in the government service had great advantages. Whatever the regulations governing schools and jobs, men with connections could arrange that their children and nephews received favorable attention.

---

5   Memorie van Overgave, Resident of Sumatra's West Coast, Le Febvre, *Mailrapport*, No. 2904/'19.
6   N. Graafland, "De Reorganisatie van het Inlandsch Onderwijs," *Verslagen van het Indisch Genootschap* (1889), p. 92.
7   Memorie van Overgave, Governor of Sumatra's West Coast, Whitlau, April 1926, *Mailrap port*, No. 2488/'26.

Whereas in the nineteenth century, the Dutch administration had frozen entry into the adat elite, one could now see a parallel development with regard to the bureaucratic elite.

Not only did civil service families have a greater chance to enroll children in West Sumatra schools, but, by virtue of their networks of relations outside Minangkabau, they could send children to other areas and thus take advantage of the relatively lower competition there. A 1909 report by the education inspector for the West Coast area concluded that such was indeed happening in Aceh. The government had recently erected fifteen schools there only to find the greatest number of pupils were not in fact Acehnese. The inspector believed that many of these non-Acehnese students were in fact Minangkabau.[8] Many men from Kota Gedang, for example, served in the civil administration for Aceh, and their children did attend school there. These included not only their children by Acehnese wives but, in many cases, their children brought from Kota Gedang as well. The Dutch were understandably disturbed by this, because they had planned the schools as training centers for the Acehnese elite.

To a certain degree, important merchant families, because they had contacts throughout the western archipelago and similar close ties with the civil service, could place their children in government schools. Beginning in the 1930s, such families were indeed becoming more and more interested in advanced education. For example, two villages in the IV Kota, Agam, had their first STOVIA graduates in the 1930s. All four students (one from Sianok and three from Koto Tuo) were children from rich merchant families that had not previously displayed any particular interest in education.[9]

As part of an administrative reorganization in 1914, the Dutch regime wanted to replace the old quasi-adat larashoofd and nagarihoofd with a new, merit civil service administration made up of graduates from the secular schools and the new civil service academy, the OSVIA. Daily village administration would be "returned to the true village leaders"—the core penghulu, or founding families. The government planned to absorb

---

8 Inspector of Education Grivel to the Director of Education, November 30, 1909, *Verbaal*, September 7, 1910, No. 32.
9 Interviews with the elders of the IV Kota, October 1967, in Koto Tuo.

the former larashoofd who were qualified into the new administration as demang (the civil service title for the equivalent position) and then post them to areas outside their former nagari. Padang officials discovered to their dismay that the larashoofd were almost always too ill-qualified to handle the new administrative functions, and, in many cases, they were totally illiterate.[10]

During the nineteenth century, rather than study themselves, the chiefs had simply hired former nagari school pupils to serve as their private secretaries and treat any aspect of administration which required literacy. Consequently, the graduates of the new civil service courses had been overwhelmingly the children of merchant and civil service families. In 1907, for example, only four of the fifteen candidate officials at the Bukittinggi Civil Service Academy were the children of larashoofd, and, more important, not one was the heir (kemanakan) of a larashoofd. Even those chiefs who saw value in secular education expected that the future of their kemanakan would be assured by virtue of birth. If they sent anyone to school, therefore, it would be a son.[11]

With the 1914 reorganization, the chiefs' job security should have disappeared, but Dutch officials continued to prefer the kemanakan of larashoofd even over a more educated middle-level villager. The Dutch professed to believe that, unless they had appropriate bloodlines, new officials would carry no weight in the village—even though they served outside their home nagari. Nonetheless, the majority of OSVIA graduates continued to be of commoner origin *(orang kebanyakan)*.[12] Obviously, this situation would create difficulties for the regime, if not immediately, then certainly in a few years when graduates fully realized that their education made little difference.

In addition to Dutch predilections for aristocratic demang, they also allowed incumbent larashoofd to continue in office until death or retirement. Only then would a demang be appointed to the district. As a result, few positions were available for the new OSVIA graduates. One

---

10 Resident of Sumatra's West Coast Le Febvre to the Governor General, July 6, 1918, *Verbaal*, March 4, 1919, No. 23.
11 Governor of Sumatra's West Coast Heckler to the Governor General, October 17, 1907, *Verbaal*, October 21, 1908, No. 44.
12 Memorie van Overgave, Governor Whitlau, 1926, *Mailrapport*, No. 2488/'26.

official predicted, in 1908, that the vacancy rate would be only about three positions per year, while the Bukittinggi OSVIA alone graduated some ten candidates each year.[13]

The OSVIA graduates were over-qualified for most other civil service posts. Also the upper-level jobs in the indigenous ranks of the administration were determined by seniority rather than formal education. The Indies government, mean-while, had abolished many top positions both by ending the coffee cultivation system and as part of a more general economizing drive in all departments.[14] The upper-level civil service families, though they could provide their children with a quality education, might not be able to assure them of a good job. Surely it is no accident that an interest among Kota Gedang civil service families in enrolling their children in the professional schools (specifically the STOVIA) appeared during these same first two decades of the twentieth century. In the nineteenth century, few, if any, people from Kota Gedang had even enrolled at the doktor djawa school. Between 1900 and 1910, the village had two graduates. In the next decade, eleven students from the village graduated from the STOVIA, and, during the remaining years before the war, another twenty-seven.[15] The competition to enter the STOVIA was especially keen, and only those with top qualifications and good contacts in government circles could be sure of matriculation.

In the early twentieth century, at a time when many more elements in the Minangkabau population were awakening to the values of a secular education, the opportunities for obtaining it were perceptibly decreasing, as the Dutch concentrated on education for the more underdeveloped areas. Academic entrepreneurs established private schools, many of which were short-lived, and some villages established community schools, reminiscent of the early nagari schools. One such village was Kota Gedang, which, in 1910, collected an education fund by assessing each family 3 percent of its income. The money was used to build a local Dutch language elementary school and to send Kota Gedang youth to

---

13 *Verbaal,* October 21, 1908, No. 44.
14 Governor of Sumatra's West Coast Heckler to the Governor General, October 17, 1909, *Verbaal,* October 21, 1908, No. 44.
15 Interviews in Kota Gedang, October and November 1967.

the Netherlands to train as teachers.[16] In some areas, lineage families banded together to raise money to send their more able members to school in Batavia, and even Europe. In many ways, the families' response resembled the traditional practice of staking promising adolescents to careers as artisans or merchants. These local solutions, however, could not completely defuse the tense atmosphere created by the over-supply of interest and undersupply of opportunity.

Through a combination of native wit, good fortune, economic necessity, regional family networks, and a tradition of seeking the future outside village society, many Minangkabau families arrived in the twentieth century in a better position than most other people in the Indies. The 1840s graduates of the West Sumatra schools had played the colonial game with great profit to their families and, in so doing, had pointed out the path of opportunity to others. Those who took up the challenge were the same families that had traditionally lived on the geographic and economic margins of Minangkabau life. Historically they had needed extra money and prestige to overcome the handicaps of being born in a family or village which did not have quite enough to achieve the ever-beckoning dream.

The Minangkabau entered the civil service, not in the spirit of the upper-class Javanese who were acculturated to the glory of service in the bureaucracy of the king (whatever his ethnic group), but more in the spirit of the entrepreneur who must first identify the name of the game and then play it to the greatest personal advantage. It was money and patronage and the power it brought which beckoned to the families of villages such as Kota Gedang, not some intangible glory inherent in serving an all-powerful ruler.

The Dutch government only occasionally helped the Minangkabau attain education in the nineteenth century, and then usually through the efforts of individuals. Men, such as Steinmetz or van Ophuizen, inspired certain villagers at certain times to begin the educational experiment, but it was local situations and interests which determined the ultimate success or failure of these attempts. When the interested Dutch officials were transferred, the interest in education remained in those areas

---

16   Ibid.; and XY, "Inlandsch Onderwijs," pp. 402-3.

where it filled a recognized local need. In other areas, however, the students wandered away when ials' backs were turned. It was, therefore, the Minangkabau people themselves who created the great intellectual flowering which would be evident to everyone else later in the twentieth century.

The Minangkabau came to grips with the new, secular, colonial order on their own terms; they took what they needed and adjusted it to their particular (and sometimes traditional) purposes. Though they worked for the Dutch regime, they did not identify their fate with that of the colonial order, as was often the case with the Christians of Indonesia. Many Minangkabau were famous and ardent nationalists, organizing autonomous non-European activities before other, often more vocal, people had come of age. From the beginning, the educated elite of Minangkabau had the self-confidence and self-assurance to stand alone without the Europeans. When it came to open warfare in 1945, the Minangkabau quickly identified the new path and strongly supported the Republican forces. The mountain fastnesses of West Sumatra provided the site for the Emergency Government of the Republic after the Dutch occupied Java, in 1948, and captured the Revolutionary leadership in Yogyakarta.

Clever manipulation and a unique interpretation of the ground rules established by the colonial regime assured the Minangkabau of their ultimate success. A small and weak people, they managed not only to avoid being swallowed up by a more powerful one, but also to use the very strength of the colonizer to the advantage of the colonized. Without the integrated administrative network with which the Dutch governed the Indies, the Minangkabau would not have become the common figures they are in Indonesia today, prominent on all levels and in all areas of archipelago life. When the Dutch regime began to waver and the new opportunity appeared, the pragmatic Minangkabau were the first to abandon the sinking colonial ship.

GLOSSARY

Adat	Body of lore and traditional customs which governed the organization and operation of precolonial society. In this case usually referred to as the Adat Minangkabau.
Anak Buah	A person's followers or dependents. In Minangkabau, usually the constituents of the penghulu suku or the mamak.
Bodi Caniago	One of two political traditions of Minangkabau. It stresses an egalitarian approach to the relationship among penghulu and between penghulu and their followers.
Cerdik Pandai	The "intelligentsia" of the nagari.
Chatib	Adat religious functionary.
Darat	The upland interior of Minangkabau. More specifically it means the heartland where the Minangkabau ethnic group originated, in opposition to the rantau.
Datuk	Honorific title for a penghulu.
Demang	Post-1914 title for a district chief in West Sumatra, theoretically chosen on the basis of ability rather than birth.
Doktor Djawa	Graduate of the Indies Medical Institute in the period before 1900. Not a trained physician but rather a medical technician.
Haji	Title of address for a man who has completed the pilgrimage to Mecca.
Harta Pencarian	The goods and wealth which a man acquires by his own labors during his lifetime.

Harta Pusaka	The goods and wealth which belong in common to one matrilineal family unit. Usually abbreviated to pusaka.
Imam	Religious leader of a community, either a village or a lineage. More recently used to refer to the particular leader of a specific mosque, such as the Imam of Bonjol.
Induk Nagari	"Mother nagari" of a nagari federation. Usually took precedence in rituals and in confirming penghulu in its dependent nagari.
Jaksa	Public prosecutor and attending investigator established by the Dutch to advise them on legal matters in West Sumatra.
Kaum	Group.
Kemanakan	Term for sisters' children. Also used to refer generally to one's dependents.
Koto Piliang	One of two political traditions of Minangkabau. It stresses a hierarchical arrangement among penghulu and a more authoritarian approach to dependents.
Ladang	Nonirrigated, generally hillside, fields.
Laras	Territorial districts set up by the Dutch in the nineteenth century. (Also refers to the two adat political traditions, Bodi Caniago and Koto Piliang.)
Larashoofd	Dutch-created position. Ruler over a laras district.
Luhak	One of the three original Minangkabau settlements, called the Luhak nan Tigo—Tanah Datar, Lima Puluh Kota, Agam.
Imam	Religious leader of a community, either a village or a lineage. More recently used to refer to the particular leader of a specific mosque, such as the Imam of Bonjol.
Mamak	Term for maternal uncle. Also used to mean guardian and leader of a lineage group.
Merantau	The process whereby young men leave their village in search of fame and fortune.

Nagari	Historic political unit of Minangkabau, usually comprised of a major village and its satellite settlements. Ruled by a nagari council composed of the community's penghulu.
Nagarihoofd	Dutch-created position. Ruler over a territorial subdistrict.
Orang Datang	Outsider who came to live in the village and was adopted by local lineage as an associated person.
OSVIA	Opleiding School Voor Inlandsch Ambtenaar. Training school for Indonesian officials.
Patut	That which is morally proper.
Pedati	Buffalo-drawn cart used for hauling bulk goods.
Pegawai	Official.
Penghulu, Penghulu Suku	Head of a matrilineage.
Penghulu Pucuk	Paramount penghulu in a nagari. Generally associated with the Koto Piliang adat style.
Perantau	The individual who leaves home to merantau.
Pusaka	See harta pusaka.
Rantau	Fringe areas of the Minangkabau. More generally it means any area outside Minangkabau or just any area outside one's home village.
Sawah	Wet-rice fields.
Serayo	Traditional labor service owed by members of a lineage to their penghulu.
STOVIA	School tot Opleiding voor Indisch Artsen. Indies Medical Institute, formerly the doktor djawa school.
Suku	Matrilineage.
Surau	Lineage Quranic school or Islamic study center under the guidance of an ulama.
Tambo	Traditional chronicles of Minangkabau.
Tarekat	Literally, the "way" or "path," refers to mystical Islamic brotherhoods in which members seek union with God under the guidance of a holy man.
Ulama	Religious teacher.

www.ingramcontent.com/pod-product-compliance
Lightning Source LLC
Chambersburg PA
CBHW030342240426
43661CB00052B/1715